THE MAKING OF
NEW GERMANY

Photograph by Max Nehrdich, Kassel

PORTRAIT OF SCHEIDEMANN

THE MAKING OF
NEW GERMANY

THE MEMOIRS OF
PHILIPP SCHEIDEMANN

Translated by J. E. Michell

VOLUME I

ILLUSTRATED

NEW YORK
D. APPLETON AND COMPANY
1929

DD
231
S 35
A 33
vol. 1

6.67 (Carnegie) Steel（...）

Cop. 38

TO MY WIFE

JOHANNA

PREFACE

At the end of 1922 I decided to whom my notes should be handed for revision and publication after my death. Readers of my *Memoirs* will learn the reasons which gave rise to that decision and accept them as sound. Having disappointed all who had such high hopes of me, as I have not succumbed to serious illness, or died of nationalistic persecution, or been called to a better world by being well squirted with prussic acid, I was in a position to publish my *Memoirs* myself.

My personal experiences, *i.e.*, the explanation and criticism of my political life, would have been in better hands, no doubt, if a candid friend had edited my notes for publication. The impartial reader will certainly admit that some one else might have been more prudent than myself. I will not disguise the fact that I was repeatedly in doubt whether I should say this or that. Many, I was perfectly sure, would impute to me here and there shady motives, as happens so often in political life. Such misgivings must be passed over unnoticed, and only the purpose of this book made quite clear.

This purpose is to give conscientious historians material and enable them to describe as truthfully as possible an eventful period and the prominent men concerned in it. As time goes on their numbers grow less and less, and for those still surviving the duty of helping to make plain the path of Truth becomes more and more pressing.

In the Preface to my book, the "Zusammenbruch," [1] I wrote,

[1] French version, "L'Effondrement."

in reference to war books already published, "It is the duty of impartial study to state the truth about the War and the changes caused by the collapse, and the writings of those who feel the necessity of gratifying, excusing or defending themselves are to be carefully noted. The author of this book feels no such necessity."—And to-day less than ever. My actions as a politician and a party man stand clearly before the public, and I shall record in this book those negotiations and proceedings that for cogent reasons were not revealed, only as far as the public interest is concerned. Politics will not be my only subject of conversation; I shall also tell the story of my life. In my early days my father taught me to keep my head up. "Youngster, keep your head up"—that was a constantly recurring exhortation, and I took it to heart. I have been as poor as a church mouse. My present affluence—money, town houses, and châteaux in all the countries of Europe, horses and motor cars— unfortunately exists only in the imaginations of my fanciful opponents. In my young days I was starved as far as a man can be starved.

As a Democrat who has to conform to the opinion of the majority, I have had often enough to submit to many things that went against the grain, but never have I bowed my head before any King or President. Being always anxious to do my duty, I had the right to hold up my head, and a good conscience has always enabled me to look down with scorn upon all backbiters, tuft-hunters and detractors, who have crossed my path in great numbers. My book will not please all those who read it. That is not its purpose, which is to serve the truth.

Many, with great zeal, have stripped the Hohenzollerns stark naked in order to show them to a gaping world as they really were. This has been useful in face of the efforts made in Royalist circles to rig them up as demigods, but not altogether in

PREFACE

good taste. But is it not ridiculous, and in the highest degree dishonourable, while gloating over scotching one yarn, to go round spreading others?

With regard to the "critical" passages in my book, I would ask the reader to consider with me Alfred Kerr's telling words: "I will get down to rock bottom. No one else will do it. It will take a long time. Let's call a spade a spade."

PHILIPP SCHEIDEMANN

Berlin

CONTENTS

xi

CONTENTS

CONTENTS

ILLUSTRATIONS

VOLUME I

MY CHILDHOOD

I WAS born in a ramshackle house in the narrow, bumpy Michel's Alley in Old Kassel. As if bent by age, the four-storied, half-timbered block leant out over the street. The house opposite did ditto, and you got the impression that the two old things were bowing to each other, as in the good old days, preparatory to dancing a minuet. Had I died of laughing at the sight of my surroundings on the 26th July, 1865, when I first saw the light of the world, that would have been perhaps the wisest thing to do. I should have been spared many later vexations. But I had a comic sense of what was round about me, kicked my legs about, all forlorn, yelled my hardest without cessation all day long, clenched my fists, and failed to make those round me understand. Three cheers for Michel's Alley!

1865-66 were and remained the most satisfying days of my life. I lived entirely on milk. This in the long run became monotonous, in spite of a mother's love, and came to an end finally with Prussia's campaign against Hesse in 1866, that I went through as "a one-year-old." I had then ceased to take any further interest in milk.

On hearing later on in life that the Prussians had driven out my hereditary Sovereign Lord, the beloved and, to many, the unforgettable, thick-headed Elector of Hesse and the last, righteous indignation seized upon me. I then determined to watch events with a view to sending the Prussians about their business at a suitable opportunity.

But joking aside, I have been able, as a matter of fact, to rely on an excellent memory from my earliest childhood in describing past events. Childish happenings that occurred at the time of the Franco-German War remain as clear in my memory as if they only occurred yesterday. When I returned to my home in 1905, at the age of forty, after nearly twenty years' absence, to take over the editorship of the Kassel *Volksblatt,* I began at once writing my childhood's experiences in pure Kassel patois, as if I had been only twenty days compulsorily absent.

Many of these dialectical sketches were collected and the pamphlets sold by the thousand. They attracted the serious notice of the Society for Hessian Folklore and History, as I learnt to my horror—things I dashed off literally anyhow, and were intended to take the place of the usual Sunday Talks —principally because this was the first time any attempt had been made to write the Kassel dialect. This acquired knowledge was very helpful to me. I wrote according to phonetic principles and as closely as possible to the actual local way of talking. The first edition was published by Heinrich Bechmann & Co. in Kassel, the second in the same year in what was then the Court Book Shop of Carl Victor, with the title "Kassel Youngsters—Short Stories in Local Dialect by Henner Piffendeckel." Another collection was later published by Dr. Helphand in his sociological library, with the title "Philipp Scheidemann, Zwischen den Gefechten." This was one of Helphand's whims, which I tried in vain to oppose. Parvous, a Russian by birth, had learnt to read quite easily the patois of my native town because he found great pleasure in my wretched stories. He had come across the selection the doctor had published. It was again published in 1926 by the Weser-Main publishing firm (J. Kampfer) in Kassel.

2

Later on I was to find out that one can remember no experiences so vividly as those of childhood. Directly I made this discovery I set about describing those experiences that seemed to me specially important. For all facts reported in this book I rely on my memory as far as I can rely on it, or I refer to my own notes. The rest I get from sources that are accessible to everybody.

My Parents

My father was a master carpenter, paperhanger and upholsterer, working for himself, a capable and respected citizen of Kassel. My mother was likewise born in Kassel. My parents came from the middle and working classes. The Scheidemanns—there have never been many of them and the name seldom crops up—probably came from the Northern Watershed, went up the Weser and then, starting out from Münden, betook themselves, some up the Werra, others up the Fulda. Namesakes of ours and researchers have traced our family back to the fourteenth century; we are able to show quite a respectable family tree. The "scratch" man has been incidentally mentioned in a Marburg Ph.D. thesis (Alfred Herbst, 1913). The oldest scion of the Scheidemanns is here spoken of, but minus his Christian name. Yet we may gather from his title of *dominus* that he was one of the most respectable citizens of Hersfeld. Thanks to numerous documents we are able to give the names of various members of this most respectable family that flourished in Hersfeld in the fourteenth century. Among others may be mentioned Henry Scheidemann, who was a petty magistrate in 1320, Rheinhold Scheidemann, Vicar of Hersfeld, Stephen Scheidemann, the village Mayor, and Citizen Jordan Scheidemann. Finally in a thesis on "The Taxpayers' Roll in Hersefeld in the Fourteenth Century"

Ludwig Scheidemann is mentioned as a Canon of Mainz in 1371. If people of this name filled official positions of this kind in the fourteenth century we may naturally suppose that the family could easily be traced by a keen researcher as far back as the thirteenth century.

One fact, however, is clear, and I give it with every sign of satisfaction; it is that the Scheidemanns had settled in Hesse at least a hundred years before the Hohenzollerns in the Mark of Brandenburg. My forebears unfortunately were not so thrifty as the Hohenzollerns (see Professor Dr. Bredt in his work on the "Discussions on Real and Personal Property between the Prussian State and the Royal House," Stilke, Berlin, 1925), otherwise they would have to will to me, if not many castles, lands and many millions sterling, a modest little cottage at any rate. Nothing doing! Ah, these old Germans were a thirsty lot of slackers!

My old grandfather who held me at the font while the parson dashed water from the Fulda into my eyes I knew intimately; the merry old soul was very dear to me. He also knew my first-born child. He almost reached the age of eighty, and could drink his beer and enjoy life right up to the end. My father served in the Elector's bodyguard during the campaigns of 1866 and 1870-71; in the latter he was in the 81st Regiment of Infantry. He was an extraordinarily imposing figure, and in normal circumstances would have reached an advanced age, but he was attacked, like many others, during the siege of Metz, with cholera that lasted many weeks, and this was followed by acute inflammation of the lungs. Though seemingly perfectly fit, he returned home after the war with the germs of death in his lungs. He died in 1879, less than forty years of age.

4

The small tradesmen who had been through the Franco-German War had a very bad time about the middle and end of the 'seventies. All the work my father had to do could be done in his workshop with the help of an assistant and an apprentice, though in his trade he was considered an artist and was patronized by all the best people at the Castle and the aristocracy of Hesse. As a bachelor he had been employed in the so-called upholstery department of the Elector. Various distinguished personages made his acquaintance and date back to this time and his soldiering days, as, for instance, General von Lossberg, who was a close friend of Prince Maurice of Hanau, son of the last Elector. Prince Maurice, as eldest of the family, was at that time Lord of Horsovice (near Prague), the Electoral Palace. He had repeatedly tried through General von Lossberg to get my father to migrate to Horsovice and take over the control of the Castle. At first the invitation was definitely declined. But the worse trade became the more frequent became my father's illnesses and the weaker became his opposition to the Prince's offer. One day, after the General's carriage had stood for hours before our house in the Holzmarkt at the corner of Leipzigerstrasse, I heard that the agreement was signed and we were to leave our home at short notice. I was in Form II at the town high school in the Hedwigstrasse when I left. The journey was probably a very fatiguing one for my parents, owing to my younger sister, but more especially to me. To me it was one huge delight, only spoilt by father and mother. The railway bridge over the Elbe near Riesa had broken down; consequently we had to be taken across in boats. What a lark! During the crossing a quarrel took place between an officer and some quite decent travellers—a regular row leading later to arrest because one of the parties took out his pistol. All this so excited my imagination that I hoped very great things of Horsovice. At first I was hugely pleased with everything, because I hadn't to go to school. This seemed an enormous step in advance when contrasted with schooling in Kassel. But things generally speaking turned out to be impossible, and the longer we stayed the worse it got. My father was supposed to greet the Prince, as was every servant on the staff, with the words: "I most humbly wish your Highness good morning." My father refused, and then and there made up his mind to go back to Kassel as soon as he could. After staying about five months in Horsovice I was sent back alone to Kassel, and was boarded with a retired Court pyrotechnist with two sons, one of whom was an artist in Berlin and the other a parson in a small country town in Upper Hesse. I probably learnt printing from the parson and piety from the artist. My stopping on in Horsovice was rendered impossible because there was no means of getting a regular course of education. The only tuition I got was from a student who had been sent down from a German University, who came to me for one hour a day. We were housed in a fine roomy suite of apartments in the Castle. One hour of school discipline was quite ample for me, because I had lots of time on my hands to go about what seemed to me more important business. Scampering about the fields and forests, shooting at targets, birds and wild cats pleased me far better than this ridiculous tuition. But my people had become convinced that this sort of life was not the right one for me, and I was sent home on that account. I may mention, too, that fits of depression came over me fairly often—I was homesick.

In Kassel I could at once return to the same class I was in when I left. My form master, Dr. Ide, a dignified man of colossal size who liked me very much, received me with open arms. When he was suddenly carried off by inflammation of the lungs, while still a young man, the whole school was in tears. In Form II I got as my form master Credé, a senior assistant master. He was a priceless person, and later on in our conversations I gave him something to think about. Credé was a bachelor. He wore a top hat of the most comic shape summer and winter. His sister, an old maid, who ran the household, cut his lank hair, and we youngsters swore that she practised the barber's art in the following way: she rammed down a pudding basin on the top of his head and cut off all the hair that obtruded. A relation of Credé's, a town magistrate called Wagner who knew of my talks with Credé, told me ten years later in the Kassel Town Hall how his great-uncle once bought at an auction at a hatmaker's, who wanted to get rid of his out-of-date stock, a dozen top hats which cost him only a mark each. With these dozen hats Credé's wants in the hat line were satisfied for over thirty years. More important for me was my acquaintanceship with Dr. Hugo Brunner, who taught our class French. My acquaintanceship with this man, an uncle of the future Mayor of Kassel, was to develop in course of time into quite a regular friendship—a secret friendship certainly, that lasted after he became Librarian of the National Library and I had long become notorious as a Social Democrat; it only ceased with the death of this clever man, though later he grew disgruntled, embittered and obstinate. I still remember with pleasure an article, "Monarchy and Republic," which Brunner wrote for the *Volksblatt* in 1906 or 1907. This article, naturally anonymous, was so rigorously worded against the régime of William II. that I should have been sent to prison for years for high treason had I not got furiously to work with my blue pencil, as Brunner used to do on my French exercises thirty years before. Brunner told me repeatedly, in the friendliest way, that I had always been one of his most unsatisfactory scholars.

The Children Are A-Hungered

My father being in a hopeless condition, I had to leave school. In my last year at school I carried round the breakfast rolls throughout the summer and winter—ugh!—the first thing in the morning between six and seven, to earn a copper or two. The few pence I got for this gave me the greater pleasure the more I froze toiling up and down those dark staircases. When I now look back at it all, I regard it as a form of primitive athletics that certainly did me no harm. I was not fourteen when I entered the printing business of Gotthelft Bros. as a compositor apprentice. The working hours, that were not fixed at that time for young apprentices, were at least twelve to thirteen hours a day, and on Saturdays, especially during the winter months, fifteen or more. I recollect having to work at Christmas time from 6 A.M. till past midnight. This work consisted mainly of manual kind that had absolutely nothing to do with printing—folding up the papers and sticking in the supplements. Folding presses and rolling machines were at that time unknown in Kassel except as imaginary fairy tales. In the first year of apprenticeship the wages were 2 marks a week, with rise each year of 50 pfennigs per week, and in the fourth year 3 marks 50 per week. For frequently working overtime one got a Christmas box of 5 marks. I don't say this to run down the firm that instructed me in the "black art." Working conditions were then hopelessly bad in nearly all trades. I mention them to

SCHEIDEMANN'S BIRTHPLACE

From an India-ink drawing by Prof. Sautter, Kassel

remind younger readers of what Trade Unionism and democratic organizations have accomplished during tens of years of bitter struggle.

My four years of apprenticeship, like my last years at school, were my hardest times in the true sense of the words. I literally froze, especially in the winter of 1879-80. When I left home in the morning before six to go to work my hands were stiff with cold and my nose was frozen when I got into the street. The terrible cold of this winter was for me especially grievous, as I had no cloak or gloves to call my own. As long as my father had to keep to his bed my mother was confined to the house and could earn nothing, and many a time I had to borrow a few coppers from my parents' friends to get bread, and often had to pawn pots and pans and my mother's clothes, that were redeemed when times got better. Certain things I was always pawning, and when payment was due I would fetch out something else for the pawnbroker— a black silk dress of my mother's, her big Oriental shawl and my father's watch. The worst thing was when I had at times to go to school, during my father's helplessness, in his or my mother's shoes while my only pair were being mended. In spite of these poverty-stricken years my childhood on the whole was quite a happy one, for I had a mother I would wish all children had—and probably don't have. In all woman's work she was a veritable masterpiece, and was in consequence greatly appreciated; she was also interested in art and literature; she read good books and went occasionally to the theatre before bad times came upon us. Naturally that had to stop. I remember well her taking me as a schoolboy to the picture gallery in the town, showing me the Rembrandts and telling me all sorts of interesting things about the great Dutchman. I came later to the idea that my mother was trying to interest my youthful mind in certain things in order to counter other influences.

My father had no definite Party leanings. One of his best friends, and of the same trade, called Edward Auell, was a Social Democrat and an enthusiastic admirer of William Pfannkuch. He was a bachelor. In times of bitter need he was a real help to my parents, and I remember him coming to see us every evening. Bad times were almost always the topic of conversation—the distress of the small shopkeepers, with Social Democracy to end up with. I listened most attentively, though most of it was lost on me. My mother—I know it well—frequently contradicted when Auell said that Social Democracy would put an end to all our troubles. The discussions became particularly lively about the time of Hödel's and Nobiling's attempts on the life of the old Emperor, William I. A democratic paper did not exist in Kassel at this time. My parents read the *Tageblatt* and got their impressions from the reports in that paper. Nowadays any Tom, Dick, or Harry would know that the Christian Socialist, Hödel, and the National Liberal, Dr. Nobiling, were not in any way connected with the Social Democrats. But then! At all events Auell had a bad time with my mother.

But increasing hard times all round and my father's prolonged illness intensified our privations at home, and when finally there was no bread in the house and my mother sent me to borrow 50 pfennigs from Auell to get a loaf, my father would say: "That Social Democrat will help us." After my father's death my indefatigable mother would work on from early morn till dewy eve. Besides looking after the home and us children, she did dressmaking jobs for people outside. She was everywhere most popular among her acquaintances because of her sound sense and skill. Rarely did I hear her complain of her fate, but I often noticed she had been crying. She even forgave my worst escapades after giving me a very serious talking to, and I'll confess she had to do it frequently. The better to understand my progress from my school days till well past my years of apprenticeship and wanderings, I will relate a childish experience.

Early Imperial Enthusiasm

I can still see most clearly how people assembled in dozens to read the special editions of the newspapers on the notice-boards reporting the attempt of the alleged "Social Democrat," Hödel, on the life of the Emperor. And I know still quite well how our form master, Dr. Credé, later on told us of the more successful attack of Dr. Nobiling in all its ruthlessness, and how in the Scripture lesson Hödel and Nobiling were described in the most appalling colours as Social Democrats. It was therefore hardly to be wondered at that we were worked up to a state of chauvinistic excitement, and the more so as our history teacher never failed to extol the Emperor as a demi-god who had not only founded the New Empire, but was to be even thanked for the air we breathed.

Besides, our fury against the miscreants was intensified because suddenly in the Scripture lesson we were called upon to learn by heart, to say for the next Scripture lesson, the texts that we were only supposed to cram up. This had up to date never been set us, but now, as two men had shot at the Kaiser, the Scripture lesson was to be run under forced draught, so that nothing like it should ever happen again. Our patriotism reached its zenith when the news came that the Emperor was coming. The wounded Kaiser coming to Kassel! Now we knew in truth that Emperors and Kings were only men, after all, in spite of the essays we had to write.

Anyhow, we were convinced of it, for we saw every day the Royal children, Prince Henry and William—the last Emperor—going together to the gymnasium, which was only a few minutes distant from our school. But to see an Emperor whom a doctor had shot at was something out of the common, to be sure, and when we were told that all the schools and clubs were to march past the Castle in which the Emperor was living, on the Friedrichsplatz, with bands and colours flying, we got completely out of hand. The day at last came when we were to march past the Kaiser and cheer him. Weller and I were to take turns in carrying the form colours, because we were the lankiest in the form. Everything went all right till we approached the Castle. I had let Weller carry the flag up to there. I wanted to carry it before the Emperor. Weller refused. There was an unseemly scrimmage in the procession. Our master saw the struggle just at a moment that must have made my rival appear in an unfavourable light. The master decided in my favour. I was just as pleased as Weller was displeased. With what enthusiasm did I wave the flag! There stood the old Emperor with one arm in a sling. He saluted us, and there could be no doubt that the salute was obviously intended for me. Of course! Ah! If I had only got hold of Nobiling—and I kept on waving the flag round about in the air with such extraordinary patriotic fervour that I had to give it up again to Weller on the master's order to prevent us breaking each other's heads.

A year later I entered on my apprenticeship, and saw and heard all sorts of things. Life was quite different from what the school had taught us. Yes, who would order his goings according to all those fine texts I had to learn! Clearly, no one; certainly not the working man whom I was getting to know. My poor little mother went out dressmaking in the morning; in the evening she would be at her accounts, when we children sat with her.

More and more the scales fell off my eyes. Was not my father a brave soldier who had fought with distinction and had sacrificed his health for his country? Was he not a respected citizen who thoroughly understood his job and had worked hard? To be sure, he was. And yet our mother had to work for strangers to save herself and her children from starvation.

Yet—it was a fact. Wherever I cast my eyes round me, it was everywhere the same—at the Schmidts', Müllers', Lehmans', etc., etc.! No, not at everybody's. The few manufacturers living in the neighbourhood were always increasing their works and always building finer mansions.

The printers among whom I was learning my job read all sorts of stuff, which they carelessly left lying about. I read everything with interest. I learnt from Lassalle's works that there were class differences: that is to say, there are men who have to sell their capacity for work to feed themselves and their children, and there are men who buy it to make all the profit they can out of it. The latter are the Capitalists of towns and countries, manufacturers and big landed proprietors; they are only a tiny fraction of the population, but are more powerful than the whole mass of workers. As long as the worker can sell his capacity for work, so long has he the chance of being just able to feed his family. When he becomes unable to work distress is the result. This was the case with my great-grandfather, and would be the same with his great-grandson, if the people had not come a little to their senses. I was soon cured of the patriotism that was instilled into me at school. Directly I entered the school of life I learnt what it means to be truly patriotic; it means being a Social Democrat!

Patriotism means love for one's country. No one can love his Fatherland more than we Social Democrats. Just because of this we did not cast the dust off our feet and emigrate, as was recommended us by William II. On the contrary, we stayed at home to fight on till the exploitation of Man by Man was stopped, and equal rights were won for all.

II

ON THE TRAMP

THE cruellest of all creatures is Man. A deep feeling of shame comes over me as I think what pain I caused my mother when I went on the tramp. In April, 1883, I had finished my four years' apprenticeship. In accordance with ancient custom, I was solemnly "acquitted" by the Senior Warden of the House, with the whole crowd of the compositors standing round. But my mates had not yet done with me. I at once entered the Printers' Union and became a member of the Social Democratic Secret Society, but a fully fledged colleague of compositors I could only be created on that day when they succeeded in "baptizing" me formally and for all time. It is a peculiar form of baptism. The holy water is not sprinkled on the head, but is to be discovered inside a huge sponge, which is placed on the top of a proof-reader's three-foot-high desk. One is plumped down three times with considerable force on this sponge after the officials have succeeded in collaring their victim and rendering him defenceless. Strange incantations are muttered at this ceremony. Directly the initiate has paid his footing the diploma of the guild is handed to him. The young compositor is then fully fledged and can now go on the tramp.

The official diploma is embellished as elaborately as are diplomas of the highest distinction—in five colours, which, it is stated, the Emperor Frederick III. granted the printers, as well as the right to quarter arms and wear a sword on official occasions:

15

Purple, gold, blue, silver the Kaiser gave us—
'And our type is always printed off in black.
Long live the Art!

The words that suggest the Middle Ages and the Guilds must naturally only be taken humorously, and are as follows:

Seize him and plant his stern-piece
Down on the cold wet sponge
Till both his hips are dripping;
Then give unto the thirsty soul
A shower-bath fresh and clean.
Thus ends the good old Christening
Of Gutenberg's young Son.

"BY THE GRACE OF GOD

"We, disciples of Gutenberg, of the Holy Roman Empire, bring to the notice of All and Sundry among our Craftsmen that this Disciple of the most noble Art of Printing, to wit Philipp Scheidemann, has to-day, in the presence of the Gentlemen Craftsmen of the Gotthelft Printing House, undergone Baptism by water *ad posteriora,* and has been hereby invested with the Rights and Privileges conferred upon us all by Emperor Frederick III. By virtue of the same we command all our fellow Craftsmen to acknowledge and accept the aforesaid Disciple of Gutenberg as a duly authenticated member of the Black Art fraternity.

"Given under our hand."

These certificates of baptism are signed by the officiant at the ceremony; by the first assistant, the second assistant, the sponge-holder and the other witnesses.

I worked in the apprentices' printing house till January,

1884. Then I could stand it no longer. I should have liked best to have gone away in the summer of 1883, but fought shy of leaving my mother alone with all her worries, and my sister, who was hardly ten. The idea that my going away alone, my jump into the dark, might cause my mother heart-breaking sorrow never in the least occurred to me at first. I only saw the great wide world in front of me and wanted to know it. Turn out! At eighteen I looked three and twenty, for I was 5 feet 11 inches tall, and wore thin, closely cropped whiskers. At any rate I looked so reliable and trustworthy that the leader of the Social Democratic Party, a fine fellow called Heinrich Huhn, whose intimate friend I became later on until his death in 1924, entrusted me with a tin box with a narrow slit for collecting donations for those who had been expelled from the country under the law against Socialists. I was hardly through my apprenticeship when I found myself in the innermost circle of the secret organization—and with all my heart and soul. I distributed to buyers the *Social Democrat* from house to house. The paper had been sternly shut down, it was closely watched by the police, and was published, owing to the law against Socialists, in Zürich, and afterwards in London. Other pamphlets I helped to distribute from village to village. I came back more than once on a Sunday evening with my trousers torn to bits, as the villagers had set their dogs on to us. I was present at all the most confidential discussions. I was rejoiced when they gave Grillenberger into my charge in order that he might be brought safely to the appointed rendezvous under the very eyes of the police. I greedily devoured the reports brought by William Pfannkuch from Berlin. He was then a member of the Reichstag for the Sixth Parliamentary Division of Berlin. I was often reproached by my fellow compositors for being too keen on politics for a young man, and for taking too little interest in questions relating to my trade. I tried therefore to satisfy both demands, but I was so badgered with one thing and another that I firmly made up my mind to leave Kassel. The police were everlastingly on my track. Once we were surprised by the police at a meeting in a public-house at the corner of the Wolfhager and Holländischen Strasse. The man "keeping cave" had not kept his eyes open; the door opened, and in walked an elderly "bobby" whom we all knew. "What's up here? What larks are you up to?" "We're keeping a birthday." "I don't believe it. I dissolve the meeting. And now hook it quiet!" Naturally we didn't want telling twice. We had our pockets full of the latest "wheezes"— that is to say, booklets with instructions as to how to act in case of arrest, domiciliary visits, and police-court proceedings. If the "bobby" hadn't been unexpectedly stupid he could have put us all under arrest and summoned assistance. Had he reported the matter, it is probable he would have been sharply reprimanded. As he knew most of us by sight or by name, he could have summoned some of us for cross-examination. I was quite prepared for a police visit, and told my mother. She agreed with me that the precious sheets of instructions should not be burnt, and tacked them to her underclothing with amazing rapidity. She continued, naturally, in a state of great alarm until I could give them back; this I did some time later. Two of my comrades on whom the forbidden papers were found were sentenced to several months' imprisonment. The policeman didn't show me up, though he knew me well, for we went to the same public-house.

A few facts about our secret organizations may perhaps be interesting, as it can be gathered from them what a bad time Social Democracy had under the Socialist Law and what self-sacrifice and zeal were necessary to the Party's service. I was forcibly reminded of these days when silly youngsters kept bawling through Berlin after the fall of the Empire, "Down, down with Labour treachery! Down with it." The heart and soul of our movement in Kassel had been for years Henry Huhn, already mentioned, a mechanic employed in Henschel's engineering works. He was hand in glove with William Pfannkuch; the latter, however, was, for good reasons, excluded from the purely organizing work of the Party. Huhn had five men "standing by" whom he could put to work at a few minutes' notice. Each of these five men had five other men to report on sundry matters, etc., etc. In this way it was easy, without having to draw up a list, to mobilize many hundreds of men in the shortest possible time. If we had a pamphlet ready for secret circulation, it was a mere trifle to distribute it immediately. This had, of course, to be done in the evening or early morning, before they went to work. Once, and once only, did Huhn get into the hands of the police, and that was owing to an unguarded remark made by a young workman, who could have refused to say anything if he had read his "Hints" conscientiously. On the charge of distributing illicit matter, both were sentenced to two months' imprisonment. Our chief sport consisted in diddling the town police and the county constabulary. Among other things the frontiers were barred against Switzerland, and later against England, in order to stop at all costs the *Social Democrat* from being smuggled across. But when, despite this, the current number was punctually delivered throughout the Empire, the "bosses" in Berlin got furious. They never solved the mystery. How could thousands and thousands of papers be brought over the frontier when every frontier post was shut? It was a very simple business.

The *Social Democrat* was not printed abroad, but in Germany itself. The names of foreign firms were, of course, given as the printers. In these cases the German Imperial Post forwarded the packages through the Empire with unerring punctuality. And when it was reported to Berlin from the frontier, through the police and their allies, that the current *Sozi* (we called it the "Cheese" as fitting exactly its original source) had definitely not passed the frontier, the wild savages at the police headquarters who had long had the latest number in their hands tore their hair out in despair and cursed the frontier stations that had again not used their eyes.

Round the World Away

In January, 1884, notice to leave was given to a few of the more senior printers; I was spared only because I was well up in the complicated methods still in vogue. I put in my spoke for a married mate, and after rather lengthy negotiations with the chief brought it about that he was to stay and I was to go. I was jubilant. Now at last I could get away. January is certainly not the best month to go on tramp, but what did I care! Off you get! Saying good-bye at home was a sad business. However, my mother didn't say much, though she cried, and that was awful for me. To-day I can understand what it means when a child comes to his mother and says he is going out into the world—aye, into the world. I didn't part from my mother to go to another job in Frankfurt, Hamburg or Berlin; I was going with a carpet bag on my back and a stick in my hand to see the world—here to-day, there to-morrow! But at home was a mother eating her heart out and wondering, with anxious eyes, morning, noon and night, where her boy was.

I tore myself away at last, and hurried to the station—

CHILDHOOD PICTURE, WITH PARENTS

leaving house and home for the first time. I bought a work-man's ticket to Göttingen. From there I walked briskly northwards. I wanted to go to Hamburg via Hanover. What on earth did I want? I wanted to go into the world, no matter how I got there!

The first evening on tramp I shall ever remember. I made my first halt in a little town on the railway between Göt-tingen and Hanover. In the hostel lived an old woman—what one takes at eighteen for an old woman. Only two or three fellows on tramp were there—old customers I didn't feel sure about. I sat down and wrote home that I was getting on fine, and was merry and bright. Then "Ma" remarked it was time to go to bed. She escorted the other two to their room, and then called out to me: "Come down." We went down a long passage leading to a big room with a stone floor containing two beds. The hostel mother sat down on the edge of the bed and ordered me to take my shirt off. What this meant I had, of course, found out from my mates' stories. That meant, "You are now going to be inspected." I obedi-ently undressed, retaining only my trousers, and, shivering with cold, handed her my shirt. By the bye, I had only heard of underlinen from hearsay. Nodding her head and blink-ing her eyes in a not unkindly way, she invited me to sit beside her. Meanwhile she had put on a large pair of steel spectacles, and examined the shirt-band with the greatest thoroughness. Naturally she didn't find any live-stock. Hav-ing told her that I had only left home that same morning, she shrewdly said: "Then you must be all the more careful, for clean linen attracts bugs; they are less fond of 'sweaty' gar-ments." Then she hung the shirt over the back of a chair, and I slipped stark naked into bed—brrh!

One day was as much like another as one egg is like another. Now and again there was a welcome change. One evening I lost my heart completely to the merry and bright little daughter of the mother of the hostel in Badebusch. I got myself up to kill at once after catching sight of the slender maid. After much thought, I took off the shirt I had been perspiring into for five weeks and guaranteed free from bugs, took out of my knapsack the fine new linen one, and fastened a new paper collar round my neck and a dicky that covered the whole of my manly bosom. What price, Badebusch! The damsel was very nice to me, and told me yarns about all sorts of my mates who had worked there. We told each other stories and played dominoes and dice together. Finally mamma came on the scene, beckoned to me with her finger, and disappeared with me into the bedroom. "Take off your shirt." She looked the collar band over and over again, and at last said harshly: "If I find another, you don't get into that bed; you will have to crack them." I was dumbfounded. Me with bugs? "It can't be. I've never had one yet. And to-day I had put on a new shirt!" "Why were you so stupid? Well, I can't find another. Good night!" This was for the time being the result of my youthful lovemaking: one bug and the prospect of having to sleep on a bench or in the straw. It did not suit me at all. I had a good look, too, myself, packed away the clean shirt, and next morning put on the stiff "sweaty" one again. Emmie smiled at me bewitchingly in the early morning when she gave me my breakfast. I was on the look-out for a favourable chance of giving her a kiss. I fancied I was Napoleon or Rinaldo Rinaldini—bold and unafraid. I soon noticed it required no great deed of daring to carry out my design, for five minutes later, when all was serene, she put her arm round my neck, gave me her fresh mouth and whispered: "What a pity you are going!" "Oh!" said I, starting up, ready for any mortal thing, "I won't go to-day in any case." I was willing to risk another bug.

At the Cradle of Sport

I still remember with great pleasure an evening in Burg near Magdeburg. We had drunk a lot of Berliner Weissbier in Magdeburg, a beverage not hitherto known to us. I do not remember whether on our trip to Berlin as far as Burg we walked or rode. I only know that we arrived on a Monday towards evening at the hostel, and the cobblers were at the time celebrating quarter day. It practically meant, as was apparent to us on the road, that half Burg was drunk. The fellows asked us to join them. As we had nothing more urgent or important to do, we accepted the invitation. Supper was the usual thing, every evening the same, as we were simple people: herrings and potatoes in their jackets. As I had never learnt to peel a potato—a weak spot in my education, moreover, that I realized soon enough—I had to eat skins and all; had I not done so I should never have been able to get enough to eat from the dish that was common to all. As we were far from being as exhilarated as our entertainers, they tried every now and then to liven us up with a peg. About midnight, as we thought, conviviality was universal. On entering the dormitory to go to bed, some of those we had disturbed in their sleep got nasty. They blatantly cried out for silence. We asked them in the most humble way to shut their mouths. Inside a minute there suddenly broke out in the pitch-dark room a regular scrimmage between about twenty men, all stark naked, but absolutely infuriated, hitting, wrestling, sparring, hurling bootjacks, cursing, kicking, swearing and groaning, till at last the hostel father came along with

23

some of his servants to pacify us in the friendliest fashion. For the purpose each had brought with him a stout leather belt. Next morning we saw all sorts of broken noses and swollen lips; conspicuously numerous were the black eyes. I seemed to notice that my left shin had considerably increased in circumference and looked damnably puffy. I can't get rid of the idea that that evening in Burg was perhaps one of the starting points of the German sport movement. Who can tell? Nearly all the combinations and permutations in every department of modern sport were exhibited in practical form on that evening. Goethe, who was apt to exaggerate, might have said (as he did after Valmy): "A new age starts from to-day and from here—and you can say that you were there."

I stopped a whole week in Berlin, and then went tramping on to Stettin, Lübeck, Kiel and Hamburg. In Lübeck I was very hard up, and took the advice of a mate who pointed out to me a horse-butcher's shop near the hostel, and described in glowing colours how good horse sausage tasted. After hesitating a long time, I risked my last threepenny piece. But I was so overwhelmed with disgust that I wasn't able to eat a scrap of the sausage. It tasted all right to my mate. On my tramp northwards I was once the guest of Prince Bismarck.

At Bismarck's Table

Bismarck as a host has been often described, and almost everybody who once drank a glass of wine at Bismarck's house, or smoked a cigar there, has written a book about it. If I should make a contribution to the memory of the famous statesman, the somewhat peculiar circumstances in which I was Prince Bismarck's guest must excuse to a certain extent my enriching unnecessarily a literature which is already too full of memoirs. Well, it was in the early spring of 1884, and I was on the road. To-day my heart within me laughs with joy when I think of it. Young and festive and the whole world before me. I have surely stated that I had for certain on the average fifteen "groschens" a day and one mark for travelling expenses from the organization. One got with ease half a mark extra if one said in the printing houses, "God bless the Art." Now and then came a few postage stamps from home. Why should I not have been happy and contented? Sometimes I was very short. I won't hide the fact that, in big towns, after getting our money, we lived rather above our means. I had two travelling companions who knew their way about; in short, they were going begging. It didn't appeal to me, and I had never learnt how. My only attempt failed. March, 1884, gave us a number of wonderful early spring days. We threw our knapsacks down into the ditch by the wayside and puffed away at our pipes. We discussed hundreds of things with great animation. Finally we confirmed the fact that our financial condition was utterly hopeless, and proceeded to curse Bismarck, who, in our opinion, was responsible for most of the evil in the world. We had read all sorts of things about this fellow in a broad-minded paper at breakfast time.

"Bismarck! Didn't you hear this morning what the butcher told us about there being a fine dinner provided for customers at Bismarck's place close by here? Let's be off there." So spake the Swabian Hönle.

"Yes, I heard that. But we shall have to go eight miles out of our road to get it. I vote for going. If so, we've no time to lose." So spake my Hessian friend, Stephen.

"You're both dotty. I'm not going to walk eight miles

for a plate of soup. And I certainly don't want any of Bismarck's favours." So spake I.

There was a long argument, and at last we went on. Our stomachs rumbled louder and louder. I had hoped to drive away hunger by lighting a pipe, but it was useless. Suddenly we reached the cross roads. Now we had either to go straight on to our far-distant goal or turn to the left to Bismarck's place, where tasty soup awaited us. I had a stern fight with my conscience, but I was in a minority. Though I cursed loud and long against Bismarck and his free soup-kitchen, I submitted with no great unwillingness to the democratic principle of "caught together, hung together," and went with them. The nearer we came to the place, the more our hunger increased. We tried to forecast what we should have to eat. Pea soup? Lentil soup or haricot soup? And how much bacon each would get. We told each other over and over again what we liked best to eat at home, and were revelling in the thought of the finest handout when we reached the farm on the estate. An enormous watchdog (I leave Bismarck scholars to inquire whether it was Tyras) rushed up to us, barking furiously. But we had already had experience with dogs, and knew that dogs that bark don't bite.

A farm-hand pointed to a door without saying a word. We knocked, and without more ado entered a gigantic kitchen. A middle-aged cook with enormous arms that inspired us with enormous respect pointed with her finger to a bench where we could sit down. We put our knapsacks on the floor. There was pea soup. There was no doubt about it. Our noses told us that, and my mouth watered at the thought of what was in store for us. With growing excitement we fixed our eyes on what the cook was preparing. She took a big piece of bacon, cut it into thin slices and threw the lot into

26

a fair-sized basin. I seemed to be in fairy-land. What a feast it would be if each of us got a basin full! I felt in my stomach distinct rumblings of approval. The unexpected was to happen. The cook with her feet kicked a three-legged table into the middle of the kitchen, put the basin on it and gave each of us a spoon. What was the next item? All three of us were to eat out of the same pot! That had never happened to me before in my experience. But all these misgivings surrendered to the keen demands of appetite. I dug my spoon into the pot and took my fill. Ah! how delicious it tasted. Pea soup and bacon after a three hours' tramp on a fresh March morning—and I was only eighteen years old! I looked at my companions, and saw with satisfaction that they liked it too.

But there's many a slip between the cup and the lip. As I put the spoon again to my mouth I had a look at Hönle, and suddenly felt as if I had a queer sort of potato dumpling sticking in my throat. Hönle's nose had become a dripping stalactite. I gave Stephen a despairing dig in the ribs. He was speechless, and then we beheld a dewdrop fall right into the middle of the pea soup.

Our spoons followed the dewdrop into the pot, accompanied by such words as these: "Beast! Swine! After an eight-mile walk! Everything spoilt! Starvation staring us in the face. You dirty tyke!"

On Stephen showing signs of going for him with his fists, the cook took no further interest in the development of events. She jerked the door open and shouted for a certain being called Krischan. As we had no wish to make new acquaintances in Bismarck's house, we took up our knapsacks and departed. The settlement with our "stalactite" friend was thorough though cruel. I should never have imagined that a few spoonfuls of pea soup could develop such skill and violence. We naturally parted company with the loutish fellow on the spot. The plebeian was not fit company for the patricians. I never again dined with Bismarck—on principle.

I Meet My Wife

After about seven weeks' tramping I found work in Hamburg, in the Rödingsmarkt, which was at that time traversed by a malodorous canal. After many months' work I became very well known among my fellow workmen. I was not admitted to the inner circle, in spite of the best intentions on my part. Its old and trusty servants in Hamburg were very cautious, and rightly so. They had no occasion to let such a strange young upstart pry into the secrets of the Northern district. Almost entirely free of all organizing duties, and free to go my own gait, I was one of the most festive among my mates and colleagues. One day the printing house where I was employed went broke, and I with many others was left stranded. But fate was kind to me, for a compositor was wanted in Kiel. I went there, to be near Hamburg. I had only been working a few weeks in Kiel when my Hamburg friends summoned me back—there was work to be had. Naturally I did not take long to consider, and away I hurried to Hamburg at express speed. I worked in Uhlenhorst with several of my best-known mates in a printing house with all up-to-date improvements. But after some months we were out of work again, for the job for which we had been engaged—a so-called emergency job—was finished.

While on the road I experienced a real romance, with all that it means. A valid reason for saying nothing about it is not to hand, and as I have no motive for wishing to appear better than I am or was, I will tell my story.

So I was once more an "out-of-work" in Hamburg. Should I stay there or go again on the road? I did not think long over it—I strapped my knapsack and "Away he must and farther wander." March was here; the sun meant well; my boots were sound and my clothes in trim. What did I want more?

A few days later we were lying on the grass on a small hill near Brunsbüttel, just where the north-east canal comes out into the Elbe opposite Cuxhaven. We were in the highest of spirits. My travelling companion, the cheerful Katzoff (as merry as a sandboy), had his pockets full of sausages, and I had still a few marks over from the last payday. In every big town I purchased a paper collar (*bielefelder*). Always be a gentleman!

The sun, too, shone brightly. Were these not sufficient reasons for making two healthy young fellows, with the joy of life glistening in their eyes, cock-a-hoop?

Lord, how we did howl our best songs into the balmy spring air! Then we lighted our pipes, and my mate very subtly explained to me that we could live divinely if I would overcome my cussedness and learn to beg. He could easily get sausage and bacon from his bosses; I was to get bread and beg my midday meal, and we could have all our cash for going on the spree. May "smugs" forgive me! The proposition was for me at the time a very tempting one.

Katzoff had gone diplomatically to work. He had let me see he would think me a funk if I didn't go begging. I couldn't stand that. "I'll start begging this very day!" The nearer we came to the neat little town of Marne, the louder my heart throbbed, and I clearly saw Katzoff eyeing me askance continually. I clenched my teeth and whispered to myself words of good cheer: "To be sure, you'll go begging,

29

you must; there's nothing extraordinary about it; you'll go begging in all weathers. . . ."

I now stood in front of the door of a small stationer's shop. I was trembling in every limb. Ah, good Lord! I had the latch actually in my hand; the door opened; there was a tinkle—it seemed as if all my bones were tingling. Ah, if I were only outside again—this awful feeling of shame! Not knowing what to do, I twiddled my cloth cap about in my hand. I stood still at the door, and no word passed my lips. Then a tiny shrivelled little man handed me a coin, likewise without saying a word.

"Thank you"—I don't know how the words came to my lips. I was back in the street again and fancied I was drunk. I stuck the halfpenny into my waistcoat pocket—it was to be a keepsake for ever.

"Now then, buck up!" my travelling companion shouted across at me, coming out of a house on the opposite side and disappearing at once into another. According to the rules of the game, he stuck to his side of the street.

My first attempt at begging had not been so bad, after all. The result, too, was really not bad. But I didn't dare go to the next-door house; I walked about a hundred yards further, and every time I heard the bell tinkle on the opposite side, where my friend Katzoff was introducing himself as a poor working lad, I felt as if I had been given a blow in the ribs, and a voice said, "Do what he does. Where's the harm?"

I struggled and struggled with myself. I would try once more. Once is no custom, but twice is enough for a start and the first day. So I argued.

I stopped in front of a larger house at the corner. The flicker on the fanlight distinctly showed that the passage was about to be lit up. I came nearer and pressed open the latch;

the bell rang and I was inside. Ah! would that I could have sunk a thousand fathoms deep into the earth. I can still feel to-day how the blush came into my face and the blood mounted to the very roots of my hair. I saw before me about a dozen young, bright, pretty girls with red cheeks and gleaming eyes —dressmakers!

Two were standing on tables to light the big swinging oil lamps, but before I could come to my senses the girl lighting the lamp nearest me jumped down from the table right under my nose. To the great amusement of them all, she made me a mock curtsey and said to me, "Don't be alarmed, Herr Director. What can I do for you?"

All I have written here was naturally the work of a moment. I know not how it came about, but I could have really sunk into the earth the first moment I saw the young girls, for I came as a beggar. Now that the dark girl had dropped her grand curtsey I was infected with the hilarity of the "heroines of the needle," and out the words came glibly: "Excuse me, miss, I'm a poor working lad——" Then the deuce of a row broke out. As if it had to be, or had been carefully got up beforehand, the girls, with merry laughter, formed a ring round the young dark pixie. The latter had seized a poker, and was hammering with it on the handle of a flat-iron, counting one, two, three.

And now the whole lot sang together:

> *"A nosegay in his hat,*
> *His staff in his hand. . . ."*

The rowdy hoydens gave me a regular serenade. The whole performance had so delighted me that I obeyed the imperious gesture of the pixie conducting and sang the sec-

31

ond verse with them. Then I was served with plenty of bread, butter and cheese. Hot grog was speedily brewed, and an amusing conversation began: "Where do you come from? Where are you going? Have you a sweetheart?" And the dark girl told me also the old "dummon" had gone to a tea-party, and then she had always to keep order as being the cleverest and steadiest. The others greeted this remark with hysterical laughter. This larky wench, "the most sensible and the steadiest," certainly seemed to me very amusing. In the true sense of the word the fox was looking after the geese. Finally the dark girl—Hannah was her name—pressed a few coins she had collected into my hand. I thanked her and made her a bow in my best form. "Come again soon," said my benefactress to me as she said good-bye. "This good fortune will hardly come my way again," was my reply.

My mind was in a curious state when I got back into the street. Tramping about didn't seem so pleasant; at all costs, I would give it up as soon as I could. I was bound to find work somewhere: they were advertising for compositors. It was funny I so often thought of Marne. Midsummer was here, and dozens of us got the sack. Unemployment once more! Peter Löhde, the hostel-keeper at the Kohlhöfen, had taken a fancy to me. He persuaded me to stop on till I could find work, and I stopped on for one week, then for two and ultimately for three, and then my fate was settled by dice. Rather down on our luck, and loudly cursing fortune, we were sitting at a round table at Löhde's—a round dozen of printer's devils—one Friday afternoon. Peter came in with a strange gentleman, and told us that Altmüller, the proprietor of the printing works at Marne, wanted not only to stand us drinks all round, but also to give one of us a job! Well, that was a real bolt from the blue.

32

The question of drinks was soon solved—much sooner, at any rate, than the question of employment. A few of the older men declined to leave Hamburg. Several of the younger ones were prepared to go, but no one would forestall the other. "Let's toss dice for it." Peter's proposal was approved: "Let's toss," and I won.

On the Sunday I was to go to Marne. I got an advance to pay for my journey, and we naturally started "celebrating" my departure on the spot. We began on the Friday and went on till the Saturday. And when I went off to Marne on the Sunday morning, with another advance from good old Peter, I was not only tormented by such questions as, "Will you see her again?" but also with a splitting headache.

A provincial Trades and Industries Exhibition was to be held in Marne. Another hand was wanted for the purpose. We had lots to do, and had to work overtime willy-nilly. As we were lodging and feeding with our lord and master, we hardly ever came out during the dinner hour, and when we left the house in the evening it was already rather dark. I saw nothing of the dark-eyed dressmaker, and was not able to say in what house I had begged, eaten and sung. And a fortnight went by.

The Exhibition was officially opened at noon on a Sunday, and naturally we could not miss such an important function. I strolled from room to room arm in arm with a good mate who had been working in Marne for many years—he came from happy Schwiebus, and Gustavus was his name. Gustavus was as well known as a piebald cow; no one knew me, so the townsfolk stared all the more at the long, lanky stranger.

Well, I'm blest! there she was. I suddenly gave a start, and my companion looked at me with amazement. There was no doubt about it: there she was. On the wall hung an

33

advertisement—a half-length photo, life size, of a young girl in a gipsy costume. It must be she. She looked at me just like that when I asked her for a trifle. . . .

"I say, Gus, who's that?"

"The gipsy! She's Hannah Dibbern; I know her. She's a fine piece!"

"Fine piece" didn't seem to me to be a very proper description. That she was "fine" and had devilish black hair and black eyes was again confirmed by her photograph as a gypsy.

Gustavus promised to arrange a meeting as soon as possible. That could be brought off the next evening; he could invite her quite casually to the garden concert that was to be given on the occasion of the Exhibition. It could be the more easily managed as he knew her father well.

It was a usual thing in the 'eighties to have a whisky here and there, with a glass of beer to settle it. Well, that same night about ten o'clock we had to escort two tipsy idiots through the town; at eleven I was fraternizing with about half a dozen respectable burghers' sons. (I was having a very good time in Marne.) Unfortunately, I lost my friend later on, or he lost me—we never could say exactly—and finally found myself at home, not without further adventures. I got into a narrow by-street with only a few houses, and there I came across a copper-smith, as happy as a sandboy, singing in melting accents, "O Susan, Susan, how fair art thou!" He called me his best pal and fell on my neck. I had to sit down with him on the steps of a barber's shop. He told me stories and sang again between whiles, "O Susan, Susan, how fair art thou!" Marne, so he said, was a tophole place; here only real "sports" lived; he never went to bed at night, and was always up for a lark. He was quite sad,

34

he said, because he did not know what to do with himself that night.

Well, this was the man who that night left me in the lurch. Ah, and bad luck came so soon! We espied, behind the rails on the other side of the street, two little white receptacles which no one ever mentions and yet which are found in every bedroom. They were hung up on two big wooden pegs. And over our heads swayed to and fro the gaudy barber's pole. The plan was to put the —— on the barber's pole. But was that anything funny? A council of war was summoned. The iron shop-sign of two old maids who ran a milliner's shop almost opposite where we were sitting was creaking in the wind. On the shop-sign we could clearly read "Fashionable Clothing Establishment." We were now of one mind. In for a penny, in for a pound. The copper-smith and I were to tie the Dresden china to the old ladies' sign-board. . . .

With our walking-sticks we soon got down the brittle products of the potteries, and started to climb up the wall at the risk of our lives. The copper-smith got over the garden wall; I had got on the top of a big water-butt, such as is always placed under every rain-pipe, and from which the women get their water for washing. I had just fastened one tightly up with my handkerchief, having no other substitute, when my new friend, perhaps as a signal that he had done his task, began to sing once more, "Susan, Susan, how fair art thou!" In our zeal for doing a job well we hadn't noticed two dangerous individuals softly slinking along: one of the town policemen and the night watchman. Both must have got hold of our legs simultaneously, for we sang out together, "Oh! Ah!"

With a skill I should have never thought him capable of,

35

my confederate jumped from the wall and ran off, with the old "groggy" watchman after him. I couldn't get away. I got hopelessly held up by my trousers, and had I attempted to jump might have fallen into the water-butt. So I remained standing on it, hanging on to the rain-pipe.

"What are you after up there?"

"I only wanted to see what a pot looked like on a barber's pole."

"Indeed! Well, come down, and I'll see what you look like between us two."

The old watchman came back just at this moment without his quarry, puffing and blowing. The copper-smith had given him the slip. I made no preparations for getting down from the barrel.

"Well, now, sharp about it. Are you coming?"

"No, I'm quite comfortable up here. What do you really want with me?"

"I want particulars about you, nothing more—if you are sensible and come down."

Well, that was talking sense, and I clambered down.

"What's your name?"

"Philip So-and-So."

"What are you?"

"An artist."

"Ah! none of your sauce; there are no artists in Marne."

"I must really contradict you, sir. I am a compositor."

"Yes, to be sure; I hadn't thought of that; a book-printer from Altmüllers. Do you live there?"

"Certainly."

"What's the name of your pal who has hooked it?"

"I don't know him."

"That's a rotten lie."

"Watchman, I give you my word of honour, I only got acquainted with him this evening. What he's called I really don't know."

"And you go round playing the fool with a man you don't know the name of?"

"But, sir, in matters of this sort all, surely, depends on his skill, and not on his name."

"Well, go home; we'll get on the track of your business friend."

Early Love

The dark girl did not come to the concert on the Sunday evening, in spite of Gustavus's special invitation through the seventeen-year-old daughter of our next-door neighbour. And how tactfully had Gustavus invited her! A nice young man would be there whom Miss Hannah knew because of a very merry meeting. The gentleman in question was burning to see her again, and Gustavus had assured the messenger of his being a kind man, etc. The small fair girl, out of curiosity, had had an extra look at us through the window, to see whether I was really a nice man, and she must have been satisfied. Straightaway she ran off to deliver the "invite" to her friend, who was a year older than she. She found Hannah and her father at home.

"Hannah, I am to give you an 'invite' for this evening's concert."

"Who is inviting me?"

"Gustavus Wabersky."

"What? How comes Gustavus to invite me?"

"Well, you know, he's inviting you in a way in another's name?"

"Another's? What does that mean? Who is the other?"

"I mustn't say; you are to have a surprise. It's about a young man you've already met in very funny circumstances."

Now, the old man, Hannah's father, who was sitting in his uniform at a table writing, pricked up his ears. "What a funny invitation!"

"Oh, Herr Dibbern, he's really a very decent man; I've seen him," the little messenger now assured him. "It's about a friend of Wabersky, and you know Gustavus."

"Nonsense! I'll know who is inviting my daughter. Now, what's the name of the nice young man?"

"Mr. So-and-So."

"What? What's the chap called? Works at Altmüller's?" the old man rapped out.

"Yes, quite right."

"But I don't know him at all," put in Hannah.

"Oh, he's really a nice young man," declared the constable, assuming the official manner. "You will hardly know the nice, decent young man, to be sure, but I know him. I made his acquaintance last night on the Steindamm between two and three—a nice young man. Such a saucy fellow! What a cheek he has! Of course you won't go to the concert. I'll give him a bit of my mind when I meet him."

We walked round and round the concert garden looking everywhere. She wasn't to be seen. Suddenly a policeman whose face seemed extraordinarily familiar to me tapped Gustavus on the shoulder and said: "My daughter begs to decline invitations from certain 'nice' "—he laid marked stress on "nice"—"from certain *nice* young gentlemen." Thereupon the angry, moustachioed constable disappeared.

Gustavus was speechless.

"What does the gent want?" I asked.

"What does he want? Why, that's Hannah's father!"

"Are you dotty, man? That was?"

"That was Hannah's father."

"Ah, Lord, it's all over! That policeman wanted to run me in last night."

"Run you in? Why?"

I then told Gustavus how things stood, as far as I knew them. He shook with laughter.

"The old man will never forget that. But it will do you no harm with his daughter; she is up to her tricks, where and whenever possible."

We first met on a Sunday afternoon. Gustavus had arranged a rendezvous with diplomatic skill. We met outside the town near her father's cottage, that stood in a pretty garden. I could have yelled with joy! She knew me at once, and she was pleased.

We then met oftener. One fine day in October we walked out to Neufeld, a small seaport with a lifeboat station. She showed and explained to me the whole arrangement. On a small hillock about thirty yards from the shore stood a small shed from which ran railway lines straight into the sea. In the shed itself stood a boat fully equipped, ready to put out to the rescue of those in trouble on the sea.

The girl, in a black velvet costume, spoke as if she knew all about it, like an old sailor. I was seething and boiling inside like the tide which was driving the huge roaring waves towards the harbour at our feet. But to-day of all days my tongue seemed to have gone on strike. We walked in silence along the embankment which protected the shore-dwellers from the stormy elements. It was a glorious autumn day. The air was so clear that we could make out Cuxhaven away over what seemed to be the endless surface of the waters.

Like a huge toy deprived of its works, a proud sailing-ship

39

drifted slowly up on the tide towards the Elbe, and still further off we saw two steamers bound for the North Sea. We sat down in silence. A solemn stillness came over us. I put her hand into mine. Then there was a long pause.

"Miss Hannah, you've described the lifeboat station to me so well; it's the first I've seen. . . . That is to say the first of that kind . . . but I've seen another kind already."

She looked at me inquiringly.

"Do you still recollect now I came to your house as a working lad?"

"Recollect it!" she cried, with a merry laugh.

"Well, you see, Hannah, that house was for me a lifeboat station. Your girl friends belonged to the crew, and you were the coxswain."

"There's a flaw in the comparison."

"Let there be a flaw! Don't you see what I'm driving at? One can't stop for ever in the lifeboat; one must think of the harbour! Ah, excuse me from talking; to-day nothing will go right."

She jumped up quickly and turned away slightly, and I fancied she wanted to run away. But she stopped still, swinging to and fro her big straw hat, just as I did my cloth cap in the passage when I tried to beg.

I took her hand again, which she gave me without drawing back.

"Are you angry with me?"

"No."

We were happy. The nearer we got to Marne, the more our consciences smote us. What would the old man say? At first he wouldn't hear anything of our early love-making.

"Father will never forget your escapade that night on the Steindamm. He said at the time, after Betty (who brought

40

the invitation to the concert) had gone, 'A man who plays the fool like this is capable of anything.' "

We trembled in our skins owing to my worthlessness. To console ourselves we kissed each other once—perhaps twice— perhaps more than twice.

Back in the Old Home

As I want to say all sorts of things about my life, yet with no intention of writing a love-story, I will end the Marne chapter. I soon left the place and gave up tramping. I thought more of the future, and was determined within a reasonable time to make a home and found a family with the happy girl from Marne. The old man—I am anticipating events by several years—was ultimately reconciled. After finding a billet that could be considered reasonably fixed in Marburg, arrangements for our marriage were discussed.

Among the companions of my young days in Marne, besides Gustavus Wabersky from Schwiebus, who ten years later edited the Hamburg *Echo,* was Fritz Lesche, whose colleague I was later on for many years in the Reichstag. The three of us were kindly disposed to each other in our young days. In the end no one of us came to grief, although there was not at that time any temperance movement through which we might have been made aware of the right way to go.

I had finally to go back home to try to get off military service, for there was a prospect of my being excused on my mother's representations. As a recruit I was assigned to the infantry of the Guard in Berlin. It was a hard job, but I did actually succeed in getting off as being my mother's sole support.

III

THE PARTY PRESS IN MY EARLY DAYS

WHEN, in spite of the Socialist Law and our pitiable poverty, the attempt was made to establish in Kassel a Social Democratic paper, I was naturally concerned from the very first day. That was in 1886. The printers were two Socialists called Eckert and Niehus. A confectioner's shop was rented for the office at the corner of the Weisser Hof and Artilleriestrasse. The office was divided by a screen into two parts: the compositors' room and the printing press. In front of the screen stood a shop counter. The editors' rooms were fixed up by covering a compositor's board with pasteboard, the scissors got from the counter drawer and a glue-pot from the printing machine. Folding the sheets and the entire work of despatching the papers were done on the counter, and we had our breakfast on it as well. The machine that we turned by hand in turn was hired, and was soon protected from the violence of unauthorized persons by the charming stamp of a Royal Prussian official. Opposite our printing, distributing and editing offices on the far side of the Töpfermarkt, William Pfannkuch ran a cigar shop which didn't pay, and from where he had to circulate information of all sorts from early morning till late at night. If he satisfied the inquirer with his information, it was customary for this "good friend" to get "tick" for a few cigars till the next pay day. The next pay day Pfannkuch only rarely experienced. If his information was insufficient—that is to say, if it did not satisfy the inquirer—the latter would loudly protest, and tell

Pfannkuch that his information was quite as bad as his cigars. Pfannkuch would sometimes dash off an article for our paper in this shop.

As a rule the articles for the *Volksfreund* were taken from the *Vossische Zeitung,* which had also to provide almost all the rest of the matter. Beside *Auntie Voss,* we took in the *Frankfurter Zeitung,* from which we obtained the "special reports" on the Reichstag. Some Social Democratic organs were sent us gratis, but as these mostly took their "special reports" from the papers above mentioned, they were less important to us as sources of information. Our official editor was Henry Zappay, who died subsequently in Brandenburg. As a matter of fact, we all had a finger in the pie. Every single one of us thought himself much cleverer than all the rest put together. The paper was often like the well-known *Arizona Kicker.* Once in the editors' rooms there was a regular row that not unnaturally spread very quickly to the compositors' and printers' rooms. I had witnessed an amusing scene in front of the coach-house of the "Weisser Hof," and composed a local article without writing it out or discussing it. In a peasant's cart lay a drunken woman who was being dragged out amid the jeers of the crowd. Those with her were all in a very exhilarated condition, and the sight was uncommonly entertaining—a living picture by Jan Steen. There was no coarseness at all about the scene. When our chief read this paragraph in the current number he kicked up a row. I was naturally protected against this tyranny by the rest of my colleagues; we sent out for some mugs of beer and sang songs of freedom. We solemnly swore that tyranny had its limits.

In the evening from six to twelve we drank to reconciliation in an inn close by. Next morning we "tossed up" who should take on the editorship, as our chief, so his wife said, must have caught a terrible chill the night before, and she could not get him to move. Bad were those days when no subscriptions or advertisements came to hand. We were, of course, sorry when any friend died and his subscription lapsed, but—truth before all things—every death announcement brought in at least three marks, and we wanted them so badly every day, because the paper for the printing had to be fetched from Messrs. van der Linden & Neubert and paid for in cash. A dead subscriber was in certain circumstances more profitable than a living one. Our sorrow for the departed was considerably mitigated by the fees paid for the announcement. It was not surprising that we craned our necks to see as soon as we could when the office door opened how much there was in the till and whether we should get a few coppers. Only in one place had we unlimited credit; that was in a public house close by, where there was a fine tap of beer. If there was no cash for days together the "proprietor of the Book-printing Establishment" (his colleague bolted after the concern had been going a fortnight) distributed amongst us beer tickets which were good for ten or twenty glasses. One glass or mug $=$ 1 litre, which cost 25 pfennigs at that time. Though the landlord swore that day in day out he made a profit only on beer, and none on food, he nevertheless sometimes gave us meals and cigars for our beer tickets. When we hadn't 15 "groschens" or even five for lubricating oil, no ink and no more beer tickets, and almost our last subscriber had died or bolted, we had a serious consultation with Pfannkuch. It was high time to die with honour and glory as "the victims of Bismarck's disgraceful law against the dangerous efforts of Social Democracy." Without turning a hair, Pfannkuch shoved his hand into a drawer and took out an article that had led to the immediate shutting down of other Party papers. "It's to be hoped you have paper enough to be able to print this article—at least for the police or the National Library."

"Yes, we have enough waste paper." Forty-eight hours later we all appeared punctually in the *Volksfreund* office in great trepidation lest the article might be overlooked by the lordly police and the still more lordly Government; and that we should not have to die with honour and glory, but expire in the ordinary way as drab victims of the grindstone. Then we saw the girl messenger who brought us the *Frankfurter Zeitung* coming across the Square. We breathed again, for this paper contained a telegram according to which the *Volksfreund* in Kassel had been duly prohibited by law, etc., etc. God be praised! Our desire was fulfilled; we had been brutally suppressed. We suitably celebrated the event, and I may say buried the *Volksfreund* well and thoroughly.

As there were no trade tribunals nor many others in existence at the time, we at once formulated to the right quarter in the Town Hall our rightful demands. As there was next to nothing there, we only received a few pfennigs. Before this splendid year in the Social Democratic *Volksfreund,* which I served zealously from the first day to the last, I had been through a bad time in a National Liberal concern—in the Hessian *Morgenzeitung,* that had been energetically run and respected for many years under the editorship of Dr. Friedrich Oetker. After a year with the Social Democrats, I entered the Democratic Independent *Kasseler Zeitung,* whose editor-in-chief was Franz Zwenger, the founder of the *Hessenland.* Here I fared no better than in the other concerns. Franz Zwenger was relieved by a Democratic Swabian called Allgaier, who was closely connected with us Social Democrats, and occasionally went out with us compositors for a glass of beer. One day the owner of the paper disappeared, and we once again stood in the street without a penny to our names.

Happy Years in Marburg

After being rather a long time out of work, I had the choice of Berlin or Marburg. My friends were astonished that I preferred Marburg; but my decision was well considered, and proved to be the right one. I was now in my twenty-fourth year, and had seen a bit of the serious side of life. Moreover, I was not only really young and gay, but worked, if I may say so, quite hard. "If you go to Berlin you'll only be a grain of sand in the desert; if you go to little Marburg you will have a chance of improving your mind." The latter seemed the better course. I worked in Marburg for thirteen full terms, *i.e.* six and a half years. I can say that these were the happiest years of my life. Here I set up a family; here I came to know educated friends, respected professors and good colleagues. When I came to Marburg on 3rd September, 1888, the work I had to do in my line gave me great pleasure: occasional work of really artistic value, almost always painted in the colours of the Students' Corps, as well as scientific theses of the most varied kinds: Ph.D. dissertations from every Faculty, sometimes in uncommonly stiff language, as well as Natural Science, Mathematical and Classical treatises in Greek, Latin, Hebrew, etc. I learnt quickly what I couldn't do. When I could read Greek, without understanding the language, as easily as German, the writings of the Professors, often illegible, gave the most pleasure of all. Ultimately I was considered by some Professors as a successful solver of riddles in barely legible manuscripts.

As no kind of Social Democratic organization existed in Marburg, I at once founded a club with the harmless name of

"Gemütlichkeit." Under this title, as we thought, the police would not suspect anything dangerous to the State. We did all our Party work from this club, wrote and circulated pamphlets and went round agitating on Sundays in our own way in the neighbourhood. The police eventually smelt a rat, and our regular meetings were placed under the surveillance of a policeman. This policeman, a Berliner with a large family, as all Marburg was aware, knew every one of us, as he came to our regular table in the inn on the Hirschberg, the landlord of which was Konrad Müller. Of course he knew very soon what we were up to, but he observed a benevolent neutrality and noticed nothing. One evening while we had been discussing an article in the *Neue Zeit* he had gone to sleep—and no wonder. Waking up about midnight, when a consumptive tailor was holding forth on Hegel's philosophy; Policeman Schulze smote on the table with his fist and asked whether this twaddle was ever going to end, adding that if we were not soon coming to the convivial part of the entertainment he was off. We naturally at once adopted his suggestion. Schulze stopped on and played "skat" with the Hegelian philosopher.

In Marburg I made the acquaintance of Henry Lauer, a rich and well-known landowner in Niederwalgern, who openly declared himself a Social Democrat and was a candidate for the Reichstag. Lauer had been for many years in America, and when advanced in years had had to take over the family estate. For a time I went to see Lauer every Sunday, and there met the most remarkable people. His house was the most hospitable in all Hesse. Whoever entered his house was always invited to take pot luck at all times, morning, noon or night. I wrote the broadsheets which we had printed in Kassel, and distributed them conscientiously. Lauer had a game leg owing to some accident, and this compelled him to

47

walk with a stick. He was about seventy years old, but his face bore the ruddy flush of youth; he had bright blue eyes, a magnificent crop of white hair on his head and an equally magnificent beard. A more sympathetic man than this old Hessian landowner one could hardly imagine. In Marburg I came into close contact with the Radical Professor Stengel, the modern language scholar, and later a member of the Reichstag. But he was "fed up" with Marburg, as was also Schücking, the Democratic Law Tutor and member of the Reichstag. Invaluable to me was the acquaintance, let us rather say the friendship, I made in Marburg with Paul Bader and Kurt Eisner. These two men published the *Hessische Landeszeitung,* then engaged in a violent campaign against the Anti-Semites, led by Dr. Otto Böckel in Hesse. Neither of them was a Social Democrat when I knew them. Eisner would have nothing to do with class warfare. But gradually a change was coming over them that was neither fitful nor reactionary, but based on fixed principles of real knowledge and accurate observation of the entire political world and its economic development. I have much to thank these two men for, for they introduced me to subjects which had hitherto been as good as unknown to me: they opened to me the gate of literature and roused my taste for many kinds of fine arts. At the time I was reading Gerhart Hauptmann's "Weavers," and was pleased to find a perfectly impossible stage direction there. Hauptmann is describing the one-armed weaver Hilse, and later on asks the wretched man to fold his hands. Eisner advised me to tell Hauptmann of my discovery, but I did not do so, as I thought it presumptuous.

On day William Liebknecht inquired of me whether Eisner would be willing to do work for the *Vorwärts.* Eisner did not think twice about it. I had already carefully sounded him when, to my surprise, I received a message from Liebknecht telling me that Eisner had decided to enter the editorial office of the *Vorwärts*. Bader subsequently edited the Magdeburg *Volksstimme*. Later on in a letter Liebknecht was loud in his praise of his new colleague Eisner, and blessed the day when he travelled with me from Giessen to Marburg to make his acquaintance. It was always a mystery to us that Eisner, a man of fine intellect, could come to such grief politically in the course of the War—especially after the collapse, as his friends saw with blank amazement. I got to know through Eisner the distinguished philosopher, Professor Hermann Cohen. I attended his lectures when I became an editor in Giessen.

In Marburg I was, up to the repeal of the Socialist Law, President of the political club mentioned above, and till my going to Giessen, District Chairman of the German Printers' Union and Vice-President of the General Sick Fund. *Some* position! These offices, however, did not give me much to do, so I could pursue my studies. I was specially studying political economy and history. I was occasionally writing for Social Democratic papers, and regularly for the *Volksblatt,* now re-started with my assistance. The *Hessische Landeszeitung* also printed many of my contributions. My chief gave me a free hand in conducting the paper. He had convinced himself that he was not doing badly with me and my colleagues, who loyally stuck by me. Ultimately I was persuaded by the eloquence of Dr. Edward David, the adored Social Democrat, at the time a master at the Giessen Gymnasium, to take over the editorship of the *Mitteldeutsche Sonntagszeitung,* and when I told my chief that I intended leaving Kassel in order to place all my energies at the disposal of my Party, he, though a National Liberal, actually cried bitterly.

IV

IN THE SERVICE OF THE PARTY

FROM the official list of wages and salaries paid by the organization in the 'nineties it appeared that I was the highest-paid compositor in the whole of Hesse-Nassau (30 marks a week, my Marburg pay). Frankfurt newspaper compositors on piecework earned, naturally, considerably more. Perhaps what those 30 marks meant will be to a certain extent clear if I state the rent I paid for my flat. I lived on the third floor of No. 18 Zwischenhausen, a street running parallel to the much-lauded Ketzerbach. I had one parlour, two bedrooms, a kitchen, cellar and boxroom, and paid 13 marks, 50 pfennigs a month. This "fat screw" ceased when I settled in Giessen and entered the service of the Party, for in Giessen I had to be content with a monthly salary of 120 marks. Unfortunately, no allowance was made for my having to pay more taxes and considerably more rent in Giessen through living in the Grand Duchy of Hesse. The house rent was bigger because I had to provide accommodation for the offices of the paper and pay out of my wretched salary for fuel, light and cleaning. It came very hard on my wife that of the 120 marks only 80 could be relied upon. This amount per month was guaranteed by the Party Executive. The deficit of 40 marks I was to get out of the paper, apart from the costs of printing and distribution. The prospect was therefore not specially bright when I started work at Giessen.

I may incidentally mention that the notorious **Prison Act** was seriously being prepared as a substitute for the Socialist laws. However, I was desperately keen to go into harness. It would have been child's play to run the weekly paper if the entire work could have been done in one or two days and if the paper had been printed in Giessen. The printing, however, was done in Frankfurt-am-Main. According to contract, all matter from day to day had to be sent in fixed quantities. It was printed on Thursdays and delivered from Giessen on Fridays, so that every district should have the paper on Saturdays. Printing on Thursday naturally meant that work on the paper had to end on Wednesdays. The hardest thing to do was to reserve as much space as possible for the Wednesday, so that the latest news might be given in the political "outlook." At first the awkward methods of running the paper were very tiring to me, especially as I could not be away from Giessen except from Saturday to Sunday. For my business in Upper Hesse was very important, as I very soon noticed. In the shortest space of time I was maid of all work, with less prospect of getting high wages, but my treatment by my colleagues was really most friendly and good. I was the editor, distributor, Press and Party secretary, advertisement "tout" and treasurer (otherwise I should never have got together those 40 marks per month).

I wrote all the electioneering leaflets and set them up in type if they had to be ready over-night in Giessen; I helped to fold them and—what was the chief thing—personally distributed them, mainly among distant villages where the Party had not yet got a footing. I would put on my knapsack, jump on my bicycle and treadle away from place to place.

As there was no law against meetings in Hesse and the country knew no restrictions beyond those of common law,

51

a preliminary announcement of a meeting was not necessary.
I could therefore get the town-crier to give notice of a meeting in any village, other things being favourable, for the same
evening. In this way I held hundreds of meetings in Upper
Hesse from 1895 to 1900. I had no lack of work to do in
Giessen, as I was very soon put forward as a candidate at
every election, whether for the Town Council, the Hessian
Diet or the Reichstag. I was a favoured being in the matter
of defeats. Probably no other Social Democrat in Germany
has been defeated so often and so continuously within a period
of five years, including those at second ballots and those running two candidates of the same party. But at that time I was
not to be daunted; I talked till my tongue ached and wrote
till my fingers were stiff. We had to develop a skill in saving
money that was quite remarkable. Some accounts of the year
1895 that lie before me remind me of the fact most unmistakably. My colleague, William Hugo of Eschwege, who was
very well acquainted with country conditions and could make
an incisive speech, helped me for a week at a Reichstag election. The following amounts were paid him:

	Marks
Allowance for railway tickets, fourth class	18.05
Reimbursement for bill-sticking at Rüddinghausen	0.50
Board and lodging for eight days, at 6 marks a day	48.
Allowance for past services	15.
Marks	81.55

Hugo's work began on a Sunday and ended on the evening
of the following Sunday. He had spoken at eleven meetings
within the week. Twice he had to walk all night because they
refused to give him a bed; once he was thrown out of the
public-house after the meeting, and once he was "hammered"
during the meeting. We who regularly ate the bread of the

Party were naturally not so well paid as outside reporters like Hugo. As we should have our meals at home, only railway expenses and allowances for lodging were paid. I have before me a record according to which I held twenty-nine meetings successively at a by-election for the Reichstag in 1896. For travelling expenses 28 marks 20 pf. were paid; for twenty-seven nights' lodgings 30 marks 30 pf. I must have been splendidly housed in Effolderbach at the time, for the night's lodging cost 2 marks. For the two fights and torn shirt collars no special allowance was to be paid. Although it was a hard matter to find the right place where we could speak, so quick were we sometimes in our movements that we were out of the place almost as soon as we set foot in it, though there were as yet no aeroplanes.

Propaganda among the Peasants

The *Mitteldeutsche Sonntagszeitung* had been started by Dr. David in 1894 for the express purpose of interesting the country population in the cause of Social Democracy, especially the farmers. David, supported at first by Simon Katzenstein, had edited the paper with this in view in a truly ideal way. His thorough study of agricultural questions, his knowledge of Socialist traditions and his outstanding gifts as a teacher fitted him for his job. David's position as a schoolmaster at the Gymnasium became finally untenable, because he publicly declared himself a Socialist and the responsible editor of the paper he had started. How much he was appreciated by his Head Master, Professor Schiller, an eminent figure in the scholastic profession, is evidenced by the fact that Schiller always referred parents, when asking advice about their sons missing their removes, to Dr. David long after he had resigned his mastership and gone over entirely to the Social Democratic

53

Party. To run the *Mitteldeutsche Sonntagszeitung* as David had begun was for me an impossible task, for I could not rely on any pedagogic gifts nor had I any special knowledge of agricultural conditions, but I "sat tight," and in a short time had highly successful discussions with Anti-Semite agitators at village meetings. The success of the *Mitteldeutsche Sonntagszeitung* and the agricultural propaganda in their spheres of influence was unmistakable. Herr von Gerlach and the Rev. Frederick Naumann, with whom I often crossed swords, not only wrote in 1898 in the *Politische Wochenblatt* most appreciatively about the editing of the *Mitteldeutsche Sonntagszeitung,* but also gave me great credit for considerable knowledge of the agricultural problem. From week to week I was becoming an ever-increasing nuisance to the Anti-Semites, for they could hardly hold a single meeting without having a row with me. I followed them from village to village, not caring in the least who their referee might be, whether he was Philip Köhler, Zimmermann, Bindewald, Hirschel, Pickenbach, Ahlwardt, Boeckel, Liebermann, Werner-Hersfeld, or anyone else. The longer the fight lasted the more bitter the gentlemen became. But I can't have done so badly, for they took to announcing by the town-crier the meetings they intended holding only just before they were timed to commence, so that people from Giessen could no longer turn up in time. As the Anti-Semites could get any room they wanted at any time and season, their little game became perfectly obvious. As soon as I was sure of my ground on the small freeholder problems, and was able to explain clearly the differences existing between the big landed proprietor and the small fry, with special reference to the incidence of taxation, Köhler and Hirschel turned up together as referees. On turning over the old copies of the *Mittel-*

deutsche Sonntagszeitung I have come across, among other instances of our battles in those days, a letter written by me which I will quote, but I must state this before I do so. While I went to every Anti-Semite meeting, the Anti-Semites only came to me when they were compelled to do so. All Social Democratic meetings, previously fixed, were advertised in the *Mitteldeutsche Sonntagszeitung* and in other local papers, and free speech was guaranteed. Prior to the Reichstag elections in 1898 we knocked out according to all rules of the game the Anti-Semite Mayor of Langsdorf, who was opposing me. I spoke in all the bigger villages near Langsdorf, and sent Köhler himself the announcements of every meeting along with a special invitation requesting his presence. We gave notice weeks beforehand of one meeting in Langsdorf itself, and publicly challenged him to attend, as it was to be held in his own village. The letter already mentioned has this object in view, and ran thus:

"MEN OF LANGSDORF,

"You state that Köhler, a member of the Reichstag, did not come to our meeting in Lich because he didn't dare to stand up against an opponent alone and could not get anyone to help him. Our previous experiences support your statement. To give Köhler, your member, every possible opportunity of getting timely assistance, we send you word to-day that we shall hold a meeting next Sunday in Langsdorf. We trust that Köhler and at least one of his supporters will be present."

Anti-Semite Abuse

Köhler would have forfeited everyone's respect had he been absent from this meeting. He got Hirschel, member of the Reichstag, to come and support him. A long account of the

55

meeting appeared in the *Mitteldeutsche Sonntagszeitung* (20th Nov., 1898). According to this, the two Anti-Semites had a bad time. In the Marburg *Hessische Landeszeitung,* there appeared a report, a column long, of the meeting, that caused the greatest sensation everywhere, being written in the Upper Hessian dialect and obviously composed by someone in Langsdorf. It stated how the Anti-Semites had been forced to come directly by the *Mitteldeutsche Sonntagszeitung,* and then continued:

". . . Ean he (Köhler) hott sich wohrhafdig ean (Redestütze) ohg'schaffd. Wer warsch? D's Hirschelche voh Offenbach. Mir glaabte juo: earmer Scheidemann awweil beaste verlor'n, etzt hummse däch. Oawwer was hare mir ins v'rreachelt; dessi' oss'n G'witterhond, do kammer d'r Deuwel off'm flache Feald met fange. Mir mahnt g'rad, der hätt e Schwätzmeaschin gefreasse. Aich glaawe, der ioss freuer emmol balwirer geweast, so horre se ingesääft. . . ." [1]

The rage of the discomfited was put clearly enough in their own paper. The editor of the *Hessische Landeszeitung,* Paul Bader, who was then the candidate of the Democratic citizens and peasants in the constituency of Marburg-Kirchhain-Frankenberg-Völh, had simultaneously a collision with Hirschel at a meeting. The latter got his own back over it by soundly abusing Bader in his paper: "Arrant deceiver of the people, the paid agent is unblushing enough, a stray Pomeranian. Bader, the deceiver of the people, lied and slandered. Bader with his Pomeranian yap," etc., etc., etc.

[1] And upon my word Köhler did get a backer. Who was he? Why, little Hirschel from Offenbach. We thought, "Poor Scheidemann, now you're done for, they've got you now." But what a mistake we made! He is one of those coursing dogs that could run down the devil in the open. One might think he had swallowed a talking-machine. I think he was once upon a time a barber; he talked them over all right. (Prof. Fiedler of Oxford, and H.B.M. Consul-General at Frankfort elucidated this passage.)

As a fair sample of the tone of the Anti-Semite organ, printed in Friedberg in Hesse and edited by Architect Hirschel, the following extract may be quoted from the *Mitteldeutsche Sonntagszeitung:* "Scheidemann, the creature who plies his trade in the *Mitteldeutsche Sonntagszeitung;* he blows off the steam of his blood-red soul." The answers in the *Mitteldeutsche Sonntagszeitung* were naturally of the same type: "Köhler has, where normal people keep their tongues, a dishclout." He was mostly spoken of as the "mad Mayor of Langsdorf." A peep into the back numbers of the *Mitteldeutsche Sonntagszeitung* is a source of pure delight every time.

Country Meetings

Younger working men can hardly have a notion of the bitterness we had to encounter in the 'eighties and 'nineties of the last century during our agitation throughout the countryside. How often were we chivvied out of the villages by dogs! When I was on the war-path in Upper Hesse, with Giessen as a centre, Social Democrats were few and far between; the same was the case from Frankfurt as far as the blessed land of Wetterau, where the richest peasants lived. Real roots were rare. How the Hessian peasants abused the poor factory worker who toiled in Frankfurt or Giessen but lived in one of the flourishing villages in Wetterau, because his parents had left him an acre or two! In one of these villages I had persuaded a landlord, who probably had a sense of humour, to let me have his big room for a Saturday. Though his regular *clientèle* vociferated loudly, he was too much of a man to cancel his promise. He thought, I suppose, that I shouldn't be able to get a word in, and if I did, I should be flying out again five minutes later for a certainty. I summoned the meeting by handbills, which I took round from house to house in the forenoon. I had, of course, to open the meeting myself, as I was the one and only Socialist in this village. At first it seemed quite a handy arrangement that the music platform could only be reached by stairs leading from the yard; later it proved the reverse of handy. The meeting was seething with excitement. The place was more like a smoke-room than a meeting-hall. When I from the rostrum declared the meeting open, I saw below me absolutely nothing but clouds of tobacco smoke and a few smoky oil-lamps. I didn't know if the audience could see me. No matter—a deuce of a shindy broke out at once when the poor peasants heard my opening words. Then I was less nonplussed than later on in life, although I have learnt a thing or two in course of years. At first I let the audience howl, took my beer glass in my hand, and when the first hubbub subsided I shouted down into the room, "Prosit." This impertinence surprised most of the people so much that I could say a few words. "It will be no use talking to-night about land-sharing —that I see clearly already." Hundreds began booing. I went on: "You have all heard already that the Social Democrats want you to have your share of the land." Numerous interruptions; but I noticed quite distinctly that many were curious and wanted to listen. "If any sharing is to come about, most of you must get more land, for the richest farmers in this village have more than all the rest put together." A few louts continued to shout so loudly that I had to stop sometimes, but in this respect I have attended worse meetings. The success of the rash venture lay in the fact that I had aroused curiosity and doubts. "If all Social Democrats look like *him,* then it's all lies about their having their shirt tails coming through their trousers, and no one either has seen a brandy flask sticking out of the pockets of these gents." I was so

58

sure of my ground that a leaflet we were shortly to circulate in this village was, I felt, certain to be read. When I had finished my speech, which was frequently punctuated by interruptions but not once by flying beer-mats, even a few questions were put to me, which I answered most fully, for as long as I answered questions I knew from experience no one would interrupt me. The most unpleasant surprise awaited me when I was about to leave the pulpit or the music stand. They had barricaded the door, and I was literally a prisoner. I did not want to kick up a row at once, and waited till the hall was cleared, but then no one responded to my knocking or my shouts for a long time. At last a servant girl let me out. When I asked the landlord for a bed, he refused. He was man enough to give me the hall, but he wouldn't dare put me up. It was a frosty winter's night, and nearly twelve, and Bad Nauheim was 15 kilometres away; that meant three hours' walking. I lit a cigar, and, merry and bright, started on my journey.

The chances of a debate with my opponents got rarer and rarer, for the National Liberal Professors from Giessen avoided any and every meeting. In a notice in the *Mitteldeutsche Sonntagszeitung* one was requested to 'phone or wire, immediately any opposition meeting was announced. If it were possible by rail, bike or on foot to reach the meeting, our candidate would be punctually on the spot. These battles we fought like sportsmen; we were certainly on the *qui vive* for any opportunity for speaking, as halls for meetings were not placed wholesale at the disposal of our Party. In Giessen we were scarcely able to arrange private meetings in halls of any size up to the end of the 'nineties—hence we always attended every opposition meeting. From 1895 to 1900 only one

59

opposition speaker had spoken in Giessen; with him no discussion was possible, as he only consented to a meeting on condition that no discussion should take place. This speaker was Eugene Richter. His condition came to our knowledge through the managing clerk in the office of Attorney Metz, a member of the Hessian Diet, President of the Independent People's Party, with whom Richter corresponded.

I became very quickly known in the whole of Upper Hesse on account of my public work. In 1896—less than a year since my coming to Giessen—when I was nominated as a candidate in a Reichstag by-election to stand against the Anti-Semite, Philip Köhler, everyone in these parts talked about Langsdorf Peter and Red Peter. This name was given me almost officially. I recollect a report from Vogelsberg, according to which a town-crier is said to have announced: "To-morrow evening at eight Red Peter is speaking in the Golden Angel."

Here are few figures that show distinctly the political progress of the Social Democratic Party in the Giessen-Grünberg-Nidda division in a few years of active agitation. This is the record of votes:

	National Liberals	Independent People's Party	Anti-Semites	Socialists
1887	10,918	7,941	—	387
1890	4,363	5,905	4,566	1,732
1893	4,300	1,883	5,606	2,852
1896	2,442	2,192	4,177	3,371
1898	4,174		4,703	4,577

Opposition Votes 8,877   Socialists 4,577

Specially noteworthy is the decline of the Liberal parties in this constituency. In 1887 they together received 18,859, eleven years later they had lost about 10,000 votes.

The *Mitteldeutsche Sonntagszeitung,* respected everywhere in both parts of Hesse by friend and foe, was edited by me with such robust vigour that it attracted the notice of the entire Party. In course of time I received offers from Dr. Bruno Schönlank, who wanted me on the *Leipziger Volkszeitung;* from Dr. Max Quarck, who ran the *Frankfurter Volksstimme;* Ullrich offered me the paper in Offenbach in case I should seriously think of leaving Giessen; Franz Joseph Ehrhardt wanted me for his province, the Palatinate; my Kassel colleagues repeatedly asked me to return home to take over the *Volksblatt* and become their candidate for the Reichstag. The hardest thing was having to decline the offer of my native town. August Jordan wrote me on 13th November, 1897: "My colleagues are unanimous in asking you to accept nomination as our candidate for the Reichstag for this town. You know the circumstances and are popular amongst all of us. Though you refused at the last interview, it was principally due to your standing for Giessen. That seat is certainly not to be won within the next ten years, whereas you can win Kassel at the next election. Talk it over with your colleagues in Giessen and say yes." The same day Paul John, the editor of our *Kasseler Volksblatt,* later District Mayor in Berlin, wrote to me: "Pfannkuch has put us in a very great fix owing to his retirement. You must help, for you are the only possible substitute, and the whole party is solid behind you." The Giessen colleagues refused, and I agreed with them, for I did not want to put them in a hole a year before the ordinary General Election. I therefore declined Kassel. In spite of this, a second nomination was directly forced upon me by the Party Executive —*viz.* for Solingen.

William Liebknecht, whose native town was Giessen, came and saw us every year. Those were times! In old Giessen he knew every house and in Upper Hesse every village. The more I got to know Liebknecht, the more I learnt to appreciate him—though more as a man, a poet and a writer than as a politician. Politically he lived for us who were now in the thick of the fray, partly too much in the past, partly much too much in the dim future. The present appeared to him as it should appear to us—like a temporary difficulty easily overcome. Maybe I wrong him—a thing I wouldn't do for anything in the world, for I loved him sincerely.

Imprisonment Ahead

Before ending this chapter it must be stated that I only escaped imprisonment in Giessen by the skin of my teeth. Having to be absent for several days on a lecturing tour in the Vogelsberg, I had asked a friend who was always ready to help to send off to the Frankfort press the manuscript I had got ready for printing in the *Mitteldeutsche Sonntagszeitung,* arranged in regular quantities for each day. Heaven preserve us from our friends! He wanted to act on his own and impress me with his own ability. One of his friends—Heaven preserve us, etc.!—told him a bit of scandal that more or less involved the whole of the officers in Giessen, and he, inexperienced in the mysteries of the Criminal Code, inserted the whole story in all good faith and from a conviction that he was showing up a terrible "capitalistic and militaristic canker" to the readers of the *Mitteldeutsche Sonntagszeitung.* The officers placed their case in the State Attorney's hands. Things looked bad, because no evidence could be brought forward in support, though no one in Giessen had the slightest doubt of its being true.

Dr. Gutfleisch, the counsel for the defence, was at the time one of the most respected and popular men not only in

Giessen, but throughout Hesse and even beyond. He was considered the most prominent lawyer in Hesse. He had repeatedly refused the Ministry of Justice. Any case Gutfleisch undertook was, to say the least, half won from the start. In the deliberations over the Insurance Act this influential leader of the Liberals of every shade of opinion had taken a line that was not favourable to the working man. As an independent member of the Reichstag and Eugene Richter's closest friend, he was at the time the most-talked-of man in Parliament. I had come up against him at many electioneering meetings, and had attributed to him, above all others, every political sin and reaction in the last ten years, with that egregious kindliness that marked my early years in politics. We knew one another well. In view of the many kind attentions I had shown him at election meetings, which as an educated man he would be bound to appreciate, I went and asked him whether he would defend me in the scandalous and prejudiced action brought against me. The honour awaiting him according to all probability would be so great that he would be content with a moderate fee, and might perhaps let me off altogether. Gutfleisch put off a trip he intended taking and undertook my defence, and conducted it brilliantly, as everyone thought he would.

After the acrid and virulent prosecuting counsel had vilified me in the strongest terms and boldly maintained that no meeting was safe from my intrusions, that I wrote the most daring articles for the newspapers and left no one unscathed in God's world, and hoped that decent people might be assured of my absence for three months (the term proposed), Gutfleisch addressed the Court. He described me as I really was and as can be seen clearly in these times: modest and retiring, extremely practicable in political argument, and at the same time so kindly and courteous as to be infectious. "The defending counsel is rather exaggerating." I wanted to interpose, but restrained myself. I wished to prove by my words how right he had been in his estimation of me and how modest I really was. But I held my tongue, mindful of the words that speech is silver and silence is gold. I cast one look at the prosecutor, which made him drop his eyes in shame and tremble inwardly. He was probably seriously debating whether he should withdraw his proposal and ask for a fine. But he hadn't the necessary wit to appreciate fully Gutfleisch's actual words. Perhaps he lacked the courage to acknowledge that he had made a great mistake in his estimation of the accused. Gutfleisch meanwhile, quite unperturbed, continued to describe his client as a truly ideal individual. We could, he said, think ourselves lucky if political strife were conducted everywhere in the same spirit as was shown by the man he had the great honour of defending.

I said secretly to myself that Gutfleisch would require no fee, for he would surely be proud of being able to defend a poor solitary defendant. I went even further in my surmises. No one could suppose that Gutfleisch, if I got imprisonment, would go to gaol in my place; yet it was quite on the cards that he would propose some fine, for he was known to be a rich man, and where we were to get the money from if the case were not dismissed was a real problem to my friends and to me. In the course of Gutfleisch's speech the eyes of the five judges rested admiringly on his client. The State Attorney looked at me with eyes of hatred over the top of his glasses in characteristic fashion. The fellow was not only hateful, but mean; to spare his glasses he looked at me not through them, but over them. Greed is the root of all evil. Shame on this worthy representative of a country of snobs! He had also the impertinence to contradict my honoured and truthful defender. But the latter, metaphorically speaking, gave him an undercut which laid him flat. "I know this worthy fellow-citizen you want to send to prison. I ask for his freedom and acquittal just because I know him. You, Mr. Attorney, do not know him, and only owing to that you want a conviction. The High Court—and this is my firm conviction—will dismiss the case, Mr. Attorney, and give justice to my client." Result 200 marks fine for slander by the Press.

Work in Nuremberg

At the end of 1899 I was asked to come to Nuremberg as chief editor of the *Fränkische Tagespost* through Philip Wiemer, a former member of the Reichstag, not to be confused with Otto Wiemer, the former Progressive and later Independent member of the Reichstag. The job had been advertised, it was true, but it was merely a matter of form. As soon as I sent in my application my appointment was certain, for all the members concerned knew about it. Though my political sphere of work in Giessen was ideal, I had gradually to think more and more of my family. With 120 marks a month I couldn't get along indefinitely. After talking with friends in Giessen I sent in my application, and was accepted. Unfortunately, as I found out too late, Nuremberg was then a hotbed of intrigue of the worst kind, and I soon regretted leaving Giessen. After the death of Grillenberg, whom the Nurembergers idolized, Karl Oertel pretended he was proprietor of the *Fränkische Tagespost,* although it was generally assumed that the paper belonged to the Party, and still does. No comparisons can be made between the conditions prevailing then and now. Twenty-five years have made a vast difference, and conditions generally are normal. Grillenberg had taken great trouble in keeping the *Fränkische*

Post above water during the Socialist Law. Oertel, who in Grillenberg's lifetime was called the "Crown Prince," became his chief's successor in the Reichstag, and wished to be his successor in the Bavarian Diet. Now a state of things began that Nazi Auer described very neatly thus: "Now we are getting human like the other Parties." Oertel, proprietor of the Party paper, member of the Reichstag and member of the Diet? Conrad Hermann, the Party Secretary from Würtemberg, who would have liked to be elected to the Diet, said to his face, "You'll lose the paper." A dead set against Oertel had begun when I arrived in Nuremberg on 1st April, 1900. A few days previously Oertel, a very sick man, had been taken to a lunatic asylum. Two or three days after my coming to Nuremberg he died without my having seen him. My predecessor was Dr. Südekum, to whom Oertel, obviously very ill, had authorized an increase in the editorial expenses of the paper, which were at the time considerable, for the purpose of getting special correspondents in Vienna, Paris and other capitals. Enough soon came to light to show that the paper was being run at a considerable loss. My salary was at once reduced to a ridiculous minimum. The staff consisted of the chief editor, the responsible editor, Gartner, who managed the local business; Heinrich Oehme, already an old man, who managed the Bavarian section in as far as it was not done from Munich by Segitz, the Union's Secretary and member of the Diet; and the local reporter, Westmeyer, who subsequently died in Stuttgart. I took the greatest pains to make it a decent paper in spite of the lack of funds everywhere, but was much too soon required for more frequent "speechifyings" and dragged off to countless meetings. The latter proved to be necessary because of the unheard-of ebullitions

66

of the rival *Fränkische Kurier,* that was then Independent against—yes, against whom, I should like to know—against all and sundry who were suspected of place-hunting. Against me, who had only just reached Nuremberg and wasn't even a Bavarian, and therefore not a voter, and ineligible, two veiled attacks were launched, from which it was concluded that I was seeking election to the Diet. Every day there appeared in the rival papers information about the secret machinations of the Party, also reports of meetings at which only very few of our members were present. The plot thickened; increasing irritability declared itself not only in Nuremberg and Bavaria, but through the whole Party in Germany on account of these proceedings. Dr. Südekum, who in the meantime had become Oertel's successor in the Reichstag and editor-in-chief of the Dresden *Arbeiterzeitung,* wrote me on 22nd December, 1900:

"DEAR SCHEIDEMANN,

"The last notice in the *Kurier* about the meeting in the Café Merk, the onus of which ostensibly you will have to bear, is really outrageous. But as the *Kurier* itself gives the number present as thirty, the rascal who writes for the lying *Kurier* must be ultimately run to earth. It surely can't be difficult to get the names of the thirty people present and sort out the guilty party or parties. This scandal can't continue."

Some incidents made me open my eyes. I discussed them with an old and trusty friend, and on his advice committed to paper these suspicious incidents. This evidence, at first only circumstantial, brought about one day an unequivocal conclusion. The informers of the *Fränkische Kurier* were the President of the S.P.D. (Social Democratic Party in Germany), the chief Party Secretary, and an official treasurer who was on intimate terms with them both. A Court of Inquiry was held under the chairmanship of von Vollmar, at which Gerisch and Pfannkuch were present. Our deluded colleagues who had sinned so grievously were excluded from the Party. The evil genius was the Party Secretary, who had completely deceived, that is to say, convinced the easy-going and credulous President that in the interests of the Party recourse had to be had to these unusual means. The colleague who had thus been so hoodwinked and yet had loyally and honourably served the Party for many years was subsequently pardoned and allowed to re-enter it.

The two representatives of the Party Executive, Gerisch and Pfannkuch, assured me at the time after the inquiry under von Vollmar's chairmanship just referred to, that they had been through many painful scenes in their active life, but anything like this Nuremberg affair was unique and would, it was to be hoped, remain unique for all time. However incredible it may seem, I will state this: many were the reproaches hurled at me from various sides because I had brought about the conviction of the three men concerned. In a rage I wrote to the President of the Party and asked his advice: "Will it be taken amiss in Berlin if I throw up everything here and depart?" I have before me Gerisch's answer in his big, bold handwriting:

"Though I was for a moment under the impression that it would have been better if we, Pfannkuch and I, had been informed beforehand of these things [the details of the cleverly worked attacks in the hostile paper and the difficulties of finding the culprits], I will frankly admit that your conduct must be acknowledged as above reproach. This opinion of mine

68

I have expressed most strongly here in the presence of my colleagues, who were very interested in events at Nuremberg.
"Your friend,

"A. Gerisch."

I was only two years in Nuremberg. At one meeting of the staff Dr. Siegmund Freiherr von Haller zu Hallerstein, who had been for some years a stray dog in the Party but had become at this time a Social Democratic member of the Diet, thanks to the blissful confidence of many colleagues, found fault with all sorts of things connected with the paper because the Labour organ was not sufficiently aristocratic for him, and I immediately seized the fine opportunity and asked the Press committee to release me from my agreement. "You would greatly oblige me if you would assent to my being released from my agreement. I have been repeatedly offered by our colleague Ulrich in Offenbach the position of Managing Director on our Party paper there, a position which in every way corresponds to my wishes and inclinations and renders it possible for me to be more politically active in my constituency (Solingen) than from Nuremberg. I trust my wish will be granted, as you know that the intolerable conditions in Nuremberg have long ago aroused within me the desire of quitting my post. You will not care to keep me in a position that gives me nowhere any satisfaction." As the President of the Press committee, a very intelligent printer employed on the *Fränkische Tagespost,* was occupied, I went next morning to have a personal talk with him. In consequence my wish was granted. The Press committee approved my request and thanked me in a kind letter for my efforts, with which they were "entirely satisfied. We greet you heartily, and wish you in your new post a quieter spot for work than Nuremberg."

The letter was signed "Hans Pfötschler, Secretary to the Press Committee."

My Nuremberg experiences had completely exhausted me. When I left the splendid town of Albrecht Dürer, Hans Sachs and Beckmesser, I had been a member of the Party for almost twenty years. Though I had had to see much political pettiness, I should never have thought it possible that such unsporting incidents as those witnessed in Nuremberg could occur in the Social Democratic Party. The explanation, however, was not too hard to find. The Socialist Law had in many places forced the management of the entire Party movement into very narrow sections. The Nuremberg Workers' Union, sound in body and mind, had a man for its leader whom the whole Party envied them, Karl Grillenberger. However, the conditions must have been unhealthy, because ultimately the whole movement was centred in this one man. A democratic policy was at the time out of the question as well as democratic life within the Party. Only a few of the *élite* were in the confidence of the real leader who towered over all the others, not only in stature—he was a Hun—but still more in intellect. Cliques had been formed that only regarded personal interest and selfish aims, though the natural consequences of this emergency law were felt throughout the whole Empire, even when no state of war existed. Many years after the repeal of the Socialist Law all kinds of coteries were still to be seen, now here, now there, in the Empire. In Nuremberg the slow poison Bismarck spread with his emergency law had been consuming for many years the body of the Party, but finally the worst symptoms of fever were overcome and a fundamental cleansing of the system was commenced. Then began a new revival, significant for the whole

Party, which, though divided in the War, came together again in Nuremberg in 1922.

In Hesse Once More

When I wanted to be transferred from Giessen to Nuremberg at the beginning of 1900, my superiors reproached me bitterly; Ulrich and David were furious. David wrote me in February, 1900, from the Hessian Diet and described to me in the most glowing colours what a great political future lay before me if I would only make up my mind to remain in Hesse. All this could not dissuade me from leaving Hesse. At that time I had to think less of my "brilliant" political future and more of the wretched present and my own family. Three children, with an income of 120 marks per month for five years running—it simply couldn't go on. Hardly had the news of the miserable state of things in Nuremberg become known when Ulrich, the "Red Archduke," wrote to me asking why I exposed myself to such vexations in the "wilds" of Bavaria; I should return to Hesse and take over the editorship of the Party paper in Offenbach. My readers are already aware that I yielded to Ulrich's further inducements. I worked in Offenbach for three years, not only as manager of our Party newspaper, but principally as a speaker in the provinces of Upper Hesse, Rhine Hesse and Starkenburg.

I have many memories of Offenbach, sad and pleasant alike. Ulrich was looked after by an old housekeeper—a priceless old woman, the "Lady" as she was called in Party circles in the whole province of Starkenburg. Everybody in Offenbach and the neighbourhood knew her and she knew them. She mothered Ulrich, the "gracious master"; when he was out of sight she always spoke of him as her child. They were about the same age. From morn till eve she was up and down

71

stairs, fussing round through all the rooms and slanging, in German, French and English, editors, distributors, compositors, the typesetter, the printer and the messenger, and blowing up the advertisers, tradesmen and the butcher and the baker. She swore away quite gaily, and she meant well. The more she slanged anybody the more bountiful she was in her gifts to the "missus," "ma" and "kiddies." She had vast quantities of fruit at all times of the year, which she distributed as consolation prizes, as well as cigars, vegetables, bread and sausages according to the needs of her victims. When one day I incidentally compared her in all innocence to an old dragon, I became her special favourite. Every day she would swear at the "bald head" in the editors' room, but she always brought me some titbit for breakfast as a peace offering. She was a real Lady Bountiful when some enemy of Ulrich's got hauled over the coals in the paper. Then she beamed with joy. One morning on reaching the office we found a great part of the Market Street strewn with straw. Ulrich had been taken ill in the night, and had only dropped off to sleep towards morning. In double quick time she got the straw laid down so that he should not be disturbed by the market carts. Offenbach's uneven pavements were notorious. They had called forth from Frederick Stoltze, the Frankfurt poet, a terrible curse, the end of which, appropriately illustrated, became a byword throughout Hesse. "Plague on thee, Offenbach! The stones you might throw at a dog you rolled into your streets, and you let the dogs go where they liked."

Hesse in the second half of the last century was the freest land in Germany. Petty rows, as in Prussia, were unknown. A lot has been said about this in the chapter on Giessen. In 1904 or 1905 Engelbert Pernerstorffer had consented to attend a meeting in Offenbach. To our great amazement our friend was forbidden to speak; obviously Prussian influence had been at work. The meeting naturally was held notwithstanding, and on the Prussian Day of Atonement, with Ulrich and myself as reporters. As we expected a huge audience, it was arranged that Ulrich should speak in the big hall of the Workers' Union premises and I outside in the open. The crowd was, in fact, enormous. Masses of working men were there not only from Offenbach and the villages near; they had come in their hundreds from "across the stream," from the other side of the Main, from Frankfurt in Prussia. Everyone who didn't want to fast and pray next door in Prussia crossed the border at midday into the "wilds" of Hesse. We made up our minds not to spare the police, and to make them feel very uneasy by publicly announcing that, though they had stopped our friend's mouth, they couldn't bind his legs; that he was stopping amongst us; that all Hesse would sympathize with us in this Prussian outrage, and wherever Prussia was less cock of the walk, duly stigmatize it as a crying scandal. Both in the hall and outside, the Secret Police, who were present in great numbers, got terribly excited by these remarks, which provoked huge delight among the crowd. They were hot on the chase of the "prohibited" Austrian, and were invariably ridiculed when what seemed to them a suspicious character "with a long nose and pointed beard" turned out to be a harmless burgher from Frankfurt or Hanau. Cheers for Pernerstorffer from thousands of throats rent the air every time the police made a false move. These Prussian activities were only once, and never again, tolerated by the Government of Hesse. The success of this Social Democratic demonstration was enormous. Numbers of new members joined the Party and hundreds of new subscribers to the paper were obtained. With all our dear friend's eloquence, he could not have gained the

73

success with his best speech that the Prussians had achieved by their prohibition. The political struggle in Offenbach was conducted by the foes of the S.P.D. with such personal feeling and lying as had never been known before anywhere in the Empire. Slander and misrepresentations, such as were practised rather more generally in the Empire for the first time before the Election of 1907, were rife in Offenbach in 1903. Offenbach was doubtless the trial ground of the Empire Union now in process of formation to fight Social Democracy. The *Offenbacher Zeitung* was constantly producing offensive and aggressive articles about Ulrich's private income, and indulged in personal allusions of the worst kind. Ulrich's opponent in 1903 was a Catholic National Liberal doctor, Dr. Jacob Becker of Sprendlingen. He had scarcely entered the lists when infamous suspicions began to appear in the Press about wires being placed across the streets by night to smash up the priceless doctor and his car. The united Citizen Party actually succeeded in winning the old S.D. seat with such nonsense. Their appeal to the lowest instincts was crowned with success —but not for long. The editor of the *Offenbacher Zeitung,* a typical jingo such as we have known dozens of, a certain Anton Beer, disappeared suddenly, for cogent reasons, "in the night and the rain." At the next election the seat was regained by the Social Democrats, and of course held uninterruptedly. This infamous electioneering conducted by the united householders only once came off.

Transferred to Kassel

I had been working nearly three years in Offenbach when one evening Albin Gerisch, a representative of the Party Executive, turned up (very mysteriously) at my place. He wanted to talk to me about a matter he thought just as important as the Solingen affair now concluded (this is to be described later). I held up my hands in horror and said with alarm: "What! Solingen again or something like it? No! No! A thousand times no! Get thee hence, Satan." Gerisch, a good fellow but very solemn, burst out into a hearty laugh—a rare thing with him.

"Don't misunderstand me. It's about a thing that is very important for the Party; another Solingen is not on the 'tapis.' It concerns my own town of Kassel. The Party there is in low water and our paper there the worst the Party possesses. The Executive is prepared to make a great financial sacrifice if you say you're ready to go to Kassel and run the paper."

I asked for an hour to think it over, and then inquired, while we sat over our beer, what the great sacrifice was that the Executive was prepared to make. "Thirty thousand marks," replied Gerisch, "spread over three years. Do you think you can work the paper up?" After a thorough talk it was clear that the whole costs of management, inclusive of editors' salaries, would be covered by the suggested amount for three to four years. Actually this imposing sum was only a flea-bite. The same evening I made a rough calculation, and said I was ready to take over the duty. The job attracted me. From the Main I transferred my home to the Fulda, from Darmhessen to my home in Kassel, joyfully welcomed by my delighted mother and greeted also by colleagues and friends of my youth, with whom I had shared six long years of joy and sorrow and with whom I had fought a bitter fight against reaction in its ugliest, stupidest and most brutal form, *i.e.,* against the Anti-Semites.

The Kassel *Volksblatt* had, as a matter of fact, completely gone to pieces, commercially and editorially. For a long time it had had no proper editor. A man employed in its distribution, an honest carter who understood how to drive his horses very well and in time proved to be an excellent fellow, would cut out the "politics" from another paper and sell to some shady reporters, none of whom could write a sentence properly, the news of the town for a few pence. The news was generally all wrong, like the German in which it was printed. There was quite a "character" among these reporters, who, when there was nothing doing, would invent news. If he found nothing better to do, he would write about horses falling down, dogs being run over, valuable birds flying away or burglars burgling houses that didn't exist. These reports were always saleable, for they were exceedingly cheap and were read with pleasure. For 20 pfennigs you could read about a half a dozen of the most daring robberies and gloat over a round dozen of black eyes or the same number of broken noses. The majority of the subscribers to the *Volksblatt,* according to the ledger, were readers *honoris causa.* After the names of the subscribers who had not paid their subscriptions for more than six months had been crossed out, hardly fifteen hundred remained. Directly those who were more than three months in arrears with their payments were "dunned," the circulation of the paper fell over in a very disconcerting way. The paper had only been preserved from extinction by the intervention of the Executive, which had to pay every fortnight the debts incurred. As it had been thus saved from collapse but not improved or made to stand on its own feet, the Party Executive resolved, as already mentioned, to place at its disposal a rather large amount of money under certain conditions. At my suggestion Johannes Kämpfer from Rottenburg, an energetic young colleague who knew Hesse and Hessians like no other, was secured as business manager, for the business part of the paper had been even worse than the editorial.

In a comparatively short time the paper took a big step forward. In working-men's circles it enjoyed general popularity and found its way among small tradesmen. Besides much other work that I had on my chest—since 1903 I had been a member of the Reichstag and had to take part in private meetings of the local Party associations—I wrote every week "chit-chat" in the Kassel dialect that went well at the start and brought in many readers from the labouring classes. If the Reichstag was sitting, I wrote the political part in Berlin, so that the other editor, Richard Hauschildt, had to do the provincial and local part, as well as arrange the Wolff's Agency telegrams arriving in the morning (these we cut out of the *Frankfurter Zeitung,* morning edition). His chief grievance, as he always complained in writing, was this: "Where am I to put all your 'stuff'? You are sending too much, and I am snowed up with your politics." Compared with the resources that are nowadays at the disposal of an editor the conditions were formerly really pitiable. Never mind! we had one ambition—to improve our paper, and were pleased to see our work appreciated. The greater and more visible my success was, the more bitter became the hostility of our opponents who were all on the "Right." The workers, in so far as they were alive to class consciousness, were on our side. Bolshevism had not yet been discovered and Moscow wire-pullers were not. If anyone had said at the time that German working men could be found who, by renouncing their own personal opinion, would allow themselves to be exploited from Moscow like marionettes, laughter would have been heard from Königsberg to Constance.

The Empire League versus *the Socialists*

Kassel, being a town of petty officials, had quickly become a happy hunting ground for the Empire League in its fight against Socialism. Lieut.-General von Liebert was at the head of the League. The Kassel local branch was directed by Lieut.-General von d. Böckh, a politically narrow-minded martinet. In the Kaiser's day every official was in a very dependent position, and the lists of enrolment in the League were managed by the Government offices. The head of the office would sign on, and who would have dared to refuse to do ditto among the subordinate officials! It was repeatedly declared that Kassel was the strongest local branch of the League of "Lies," as the association was invariably called among the working classes. It was said to be more than five thousand strong. The League was extraordinarily active. Its *modus operandi* at election time was this. All civilians had to pledge their word to vote against the Social Democratic candidate at every second ballot in all circumstances. In return for this pledge all civilians at a general election would enjoy the support of the League, would receive all election literature, pamphlets, leaflets, etc., and could hold meetings opposing Socialism. At the League meetings any sort of lie could be told if it brought Social Democracy under suspicion, and free speech was naturally "taboo."

The members of the League, being perpetually attacked in the *Volksblatt,* on one occasion announced a meeting with an intimation that free speech would be permitted. We had heard *sub rosa* from one of the many "impressed" members that free speech was certainly mentioned, but that as five or six of their own members were down to speak, the meeting would have to end at closing time. We warned the workers not to give any money to the League, that they would do better to stop at home and not be made fools of. Next day the League issued a notice in every paper in the town to the workers: "Your leaders are afraid." We then appealed to our own well-disciplined members, and ordered that no one should attend the meeting, adding that their leaders, as they well knew, were not afraid. That was all. Except myself not a single worker was at the meeting. On my entering the crowded hall, great excitement ensued. What ghastly impertinence! I took a seat in the middle of the hall, though it had been reserved for somebody else, just as if my arrival had been expected!

The chairman opened the meeting in a pompous speech that he considered patriotic, and then called upon the senior *rapporteur*, Mr. So-and-So. After this speaker had bored the meeting for an hour with his stories of the Colonies, the second speaker was called upon, Herr Katzenbuckel from Berlin. All through the first speech the eyes of the entire audience (a thousand strong) had been fixed on me rather than on the platform, and after I had burst out laughing at a fatuous remark of orator number two, their attention was intensified and they hardly took their eyes off me. Obviously they were being bored to death. A third speaker then got up, followed by a fourth, who was to speak on the Labour question. This speech made everybody yawn and actually murmur. When the latter was about to finish, I noticed the chairman making preparations to close the meeting. He was sipping lemonade, which was probably as weak as the speeches, fidgeted about in his chair, wiping his warrior's head with his handkerchief and then his bristly moustache. To be sure the worst was over, for me at any rate. The referee hurried over the last part of his speech; he had exhausted the subject. Then the Lieut.-

79

General got up and thanked the speakers for their instructive discourses, and was preparing for his patriotic peroration, which always ended, as everybody knew, with three cheers for His Majesty, our most gracious King and Governor. But before the cheering started I hurried through the hall and loudly claimed the right to speak, as it had been expressly stated that free speech would be permitted at the meeting. The Lieut.-General wanted to protest, but the whole meeting demanded that I should speak, and a thousand people were nearly bursting with curiosity. "What shall we see when he gets to work?"

"Agreed! Scheidemann may speak, but only for ten minutes."

I was already alongside him, and started: "After Böckh —this is here, I gather, the usual form of address—has allowed me to speak for ten minutes, I shall have to prove that, in certain circumstances, more can be said in ten minutes by one man than can be said in a hundred and fifty by four or five." I was assured later that Böckh turned as white as a sheet at my first few words. It was only right to remind him of his discourteous behaviour. I naturally didn't waste many words over the "instructive speeches." In two sentences I banished them from the minds of the audience like a man cleaning a blackboard with a sponge. Then I touched on class differences, knowing that I had men in front of me whom one had to begin on the alphabet. On the left sat dense masses of skilled and unskilled workers; on the left a small group of employers who got rich from the work of others and owed their political influence to the indifference and slackness of these same people, *viz.* the working classes. "Geese and fowls are not so foolish as to trust their luck to foxes. But you, working men, small tradesmen and Government clerks, run

about after retired generals and active employers in the belief
that your interests are in good hands. . . . Where is the
worker who ruins his own trade? He doesn't exist. The
small shoemaker has his livelihood taken from him by the
shoe factory. Who is behind the factory? The Capitalist
. . . and there's the unpatriotic attitude of the Social Democrat! It's false. Where does the saying 'bricks without
straw' come from? From the bosom friends of your chairman, the Conservatives. For purely patriotic motives they
would like to vote the ships, said to be indispensable to the
Fatherland, but only if they can buy their corn at a fixed minimum price for a long period and are given the right of de-
frauding the people by sticking up the price of bread. That's
what the world calls patriotism."

I was in the finest form. The audience listened attentively
as to a stimulating sermon, when the chairman cut me short
by ringing his bell, telling me that the ten minutes were up
and the meeting must close, of course with the final shout
of "Long live the Kaiser and King."

For days together this meeting was talked about in the
capital of petty tradesmen and discussed in every public house,
and not unfavourably to Germany's Social Democratic Party.

The Social Democrats were making headway in Hesse.
Only interrupted by my two years in Nuremberg I had steadfastly continued the fight from 1888 onwards against the
Anti-Semites. Kassel, as the last fortress of this crying shame
against civilization, must be won, and won for Social Democracy. That was our programme, and we went through
with it. At the elections in the winter of 1906-1907 the blow
was not dealt. One year of intensive work was not sufficient
to capture the fortress. But in 1912, after we had scotched
the disease by practical work, especially in the Town Coun-

cil, to which I had been elected with a few other Social Democrats, it was toppling down. With the Anti-Semite Lattmann, the last Anti-Semite departed from the Reichstag, and our candidate, Hüttmann of Frankfurt-am-Main, took his place in the Parliament of the Empire.

In the elections of 1903 3,010,800 votes were given in the Empire for Social Democracy; in 1907, 3,258,000; in 1912, 4,250,000. My stay in Kassel did not last over six years. At the Party Conference in Jena in 1911 I was elected to the Executive Committee.

V

IN THE GOVERNMENT OF THE PARTY

WHEN the Party Conference assembled in 1911 in Jena, the Obscurantists were making a great noise in Germany. Prussianized Germany was a great deal too free for them. The "Black-blue" Block ruled in the Reichstag with a steady majority. The Evangelical "blue" Junkers and big industrialists were united with the "black" Catholic clerical party—a state of things dear to the heart of the reactionist. The Kaiser was able to say to his sheep-like people with such a majority in Parliament: "I will lead you forward to glorious times." The Labour movement was deceived and hampered by the Government, especially in Prussia, in the pettiest way. The judges gave cruel sentences. In less than six months four well-known Social Democrats had been collectively condemned to twenty-three months' imprisonment for alleged high treason (*lèse majesté*), and yet the existing laws against Social Democracy were not effective, according to the Conservative Press. New special legislation was in the wind. Owing to the brutality of the "Royal and Imperial" police towards workmen on strike, rows had occurred in Moabit. "This is the beginning of revolution." "Red *pétroleuses* have thrown burning lamps at the police." Thus did the Conservative organs shriek day by day and week by week.

Some street demonstrations for equal franchise in Prussia had scared the sleepy readers of the "National" papers who wanted their "Royal Prussian" repose. Then came the cry,

"Help! Help against Social Democracy." What the Emperor thought about it is perfectly plain from the accounts that his old Court Marshal, Freiherr von Zedlitz-Trützschler, has written in his book "Twelve Years at the German Imperial Court." Unscrupulous extremists had inveighed against the Workers' Unions, and His Majesty rejoined, "Yes, before long there will have to be some blood-letting plus a little shooting at intervals." When the Berlin tramway men went on strike in 1900, which certainly did lead to some outbreaks on Dönhoff Square owing to the tactless conduct of the police, the Kaiser wired to the Headquarters of the Corps of Guards: "I expect, if the troops are called out, at least five hundred people to bite the dust."

When the delegates of the S.P.D. met at Jena the Party numbered nearly 850,000 regular paying members. Within a year more than 116,000 new members were enrolled. An unprecedented desire for battle was rife among the delegates —only a few months more, and then would come the great reckoning with the "Black-blues." It therefore behooved us to make every preparation and fill our arsenals. In place of the late Paul Singer, the Königsberg lawyer, Hugo Haase, was elected President. Singer had been Vice-President of the Party with Bebel. Ebert, Gerisch, Molkenbuhr, H. Müller and Pfannkuch were re-elected Secretaries. Otto Braun and Scheidemann were elected as additional Secretaries. Louise Zietz was co-opted on the Executive for the women.

My election to the Executive necessitated another move from Kassel to Berlin. My wife, who had now to change her home for the seventh time with bag and baggage, began to jest about getting a caravan, as then we should be spared packing and unpacking so often.

The work of the Central Office of the S.P.D. was a great
disappointment for me, in spite of the friendly relations prevailing between our comrades and fighting men in the Party.
I had had a free hand up to now in all my jobs, although I
had as editor to work with the Press Committee. I never
had any difficulties with them; on the contrary, the committee
men were always my best allies, and we stuck together through
thick and thin. The ready pen of the editor I now had to
drop for official "dossiers." To begin with, I worked with
Ebert and Müller in the same room. When a caller discussed
matters with one of us, the other two had to hold their tongues.
And what did the dossiers conceal? What did the callers
discuss? Things of little importance that did not interest
me at all; naturally I had to grin and bear all sorts of weari-
some complaints and this unending office work. I admired
the patience and industry of my colleagues, who showed me
a good example. With amazing earnestness Ebert announced
in a full sitting of the Executive that the business manager,
So-and-So, in Dortal had brought new curtains for his office;
he would not allow these high-handed acts, and the Executive was involved in these transactions. Naturally! An addition of 30 marks to his salary was approved for an employee
in the printing works at Westfälingen that had been erected
by the help of the Executive. In Erdburg an Arbitration
Court was to sit for which we had to appoint a chairman.
Good Lord! I asked myself, who had never had anything to
do with such things in my life, whether all this was work for
the governing body of a Party a million strong? The school
of the Party belonged to my department, where Dr. Mehring,
Rosa Luxemburg, Heinemann, Stadthagen, H. Schulz, Heinrich Cunow and others were teaching as well as representing
the Executive in the Press Committee of the *Vorwärts*. They

were duties which might in a way be necessary in an emergency. That was all. But I was an editor always and everywhere—the man who dashes off the news at express speed, who talks to thousands of people from day to day and stands in the middle of the whirl of life.

In Müller's place I had once to make certain proposals in a case before an Arbitration Court; it was probably about appointing a chairman. I mentioned the previous facts of the case against the offending member, and decided that the man had been rightly excluded from the Party; we should be glad to be rid of such a man. I was therefore against another inquiry in another Court, for it was a pity to spend any money which we could ill afford for the purpose.

All my friends were greatly amused, and shouted out: "You don't know the regulations of the association. According to them a second hearing must be given if requested." I frankly acknowledged I had never read the regulations, and moreover had no intention of doing so, because they were of no interest to me. It was lucky for me that my colleagues at the time were good fellows and friends, otherwise there would often have been painful scenes.

I had to study the details of a special case of a colleague who had been taken ill suddenly. I had been through the correspondence and put it into one of my portfolios. Some time after there was great excitement in the office because the correspondence with my good friend and colleague X. could not be found. Finally it occurred to a colleague that I had at one time gone into his case. Suddenly three men came into my room, which was the last of a row of rooms shut off by screens: "Philipp, old man, where have you put the correspondence with X.?"

"It's in the portfolio."

"No, it isn't there."

"But of course it is—excuse me just a moment."

I opened my cupboard, fetched out the docket and handed it proudly to one of the clerks. He first looked at the docket and then at me and said: "On it is written the word 'deranged.'"

"Yes. Where on earth could I have put X. else?"

Two years later the whole Party knew that X., whom I had rightly put in the right place, had a screw loose.

As Bebel lived in Switzerland for half the year, and Haase, the other President, was often called off for legal business and prevented from punctually attending the ordinary meetings of the Executive, Ebert was most often in the chair. He was a good man of business, and knew all about what had been done before, as he had been ten years on the Executive. He was an autocrat, in the best sense of the word, in a democratic body. What he wanted done, he got done almost always, though not without a considerable angry rolling of his eyes. Absolutely intolerable to me was the method followed in making appeals and similar announcements. During the eight years of my service on the Party Executive I had to write most of the drafts for political propaganda. A proof was given to every member and every member added his corrections. Possibly this is the only way of procedure in a democratic party, but that does not alter the fact that I was often sick at heart when I saw my own drafts after many hours' discussion in the paper. Our public announcements suffered apparently because they seemed never spontaneously written by one man and were too obviously altered, changed and chopped about by eight or ten men of widely different capacities. Though we got on excellently together, the resolution I had taken in the first year of my service on the Executive, of resigning after two or three years, stood firm, because the whole system of bureaucracy did not appeal to me in the very least. In 1914 I had been for a year in thorough agreement with my friends in Kassel as to when and how I should definitely retire. Then the cursed War broke out, and it was naturally my duty to stick on. In 1917, when we thought, a little prematurely, that the end of the War was appreciably nearer, I had to bind myself at a confidential meeting in Kassel to contest the seat and again take over the chief editorship of the *Volksblatt* as soon as I could. This agreement unfortunately could not be carried out, because the War ended in a way we were far from expecting. I was present when Ebert discussed the question whether he should accept a suitable post on the Central Committee in Hamburg with representatives of our Union after the War. The abominable attacks of all sorts and conditions of Radicals on the Party management, begun before the War and gathering strength during it till things became intolerable, sickened even him of politics.

During the years I was a member of the Executive the only oases in the desert were the Party Conferences, when things were hotly debated and where I had work to do that gave me pleasure.

The Dispute on the Second Ballot Agreement

The allied forces of agitation and organization in the Social Democratic Party were concentrated from 1910 onwards on a fight to a finish with the "Black-blue" Block at the forthcoming Parliamentary elections. In a report laid before the Social Democratic Party in the Reichstag enumerating their grievances, Adolphus Geck wrote thus:

"Scheidemann in his lively manner of speaking described the great responsibility the ruling caste incurred for the financial bankruptcy which was the result of continuous competition in armaments and of an international policy which was still flourishing. An Empire that sacrificed 98 per cent. of its net income to this warlike lunacy, along with the plundering of the working classes by a subtle system of taxation and the sparing of the rich classes, must put up with the few promises of the Government remaining unfulfilled, that had been made to alleviate the bitterest distress, as, for example, in the case of ex-soldiers and regulars. The numerous promises the Prussians have made are like the most brittle china, but the policy that you have pursued is one big basket of broken crocks, a heap of broken pledges and broken honour. . . . The Empire can deny nothing to the ever-greedy Junker, to man's covetousness, effrontery and brutality. Scheidemann indicated the cleansing of the Reichstag from the rule of the Junkers as the next objective, to which the winning of the free vote in Prussia would first and foremost contribute."

Cleansing the Reichstag from the rule of the Junkers! Destruction of the "Black-blue" Block! There was the rub! And I had been allowed to open the lists with a flourish of trumpets: a campaign of agitation that shook the whole Empire began. It was the energy of the Party leaders that pleased me: pamphlets, newspaper articles, meetings, conferences to fan the last flames throughout the provinces. The result was brilliant. This is such an interesting chapter about things in the good old time that dull, dry figures must first speak.

Shortly before the end of 1906 the Reichstag was dissolved for throwing out a vote for Colonies. A wild National electioneering outburst followed, directed against the Social Democrats. As usual, the honest German peasant fell into the trap set by the Nationalists. The number of votes recorded was curiously large; those who usually were too lazy to vote voted this time, and in favour of the National parties. The Social Democrats could command more than eighty-one votes in the dissolved Reichstag; in the new they returned with only forty-three. It seemed extremely deplorable, and gave Prince Bülow an opportunity for saying all sorts of silly things about the setback to Social Democracy—idle words that the author, Privy Councillor Hamann, whose job it was, put into the Chancellor's speech. Figures can prove.

	1903	1907	1912
Votes recorded for Social Democracy ..	3,010,800	3,259,000	4,250,400
Wins at General Election	56	29	64
Number of Second Ballots in which S.P.D. took part	118	90	121
Seats won at Second Ballots	25	14	46
Defeats at Second Ballots	93	76	75
Total number of seats	81	43	110

A casual glance at these figures proves satisfactorily how election results could be "faked" formerly. "Faked" is a nasty word—*corriger la fortune* M. Riccaut de la Marlinière calls such a proceeding in Lessing's play. The S.P.D., it is only too true, returned to the Reichstag in 1907 with only forty-three representatives, and they had left it a few weeks earlier with eighty-one. Yet this in no way meant a setback for the Social Democratic Party. The solution of the riddle is really very simple. Owing to the Party splits in Germany, an absolute majority could not be got for one candidate in many divisions at the General Election. In the 397 constituencies into which the Empire was formerly divided, very many Second Ballots became necessary: 1893, 180; 1898, 187; 1903, 180; 1907, 158. A glance at the above table shows clearly and distinctly how the S.P.D. in 1903 and 1907 had been swindled out of their seats by the burghers' parties at the Second Ballots. In 118 Second Ballots in which they took part in 1903 they only got twenty-five seats, in ninety Second Ballots in 1907 only fourteen. This makes quite plain how the S.P.D. was cheated by the Nationals before Proportional Representation was introduced. After the collapse let us quote one single constituency which may be described as typical: Kassel. In 1907 there were:

Eligible to vote	44,919
Of these voted	39,392
Social Democrats	17,073
Anti-Semites	11,788
United Liberals	9,477
Hessian People's Rights Party	739

Split votes totalled a few hundred.

An absolute majority, *i.e.* more than half the total votes recorded ($39,392 \div 2 + 1 = 19,697$), was attained by no single Party at the General Election. The S.P.D. got together a relative majority with 17,073 votes. The next strongest Party were the Anti-Semites, who won the seat at the Second Ballot, although they polled 5,285 votes less than the Social Democrats polled for their candidate at the General Election. At the Second Ballot the Social Democrats polled 18,050, the Anti-Semites 21,555 votes. As not even a thousand extra votes had been polled for the Social Democrats from the General Election to the Second Ballot, while the Anti-Semites had increased their vote by more than 9,700, it was evident that the "National" Parties and the Anti-Semite Liberals of all sorts and conditions plumped solid for the Anti-Semite. The Progressive People's Party suffered under this corrupt Second Ballot in many constituencies quite as severely as the S.P.D.

A big tactical task lay before the S.P.D. and the genuine

Democrats in the Progressive People's Party before the elections in 1912, the object of which was to prevent if possible the "faking" of the Second Ballots and generally to adopt measures which should oblige both parties to come to a mutual arrangement with regard to the Second Ballots. The table given on page 90 of the election results in 1903, 1907 and 1912 shows clearly enough how advantageous the agreement was. In the Second Ballots the Social Democrats in 1912 got forty-six seats; the success of the Progressive People's Party was relatively much greater. The agreement was naturally at first kept a secret. When it became known in Social Democratic circles many exclaimed vociferously against it. One saw principles in danger. Bebel, who was confronted with a *fait accompli,* had great misgivings. How will the Party Congress pass off? I tried to convince him that the pact was not only prudent, but politically necessary. "I haven't the slightest doubt that the majority of the Congress will agree —I am sure of my ground, and look forward with pleasure to the speech in which I shall justify the agreement." I had been appointed *rapporteur* by the Executive for this part of the agenda. Bebel remained sceptical up to the last; he had seen the most wonderful things happen on Congress days.

The Founding of the Pact

A few sentences from my speech in justification of the agreement on the S.P.D. Congress day in Chemnitz (18th September, 1912), must be repeated here. It should be specially noted that all demonstrations of applause, etc., are omitted, both during and at the end of the speech. Anyone who wants to read the speeches in full, extracts from which are given in this book, must turn to the shorthand reports.

"In no circumstances must we let ourselves be beaten. We

must do all we can to give the people a Parliament that they wish to have. On 12th January we could form a very clear idea of the Reichstag the people wanted, for the voting showed it clearly enough. But what kind of a Reichstag the people would get was quite a different matter. Immediately after the Elections, that resulted in such a triumph for us, the activities of our enemies began with an attempt to 'pinch' as many seats for the Right as possible and to rob the Social Democrats of what the voice of the people had given them, as far as they could. The object of their manœuvres was obvious. The elections were to be conducted on the Three Class system without the Three Class franchise. Now, the efforts of our enemies to pin us to the wall, as in former years, at the Second Ballots, have in the main been defeated; the machinations of the noble lords have failed. I am immodest enough to say that a small part of our success is due to our Executive. Of the 12½ million votes recorded, the Conservatives, Imperialists, Centre and Anti-Semites combined secured 3¾ million—that was 400,000 votes fewer than we alone obtained. In spite of this there was great danger of the 'Black-blue' Coalition returning to the Reichstag with a majority after the Second Ballots! These parties together had numerically, according to the number of votes recorded, a joint claim to 127 seats, but at the General Election had obtained 116. We Social Democrats, on the other hand, had a claim to 138, according to the number of votes received, but had only secured sixty-four. And the Liberals, well, they had got, let us say, about four, with 3½ million votes.

"Now, I ask you, could we be held responsible if the 'Black-blue' Coalition, despite and dead against the expressed voice of the people, returned with a majority to the Reichstag? No, we could not be held responsible. It was our duty to show up the 'fakers' who wanted to do us out of the seats we had got. It was our imperative duty to vindicate the clear voice of the people, as far as possible under the existing law, in the situation at the time.

"We were faced with an extraordinary state of things; we solved the problem by extraordinary expedients. The more clearly it was explained to the masses, the better they would understand and recognize how and why we had to reach a thorough agreement on the Second Ballot question for the maintenance of our principles and for carrying them out. It is utter nonsense perpetually talking about the impotence of the Reichstag. We know it has been impotent with the higher powers, but we know its power among the lower orders. Is the Reichstag really so impotent? The man who says it is immaterial whether seventy or a hundred Social Democrats sit in the Reichstag is no politician at all. Is it immaterial how many Social Democrats sit in the Reichstag? Most certainly not. In the Reichstag many measures of supreme importance have been carried by bare majorities of five to six votes. When the death duties were rejected it really meant that only five more votes were wanted on the Left to get a directly opposite result. In the Second Ballot agreement everything was taken into consideration by the Executive and conscientiously debated in the interests of the Party and the people.

"Naturally we had not the remotest intention of abolishing class distinctions. He would be a fool who attempted it. Our aim is, and will ever be, the realization of Socialism by the victorious Democracy of Labour. Who can say what stern fights are before us on our journey? But we have made up our minds to go on to the end, and are all convinced it will lead us to victory. We have still strong walls to scale and a strong and unscrupulous foe to defeat. Hard struggles are ahead, but the victory that beckons us on will be magnificent. Thus I think we will fight to the finish till we conquer, and

CARICATURE OF SCHEIDEMANN BY HANS LINDLOFF

right willingly we will do so in the consciousness that we are fighting for liberty and equality. So to live is a pleasure!"

In a debate of many hours the Congress discussed all the resolutions relative to this subject, both for and against the agreement, and passed to the order of the day in response to a motion of the *rapporteur* in his speech that wound up the discussion.

The outcome of the meeting was a great triumph for the S.P.D. Executive, which had done the right thing in the difficulty. Bebel and I lodged in the hotel where all the Executive were stopping, occupying an entire floor. He was down with a bad attack of influenza, and had to keep to his bed for several days. When I returned to the hotel after the meeting was over and told him the result, he was overjoyed. "There was an animated discussion, I suppose? Did they give you a warm time?"

"Not in the least! Two Radicals even praised me to the skies."

"Well, I'm anxious to know about that!"

"You shall. Schiller said that I had given him an oratorical treat, and Louis von Hagen even declared that the Executive couldn't have put up anyone better to defend it. I was the 'cutest' of the lot. Well, how do I stand now——"

"Now get out of it! I was already informed, however," said Bebel, chuckling, "you can't have done so badly."

He gave me his hand, adding: "You must really go now, otherwise you'll catch my complaint."

I left the room as proudly as if I had been decorated with the Order of the Dragon (1st class), promising to drink his health.

After Bebel's Death

Bebel had been ailing for a long time when he travelled to Chemnitz in 1912. He had to deliver his last speech from his seat. The swivel seat was tied back tightly by the Party attendant before the sitting began, so that our leader could stand in his place. To be wedged in like this didn't suit Bebel at all; he felt bound hand and foot, in contrast to von Vollmar, who always spoke in this constrained position. But von Vollmar had been almost paralyzed since he had been wounded in the 'seventy campaign, and couldn't stand for long, whereas the lively and excitable Bebel, speaking from a sitting position, fixed in between the arms and the seat, was a painful spectacle for us all. While preparing for his journey to the Jena Congress our leader died in Passug in Switzerland on 13th August, 1913. We had known for years what a state of health he was in, and received reports about his feet and legs swelling, with anxiety and sorrow. When the startling news arrived, all who knew his unique personality, or who were, like us, his personal friends, were thunderstruck. Everybody felt it: now a gap had been made that could never be filled. It is unspeakably snobbish to say that no one is indispensable. To be sure one can find a substitute for everybody and everything. But if we perceive that the noun from "substitute" is "substitution," the scales would fall from our eyes; we would easily understand what the empty words mean—"No one is indispensable; everybody can be replaced, even Bebel." In the War seventy million Germans, men, women and children, had to exist on substitutes for soap, leather, linen, wool, bread, fat and meat. The saying therefore in Germany that everything and everybody can be replaced should only be used with great caution.

Bebel has been so often described by friend and foe that a few words here may suffice. He was an inspiring speaker, who cast a spell over even those of his hearers who could not follow his train of thought. His voice was remarkably clear, sharp and metallic, and as people used to say, he had *metal* in his throat. He had no gift of humour. He would sometimes laugh heartily, really heartily, but earnestness soon assumed the upper hand. I recollect the following incident: In 1904

or 1905 the Alsace wine-growers invited the Reichstag to a
wine-tasting party that was given one evening in the corridors of the Reichstag. The passages were gaily decorated,
set out with tables and chairs. Fooling was naturally indulged
in by members of nearly all parties, especially by the South
Germans. Adolph Geck, the Socialist songster, and other
members of the Party were going to sing the "Sermon of the
Capucines," by Frederick Stoltze, the Frankfurt democratic
poet and *bon viveur*. Enveloped in huge white tablecloths,
borrowed from the restaurant in the Reichstag, covering the
entire body from head to foot, the red Apostles marched in
solemn procession, one behind the other, into the lobby.
Adolph Geck sang with his fine baritone voice the Capucine
hymn, "Hear ye what the wise Paul saith":

> *Paul, he wrote to the Ephesians*
> *Never drink from empty glasses!*
> *Now and ever more, Amen,*
> *That was against the Lord a sin.*
>
> *Wine, so wrote he to the Romans,*
> *Wine tastes always better far,*
> *And water, as mankind doth know,*
> *Does not really taste at all—*
> *This was the Lord's intention quite.*
>
> *Therefore wrote he to Philippi,*
> *Don't be only merely sippers,*
> *In wine there dwelleth veritas,*
> *Truth and naught but truth dwells there.*

The chorus, which was at first only sung by the red Apostles,
was finally taken up by all present at the wine-tasting party,
and ran thus:

98

IN THE GOVERNMENT OF THE PARTY

Hear ye, mark and inwardly digest
What wise Paul hath here confessed.

Bebel had been sitting between thin Junkers and fat Centre-
men, and when he heard of Geck's intention, came running
up to us, begging us to abstain from such foolery. The Apostles were attired in their white cloaks in the present Zeppelin
Room of the Reichstag on the chief landing. Bebel with up-
lifted hands begged us to take no part in the "rag." "Who
knows how it will be taken?"

In the evening Augustus had not a word to say; he was
simply laughed at. He could not be induced to return to the
Great Hall. He stayed in the same room till the Apostles
returned amid tumultuous applause, such as has never greeted
any Reichstag orator either before or since. "How has your
foolery been received?" he cried as the door opened.

"You missed a treat. Be quick and go into the lobby; then
you will see that they are holding their sides with laughter."

It should be expressly stated that the personal relations of
Reichstag members were quite friendly formerly, and continued so till the beginning of the Imperial League's agitation
against Social Democracy. There existed a feeling of mutual
esteem in spite of political differences and really sharp quarrels.
There was frequently quite a pleasant atmosphere of sociability,
for instance, at the reserved tables, and it cannot be seriously
denied that the general level of the Reichstag, though it had
suffered under various types of Anti-Semites, had decidedly
improved up to the arrival of the People's Party and the Communists. The speeches, at any rate the official speeches, of the
Party leaders at full-dress debates were more carefully prepared, and were in consequence more pithy, than many discourses on agriculture, forestry and pasturage which later were

delivered in the House. Compare speeches by Kanitz and Heydebrand with those of Hergt and Westarp, or compare Scholz with Bassermann, just to give a few examples. To determine the difference between the former and later level of the Reichstag, one has only to compare a few speeches on the "order of business" or the "personal statements" from the year 1914, with those of 1927, after the German Nationalists had split into the various camps of the National-Socialist and People's Party members, with the Communists, having quarrelled among themselves, had divided into three camps.

Bebel was such a gifted and skilful Parliamentarian that he naturally could intervene in debate at any time. But he was so conscientious that he prepared his speeches in the most careful way if he had time to do so. When the Party was greatly excited—generally about Morocco, and particularly about Rosa Luxemburg—a member of the Executive wrote to President Bebel, who was staying with his daughter in Switzerland, asking him whether he would not like to come to Berlin. "What are you thinking of? I haven't yet written a line of my speech." That was in the summer, and his speech wasn't wanted till four months later at the earliest.

Other times, other customs! Other times, other possibilities and duties. Parliamentary life in peace time was idyllic compared with the time during and after the War. This must be my justification for comparing the speeches we hear now with those we heard formerly. Bebel would sometimes get excited over things that nowadays we consider trifles. For months and years he would fight for principles that seemed to him, and to us as well, in danger. Let us recollect the fights between him and Bernstein over Revision. But what tiny pebbles these were compared with the huge rocks that the Social Democrats had to roll along both before and after the War. The question has often been asked how Bebel would have acted in the War. Would he have voted for or against the War Credit Bills? I haven't the slightest doubt he would have been in favour of these, because of his views on the Russian "steamroller" question, which he often talked of. Whether he would have gone on voting for them is another question. His decisions on all questions were to the point, but he always had his finger on the pulse of the Party. There were times in the War undoubtedly when it was impossible to say whether the Party as a whole was behind the Executive. Even at the risk of being in a minority the Party Executive acted solely from this point of view: How can we in accordance with our honest convictions, best represent the interests of the country? As the bulk of the German people could not be always informed of the most important facts, any other attitude was impossible.

Men who sit on a Party Executive and have often enough serious duties to perform and still more serious anxieties to bear, are frequently confronted with the problem as to what stands higher—the representation of public opinion or party loyalty that forces us not only to oppose, but also to keep silence. Bebel did not recognize party loyalty in this sense. When the Executive were furiously attacked at a conference in a hot debate, Bebel, the President of the Party, spoke in effect: "If I were not a member of the Executive, I should attack you in quite another way." At the same time everyone knew that he lived most of his time in Switzerland when the Reichstag was not sitting, and therefore could not criticize as he liked the conclusions of the Executive on questions he did not exactly know. On another occasion he even declared his intention of hoisting the standard of rebellion in the Party, should this or that not happen. Such minds are, of course, often brought into conflict with other independent characters, but get their own way with the average or below the average man. It was formerly so, and will presumably still continue till mankind solely consists of firm and highly intelligent men, made in the likeness of God.

Bebel and William Liebknecht, who had fought for ten years side by side, and whom the Socialist Party considered an ideal pair of companions, had been really at loggerheads for ten years before their death. The following scene took place in public between Bebel and Auer, a quick-witted and stalwart member of the Executive. Bebel was speaking about questions of general policy, and rounded on von Vollmar, Auer and others in the most violent way, saying: "*I* haven't begun this time." As soon as Vollmar had spoken, almost the whole of the Press Committee took up a clear and definite position against him; clamour broke out from every corner. A cry of rage arose from the whole Party. Auer said, in his usual witty way in the *Socialist Monatsheft*—the *Neue Zeit* apparently being non-existent for him—that a very trifling incident had been exaggerated into a vital question of policy. ". . . They said the matter arose from a misunderstanding on my part. Bebel, they said, suspected conspiracy. This suspicion was perhaps aroused by letters of mine to Auer [Auer: 'I haven't even read them (*uproar*). In such disputes I always lay them aside.']. I mean several letters I wrote to you four to six weeks ago and provoked by you, and now Auer says he hasn't yet read them (*Hear, hear*). I'm pleased to hear it. I am to waste my valuable time writing to you on an important matter—he told me his views by letter—and you don't read them (*Hear, hear*). As I don't write letters for pleasure, I will in future draw my own conclusions."

When the official minutes of the meeting were read, everyone present at that Dresden meeting must have thought that

serious alterations should be made, especially in Auer's outburst. The words, "I always lay aside all letters in such disputes," were added later for certain. The whole thing acted
like a cold douche. I never knew a man whose characteristics
were so like his facial expression as Bebel's. Half a lion, half
a fox. His broad, massive forehead with a thick mass of hair
on top; then his cunning eyes and a face narrowing almost
to too sharp a point at the chin; it betokened courage, brains
and craft. So was Bebel. So he looked when thousands of
men and women with tearful eyes walked by his open coffin
in Zürich to say farewell for ever to this strange man, who
had been the guide and teacher of millions.

The General Strike Debate in Jena

At the Jena Congress in 1913 I had the honourable duty of
presenting the General Report of the Executive. It meant
that I was to talk about its entire political policy in general
and the question of the General Strike, which had been warmly
supported against the express wishes of the Executive. As
these explanations—in the light of our experiences later on
in the Kapp-Putsch—had great importance in the history of
the Party, a few sentences are given from the Report.

I had drawn attention in the opening words of my speech
to the unscrupulous conduct of the police, judges and even
the Government towards the educational policy of the Party.
It was scandalous to see how efforts of a purely social and
educational kind for our youthful members were suppressed,
and I described how mighty political organizations had been
formed on country walks and at lectures on Schubert and
Beethoven.

"In 1912 we had 574 Juvenile Committees; in 1913, 655.
Subscribers to the *Arbeiter-Jugend* were in 1913, 99,540. The

number of the daily newspapers rose to ninety in 1913, the number of local clubs from 4,827 in 1912 to 4,978 in 1913; the number of pamphlets, etc., circulated amounted to 1,073 millions in 1912, in 1913 to 472 millions; the number of members' meetings in 1912 was 42,241, in 1913 36,393; the number of public meetings in 1912 was 29,685, in 1913, 11,415.

"We were still occupied with our campaign of protest against the agrarian policy of the Government when the Balkan War broke out. The risk of war was approaching. We opposed the war, which was becoming a danger to the civilization of all Western Europe, tooth and nail. The German proletariate has done its whole duty in its fight against Imperialism and the danger of war. The same is true of our comrades in Austria and France.

"The crowning triumph of our whole policy of protest was achieved by the International Congress at Bâle. We were in the midst of a great popular movement which would fill every one of us with joy and pride, when the new Army Bill was brought before the Reichstag. The Jingo politicians tried hard to fan the flame as long as villages were burning and blood was flowing in the Balkans. The Bill was introduced, and a new cry of anger went through the ranks of the German proletariate. Just as we had worked against Imperialism in general, so now in the same spirit the whole of the fighting force of the Party rose against the Bill in particular. Every possible contingency was debated. Finally—and in my opinion at the wrong time—the password was given: a General Strike. The password being given, a remarkable debate followed— a debate, I should like to say, that was by no means edifying as it proceeded, and the results attained cannot afford at any rate much satisfaction. What, then, was the final result of these discussions? All the speakers who had spoken their mind publicly about the General Strike—I neither heard nor read of a single exception—came to this conclusion: at the present moment a General Strike is impossible. We said this to each other in the Executive before the beginning of the debate, and therefore held our tongues, because we said to each other, 'Why should I tell my foe, my deadly foe, what I now cannot do?' We were of opinion that one need not say to his adversary, 'Look here, I have another weapon here; if I use it, you are a dead man. But you can be easy; I can't use it at the present moment.'

"I will be perfectly frank about the attitude of the Executive to this question. The Executive stood by the resolutions passed at Jena and Mannheim. It was then decided, among other things, that 'directly the Executive considered the necessity for a General Strike feasible, it had to put itself in communication with the General Committee of the Unions and take such measures as to ensure the success of the action.' You may rely upon it that the Executive is determined to respect this resolution passed at former Conferences and to act in accordance with it. . . . In describing the movement in Belgium and Sweden, one fact is always forgotten, and an important fact it is, about which we never talk, but which we are bound to consider. Our Belgian and Swedish friends have no need to consult us at all about the intended General Strike—they can begin their strike when they like; they need not come to any understanding with us beforehand. They can enter the fight with the comforting feeling that there is a big brother on the other side of the frontier who will help them if things go wrong. Comrades, we have no big brother on the other side of the frontier. You may have read this: 'Why were no republican demonstrations made when the Tsar, that man of blood, visited Berlin?'

"In previous resolutions at Jena and Mannheim it was stated that the General Strike was not only to be put into force to ward off attempts that threatened our existing rights but, if we could, to get new ones. We supported it absolutely. As things stand in the Empire, the Prussian franchise question is in the first place the only thing on which we can call a General Strike. We took part in the Elections for the Diet and abstained from voting at the General Election. We tried to interest the people in the Diet. Hitherto the people had taken not the slightest interest in the proceedings of this remarkable Parliament. We circulated pamphlets and held meetings throughout Prussia; we witnessed imposing demonstrations in the streets. The work was not wholly in vain. We interested not only the working classes; we also drew the attention of our overlords to conditions that seriously menaced those who refused to give the people their rights. We heard the speech from the Throne in 1908 which announced that electoral reform was one of the most pressing questions of the day. We saw the failure of the Reform of the Franchise in 1910 and the result of the last elections to the Diet. There was, in fact, no prospect of solving the problem on the basis of the Three Class vote; hence the Party resolutions at Jena and Mannheim. We will have a General Strike, but we will hold on to what Bebel said. The General Strike is the *ultima ratio* of Social Democracy. Everything in due time! The class-conscious worker knows that in the hour of stress and need he has to join up with all his body, mind and spirit for the cause he thinks right, and with his whole heart. Those who have talked and written about the masses and the General Strike are mostly those who have the least sympathy with the masses. We know the masses better than those who write revolutionary articles, but with these one can make no mass movement. I can tell you that the resolution, though called 'eyewash' and unsympathetic with the masses, is the result of anxious deliberation not only by the Executive and the Select Committee, but is the product of earnest deliberation by every corporate body in any way concerned. I cannot speak plainer, but I trust that friends will understand me when I say one and all affected by this question are behind us in a General Strike."

The best brains on the Radical side of the House took part in the debate: Dr. Gottschalk (Königsberg), Dr. Rosa Luxemburg, Dr. Karl Liebknecht, Clara Zetkin, Ledebour, the Dutch Professor Pannekook (Bremen), Dr. Laufenberg (Hamburg) and Dr. Louis Frank, the distinguished and wise politician who co-operated with us from the Radical side, but did not endorse the arguments of the *rapporteur,* and finally voted for the resolution of the Executive in consequence. In my concluding words on the General Strike debate I made a direct attack on Rosa Luxemburg. She had described me very ill-naturedly as a red, shock-headed Peter, who hatched a bogey-man in order to scotch him later on. I can solemnly swear I have never hatched a bogey-man. She meant by that, that I had created a difficulty that did not exist, and so had clutched at imaginary straws. It was untrue. Rosa Luxemburg was naturally then as innocent as a virgin—the personification of wisdom, and I was only a male ignoramus, "Thou art like the ghost that thou hast conjured up, not me." "Friend Luxemburg, you said that to me. I will answer you with another quotation from Goethe. 'When wise men speak I'm glad I understand what they say,' and I will add this: 'I am not glad when wise women talk in such a way that no one can understand them.' And just one word more about Rosa's habit of criticizing those who do not see eye to eye with her. I don't pretend to be as wise as Rosa Luxemburg—far be it! I can't be as wise, for you all know I've only been a poor working man who has had to pick up all he knows by consuming the midnight oil, and friend Luxemburg makes merry over this. I wanted to tell you, friend Luxemburg, that you have not only behaved to me in this way, but to other friends as well, yes, even at meetings."

Rosa Luxemburg and her supporters suffered an astonishing defeat. In the actual voting 142 voted for the "Radical" resolution of Rosa Luxemburg and Liebknecht, and 330 for the resolution of the Executive.

VI

ACTIVITY ABROAD

THROUGH my political activities, especially in the Reich-stag, I had become well known abroad. This will be described in a later chapter. Before sitting on the Executive I had been officially invited to many Social Democratic meetings abroad. I had to plough the fields of Switzerland from Lake Constance to Geneva. I spoke inside a fortnight at twelve meetings that were nicely arranged in the following order: Romanshorn, Berne, Appenzell, St. Gallen, Geneva, Zürich, Freiburg, Schaffhausen, Winterthur, etc. I am writing from memory, as I do not possess any notes on this Swiss trip. If the list of places differs at all from what I have written here, it does not alter all the cross-country travelling I had to do. When, on arriving at Zürich, I asked the Party Secretary in alarm about this arrangement, he told me, without turning a hair: "You've a railway season-ticket for a fortnight; so you can travel every day if you like through the whole of Switzerland."

He was a good creature, but by no means on a par with a German Party Secretary who went the length of amusing me with the following amenities. In a university town of 20,000 inhabitants, 2,000 of whom were students, the People's Party ruled the roost. From sixty to seventy regular Social Democrats supported the Secretary. All other parties were also represented. The Secretary hired a huge concert hall in 1914, before the Reichstag Election, with seating accommodation for several thousands, for a public meeting, at which I was down to speak. I agreed to say a few words, though I was under no delusions about the result of the meeting. The meeting had been advertised far and wide by the opponents of my Party—German Nationals, the People's Party, and also Communists—and the hall was crowded, and a host of at least 1,500 men and women were assembled outside. When our general, a Social Democratic Ludendorff, armed with a little bell he could put in his waistcoat pocket, entered the hall with me there was already a deuce of a row going on. For two hours students and Communists shrieked and howled at me. Everything I said was interrupted by a tornado of wild abuse. The meeting, like everything else, at last came to an end. While we were sitting very close to one another I asked the man who arranged the meeting how he had come to get up a meeting of this sort. With only a few Party friends in support he might have known that the town was notoriously reactionary, that could be no secret to a man living in the place. Likewise he should have known that the Communists would come in great numbers from the neighbouring villages. A row was to be foreseen. What was the good of a meeting which the chairman could not control and would certainly do us no good?

"What was the good?" replied the chairman. "I did raise the price for admission! We've done good business for the Party." He was fully of my opinion that he could have done still better business if he had given the audience permission to pelt the speaker with beer mugs.

I took my wife on the Swiss trip so that she might see the beautiful country. She was naturally charmed with the kindness of the Secretary, who had mapped out the tour entirely to suit the local committees, without in the least considering the speaker. Every evening after my lecture I had lively arguments, lasting often till midnight, with all sorts of highly interesting but narrow-minded people. I came across Syndicalists, Teetotalers, Anarchists, Non-smokers, Freethinkers, Cabalists, Radical Socialists, religious fanatics, and Revolutionaries preaching direct action. . . . We returned dead tired to our hotel, to start out again early next morning, so that I could arrive punctually in the evening at the appointed place for fresh sparring matches.

As a member of the German Executive, I, as well as my colleagues, was not only invited to conferences with foreign bands of brothers, but also entrusted with special duties. Thus I went frequently to Vienna, Holland, Belgium, France, Denmark and Sweden. A big propaganda tour in the U.S.A. will be separately described. These trips brought me into very close contact with the active spirits of Democratic Socialism in many European countries. Close ties of friendship bound me and still bind me to most of these men. Where the ties of friendship no longer exist, Death with its cruel hand has severed them. There is no outstanding international Socialist whom I did not get to know in course of time or learn to appreciate. With special pleasure I remember the Paris meetings with Jaurès and Jules Guesde, as well as Edward Vaillant and Camélinat, the two champions of the Commune in 1870, who only saved their heads from the guillotine by flight. Who could have wished for a better guide through the Louvre than Jean Jaurès?

Here, moreover, a little scene was to be enacted. Four of us were in the dome of the Invalides, the resting-place of Napoleon I.: Jean Jaurès, Engelbert Pernerstorffer, the Alsatian Socialist Grumbach and I. No one else was there. Jaurès was telling a story about Napoleon. Grumbach suddenly dug me in the ribs, pointed to a gentleman who had just entered on the far side of the gallery, and whispered to me, "That's surely Bassermann." Right enough, it was Bassermann, the President of the National Liberal Party. I told Jaurès, and naturally got permission to introduce the gentleman, as soon as we met. Bassermann, however, saw us from the other side of the memorial, stuck his nose a trifle more into the air, and walked towards the exit with a swagger that meant to say what a wretched bungler Napoleon was compared with him, the mighty politician. Jaurès smiled, Grumbach chuckled, and Pernerstorffer and I hung our heads in shame. I can vividly remember my many meetings at congresses and demonstrations with the Dutchmen, Troelstra, Vliegen, van Kol, Albarda, Vibaut, etc., and with the Belgians, Vandervelde, de Brouckère and Camille Huysman in Brussels, where the solemn dedication of the Ferrer Memorial made a great impression upon me. I frequently made long lecturing tours through Sweden and Denmark; my last trip was to solicit contributions, during the period of inflation, for the distressed universities and scholars, which actually flowed in in considerable sums. A very close friendship unites me to the Socialists of the Northern Kingdoms—with Müller and Engberg in Stockholm, and Stauning, Borbjerb, I. P. Nielsen, Kiefer and many others in Copenhagen.

An American Propaganda Tour

In the beginning of June, 1913, I was invited by the German Language Federation of the U.S.A. to go on a lecturing tour. It was to be a two months' engagement, inclusive of travelling there and back. As I had long been wishing for a jaunt to America, and the Executive gave its assent without any bother, the matter was soon settled. The tour was to start immediately after the Congress day in Jena.

I travelled from Jena to Berlin, packed my bag and embarked at Bremerhaven. As I went on board the *Crown Princess Cecilia* I felt as I did thirty years before, when I put my knapsack on my back to go into the wide world. A new world in truth opened out before me, coming as I did from the hard battles of political strife. I lived for a week on board this wonderful ship, as it were in the land of Cockaigne. My heart beats quicker when I think of this fine trip and make it all over again in my mind. From jottings made at the time I will give the following extracts:

"There is a continual coming and going on the foredeck. Many hundreds of steerage passengers, mostly Italians and Poles, are crowded together here in a small space. Women are in a considerable majority. The number of children is enormous. Young mothers sit here and there, comforting their sucklings, and looking sadly into the distance. Will the New World give what the Old World has denied the disinherited?

"The longer I look on at this changing scene, the more easily I can determine the origin of these men and women with some degree of accuracy. They all seem to love colour; this confirmed by the glaring shades of their more or less picturesque attire. A few young girls, unmistakably Germans, seem absolutely out of place in this motley crowd. They look out of it in this picture. All seemingly are ceaselessly moving to and fro like the beads of a kaleidoscope. Just at this minute I catch sight of a Pole on the port side with a fat bloater in his hand. Now he is standing on the starboard side near a pretty Italian girl, who is biting into an orange with her fine teeth. It is to be hoped she won't be beguiled by the dirty fellow, for she would be as bad a match for him as the juicy orange would be for the herring that now covers his stubbly moustache with salt.

"The sun has now forced its way through the clouds and everything is bathed in rosy light. A Czech has fetched his concertina from the cabin and plays dance music. What a change this old bellows makes! Ten couples or so are dancing round in step, or rather are trying to.

"More of these fantastic figures have now come on deck from the vasty deep, amidships, blocking the way for the dancers. The polka changes naturally into a comical foxtrot, and the couples try to wriggle their way through. The general merriment increases. It is not only young men and maidens and married women of the same age who are dancing; it is the elderly folk as well—here two young girls are dancing together, there two men who are 'tripping it as they go on the light fantastic toe' in a style never seen before."

All this is taking place on the bows of one of the finest ships that the North German Lloyd speeds across the ocean every week from Bremen to New York, where they arrive as punctually as an express train.

The second-class passengers have comfortably settled down right aft. The whole amidships is reserved for the first class. The first meal in common, of four or five courses, makes us acquainted with our fellow travellers. I had struck, as we say, a lucky patch. I was shown to a table by the chief steward where there was no gloomy guest. The senior medical officer sat at the head.

The first night was over and we were steaming down channel with the English coast on our right. At Southampton our ship could not anchor until the *Olympic,* the sister ship of the ill-fated *Titanic,* had been towed out of the harbour.

Two tugs tried to turn the *Cecilia,* one at the bows, the other
at the stern. In this manœuvre a strong steel hawser fell over-
board from one of the tenders and immediately fouled the
screw of our ship, and we were in a nice fix. A diver was
summoned; after some hours' work the hawser was disen-
tangled, and we were free to go on our way. Was it really a
bad start of ill omen, as many feared? Our captain knew
how to dispel all misgivings, and an hour later no one thought
any more of the *contretemps* that, however, had been already
telegraphed all over the world and worried not a little the
families of the passengers, as we should learn later. In the
same night we called at the French port of Cherbourg, where
travellers, almost all of whom came from Paris, were taken
on board. Now there was no further stopping-place between
there and New York, and we were on the broad Atlantic.
When I woke next morning the *Cecilia* was dancing a polka.
Now she reared up on end; now she went down into the
depths beneath. A truly awful grating sound alarmed the
nervous passengers when the ship buried her head so deep
that the screw in the stern whizzed round out of the water.

On the "'tween decks" nobody was to be seen; now and
then a monster wave would sweep the deck, on which had
sounded the day before the "joyous tinkling of feet" to the
strain of the concertina. On the promenade deck the first
victims of sea-sickness lay stretched out at full length in comfortable deck-chairs.

The sea continued to be rough for two days; then spring
seemed to have returned again, although the almanack told
us we were only a few days off October. On board all was
merry and bright. On the "'tween deck" dancing recom-
menced to the strains of the concertina, and the steward's
orchestra played dance music to the first-class passengers on

the gaily decorated deck. Opera stars, who were going back to America crowned with laurels or who, thirsting for dollars, wanted to fill their purses in the New World, sang and played. We passed the Statue of Liberty, and saw all the more or less known places and forts in the harbour. Then suddenly the ship stopped, still a long way off the pier. The quarantine station was reached and doctors came on board. Then the mails were taken off; post boats lay right and left of us; for a whole hour numberless sacks with letters and cards were stowed away in these boats without interruption. A whole staff of German postal officials had been employed during the crossing in thoroughly sorting the German mails. A few American post-office people had already arranged the letters for New York according to districts and streets. This stoppage off the harbour is not a pleasant memory for me personally, for simultaneously with the post boats came a whole swarm of newspaper reporters. Five men at the same time asked me all manner of searching questions. . . .

Five minutes later I stood on American soil, heartily welcomed by twenty or thirty men and women. The luggage was soon passed through the Customs and sent to the hotel. Then we rode from Hoboken under the Hudson to New York.

Public Meetings in America

A tremendous lot has already been written about the United States and its marvels, likewise about New York and its skyscrapers, its imposing thoroughfares and streets. I shall resist the temptation to increase the number of these accounts, and shall rather be content to record some of my personal experiences, and state how things differ there from those at home. Let us take one example—a public meeting in New

York: bands playing, colours flying! In front of one meeting hall I found a band awaiting me. It formed up and marched in front, blowing and trumpeting a real American marching tune. Two men walked by my side, with me in the middle, others pushing us forward. An indescribable hubbub broke out all round us on entering the hall. My hand was shaken thousands of times. At last, more dead than alive, I was lifted on to the platform. The band began once more. Cheers rang out at intervals, and then a man stated what kind of a being I was. Then he introduced another man who should take the chair. This other man described what I meant or did not mean in his eyes. He was cruel enough not to ask me to speak. He called upon a glee club that now sang a song of welcome and then sang another as an encore. Then a young lady presented me with an enormous bouquet, which I really did not know what to do with.

Finally, I was introduced and could begin my speech. But I was so nervous owing to the inflictions of the last half hour that I saw in front of me at the meeting everything I thought I had long since overcome. I saw three or four men chewing gum in every row—it was horrible. Wherever I looked, one was chewing here, another there. They chewed and chewed without stopping, and seemingly without getting tired. During my speech I began to count; four were chewing in the first row, three in the second and nine in the third. . . . I had to count, whether I would or not; three were chewing here, seven there, and in the entire hall at least three hundred.

At another meeting it was as quiet as the grave in the hall. I was told that Syndicalists, Anarchists and similar contemporaries were going to speak against me. "All right," I said, "I'm quite agreeable." It should be my utmost endeavour that these gentlemen should not be without a subject for discussion.

In my speech I stroked and fondled the Syndicalists and the Anarchists in the most provoking way. But dead silence still reigned in the hall—until all of a sudden a real live baby uttered a frightful shriek. I was silent for a few seconds, and then, as the squaller did not quiet down, I said, "Up to now only one young man has offered any opposition," looking very straight at the child's mother. She pressed the young Anarchist so tightly to her bosom that he was actually quiet for a few minutes. Then he started shrieking again, as if he were being spitted, and as the woman made no sign to walk out with her child, I then said: "The young man is interrupting again, but the real discussion only begins after my address; perhaps he could make up his mind to continue his interruptions outside," and at last the woman went out with her child. I am perfectly convinced that she took my remarks very amiss; at any rate, the twenty other women who were sitting in the hall with children followed the woman out. I was told afterwards that the shrieking had not in the least disturbed the meeting; the American pays no attention to such interruptions if his mind has once been concentrated on one definite point.

On the Platform

The speeches I have made at home and abroad are often referred to in this book. Apart from a great difference existing between speeches before native or foreign audiences, experiences on the platform have uncommonly many sides that are by no means only serious, but are even sometimes distinctly humorous.

To speak before a foreign audience is no easy thing. Whoever is not as completely master of a foreign language as of his mother tongue had better not attempt it in public speaking. Whereas the German is much amused when a foreigner mangles his language, it is real torture to a Frenchman when he doesn't hear his language, of which he is uncommonly proud, purely and grammatically spoken. In course of years I have naturally learnt how to speak before foreigners and how to avoid boring them. The first axiom is that one must take great trouble not to speak too fast, but, on the other hand, should speak clearly, distinctly and purely. By this one makes himself more easily understood, at any rate by a foreign audience, which has taken pains to learn German. I have for many years abandoned the practice of first delivering my whole speech and then of getting it translated. It must in the end bore and unsettle a meeting when a foreigner speaks for an hour without the majority of his hearers being able to follow him.

Just as wrong do I consider the method which speakers of the Salvation Army generally adopt with foreign audiences. They make the interpreter standing close to them translate at once each sentence, one by one. The speaker loses by this all his "go"; any trace of characteristic individuality is killed and the whole thing becomes automatic.

On the other hand, the following system has proved very useful. I can speak only of my own experiences. I carefully prepare a speech intended for foreigners in sections. For the treatment of the subject it is sufficient to write each section in such a way that your speech will in no case take longer than eight to ten minutes for each section. After each section has been discussed, the interpreter, to whom the actual manuscript must be handed before the speech is made, translates it. I have always succeeded in finishing off the subject with three or at most four pauses in between without losing the attention of the audience. Of course the speaker is not bound to stick

rigidly to the manuscript, which the translator must certainly
do. Whoever can manage at the end of a section to regain
the attention of his hearers by a remark that the translator
can catch at once will get good results from this style of speaking. At any rate, I have found this method the best in speaking to foreigners in Europe and the United States.

Propaganda Difficulties

Our German working man can scarcely have a notion of
the difficulty of preaching Socialism in the United States. It
is easier for Americans than for us to illustrate by glaring examples the absurdity of Capitalism. What, after all, was and
is our Krupp when compared with the many American multi-
millionaires, such as Vanderbilt, Astor, Gould, Carnegie, Ford,
etc.? But it is not enough to have these glaring examples;
one must be able to put them clearly before the masses. Picture to yourself a town in America. There is no such thing
as a proletariate speaking the same language; every day thousands of new emigrants come pouring in from every country
in the world. Along with a few stragglers from more civilized
and more highly developed countries come, or came before the
Aliens' Restrictions Act, huge crowds from Poland, Italy, etc.
Among them are a large number who imagine they are living
like princes if they (as in America) sleep only three in a bed,
whereas at home this number is five or six, and then miserable
plank beds or straw. To win these poor devils for Socialism
would be no thankless task, if one could only get at them;
but even if one could surmount all language difficulties and
find friends who knew the dozens of languages spoken in the
United States, how and where would one find those one would
like to get at? Take the circulation of tracts, pamphlets, etc.
Certain nationalities live in certain places in the big towns, but,

notwithstanding, it can easily happen that a tract written in German and English and circulated in thousands only finds a hundred readers who can read these languages. The Party Press therefore has to contend with absolutely insurmountable difficulties. As in the case of American newspapers, these tracts must be almost exclusively sold in the streets; regular subscribers are the exception.

I have given lectures in the United States: in Brooklyn, N.Y., Bronx, N.Y., Passaic, N.J., New Haven, Conn., Newark, N.J., Elizabeth, N.J., Schenectady, N.Y., Lawrence, Mass., Providence, R.I., Paterson, N.J., New Britain, Conn., Hartford, Conn., Rochester, N.Y., Buffalo, N.Y., Cleveland, Ohio, Detroit, Mich., Chicago, Ill., Milwaukee, Wisc., St. Paul, Minn., Denver, Col., St. Louis, Mo., Staunton, Ill., Springfield, Ill., Pittsburgh, Pa., Baltimore, Md., Philadelphia, Pa. To wind up, I spoke again in New York. The tour was not arranged so that I could get always from one place to another close at hand. Though trying, it was bearable. But when I received in Denver numerous letters and telegrams asking me to come to California also, I declined. It was too much of a good thing to have to travel huge distances and deliver lectures every day in big, overcrowded halls, and only have one free day a week. An overwhelming longing for my wife and children came upon me and helped me to make up my mind to turn right about in Colorado.

The whole Press, German and English, civic and Socialist, treated me in the kindliest way and reported my lectures at length. The *New York Staatszeitung* went into raptures: "This conspicuous Labour leader does not appeal to the passions of the multitude and scorns flowery rhetoric; his speeches are strictly logical and his remarks betray sound sense and convictions, and these qualities win for him forthwith the hearts of his listeners, both men and women, who greeted his utterances with demonstrative applause." The Social Democratic papers reported a brilliant success; the Syndicalists lost their tempers. In a comprehensive report the S.D. *New York Volkszeitung* stated: "Schiedemann has left behind him a deep impression. His clear delivery, and not least his fearlessness and confidence in expressing his convictions, took by storm the hearts of thousands who heard him. And more than that—many hundreds who have become weak-kneed and doubtful in the attack of Syndicalism of the traditional fighting method of Socialism, received from his championship of German Social Democracy fresh courage and fresh belief in the strength of political action. Something like a whiff of fresh air emanated from Schiedemann's entire personality."

VII

A QUARTER OF A CENTURY IN THE REICHSTAG —THE SOLINGEN SEAT

ONE of the most painful chapters in the history of the S.P.D. is headed "Solingen."

The town is wonderfully situated in the Wupper hills, inhabited by an industrious and highly skilled population, festive and freedom-loving, and is the home of one of the most peculiar of industries. Solingen is the town of the knife-grinder—carving knives, pocket knives—and the special features of the industry have naturally developed a special organization. As there is only one Solingen in the Empire, the unions of specially skilled artisans were peculiar to the place. It has happened in Solingen that workers have been on strike for several years and yet have not been out of work for a single day. It is a fact that no one living outside the Lower Rhine can understand, because he does not know the special character of knife manufacture and knife-grinding. There were naturally ages ago big knife manufacturers who only did their work at home. They, however, were exceptions. In the main small and smallish working Capitalists were concerned, who only did a part of this highly specialized work in their own homes and who (and this is the point) got the sharpening work—for which special skill is required—done by expert workmen, who rented premises with water power available and were, in their own special way, independent people. Therefore if any workman was locked out he could

123

go to one of the others and continue his work. There was always abundance of work to be had. As religious hypocrisy and fanatical free thought lived side by side on the Wupper, so in the Solingen industry did there exist also side by side the most up-to-date methods of manufacture, the most meticulous division of labour, which produced extraordinary proficiency in the specially skilled man, and most antiquated methods, *e.g.* factory work with home work and their own workmen. As the Solingen knife-grinders had, as a matter of fact, no competition to face—there was formerly very little attention paid to Sheffield—they found themselves in comparatively good circumstances. Directly a man owned a "cottage" he was independent of everybody and earned relatively good money.

In short, the Solingen workers constituted a *corps d'élite* and had, owing to their social importance, some of the features of guilds. At any rate, they took not the slightest interest in the Central Organization, because Solingen was all in all for them, both in its trade and the Union representing their interests. They kicked against the Metal Workers' Union, as it would, they said, endanger their independent position, "because it would bring all metal workers under one ferrule and further the modern system of production which must oust the 'knife-grinder' from his good position, whether he liked or not." Rows broke out between the workers owing to these opposing views that naturally can only be shortly stated here, and sometimes took very ugly shapes. Yet Lassalle had sown in Solingen itself and Remscheid the first seeds of Socialism, and found joyful approval in a population that easily enthused to every new idea of freedom. The truth of the Marx-Engels theory about the materialistic idea in history is here illustrated in an interesting way by the conflicts which broke out among the Solingen workers. Incidentally, it should be stated that the rows, which at the end of the 'nineties of the last century are connected with the name of Schumacher, had occurred before in almost the same way. They were discussed at the time under the title Rüddinghausen-Schumacher by the Party.

The Central Union *versus* the Local Organization! At meetings and in the Press the fierce struggles of the workers among themselves were a matter of great satisfaction to the independent workman. At the end there were two Labour papers and two Social Democratic candidates for the Reichstag. At the end of the 'nineties the workers, fighting for the Central Organization, did not intend in any circumstances to re-elect their previous Social Democratic member, Schumacher. All the more determined were local workers to have him. The battle took a most violent form, and was finally fought out in the most personal way. The foes of the S.P.D. all through the Empire revelled in this fratricidal strife in Solingen. At many Social Democratic meetings Solingen was the only topic of conversation.

As I was elected for Solingen in 1903 and this election opened a new chapter in my life, it must be explained as concisely as possible how I achieved the high honour of becoming the Reichstag member for Solingen.

On the Conference day in 1897 the Solingen dispute played an important part. It was exhaustively discussed by the so-called Committee of Seven at the Conference, whose President was Dr. Leo Arons, along with the members intimately concerned with Solingen, not forgetting Schumacher himself. An agreement was come to, as Gerisch had foreseen and hinted at between the lines of his speech. He said he no longer trusted the members at Solingen, who were filled with indescribable mistrust and hatred for each other. Dr. Arons, one of the worthiest of Social Democrats I ever knew, reported in a very optimistic fashion on behalf of his Committee, not knowing the state of affairs in Solingen as well as Gerisch:

"The Committee of Seven has fortunately had an easy task in concluding the Solingen affair, thanks to the co-operation of the Solingen members on both sides. I ask you not to under-estimate this co-operation, for the Solingen members were well aware that in supporting the resolution they approved they would have a bad time at home. The Committee of Seven proposes the following resolution:

" 'The Conference proposes: as Schumacher has declared that he declines to be nominated as candidate for the Reichstag, the Conference decides on authorizing the Executive to propose a candidate who has no connection with the Solingen disturbances.

" 'The Conference authorizes the new Executive to conduct the fusion of the *Bergische Arbeiterstimme* with the Solingen *Freie Presse,* as well as the transference of ownership to the whole Party, as soon as possible.

" 'The members Inger and Schaal on the one side, Schumacher and Langenberg on the other, state that they will bring this resolution before their members.'

"Now a few remarks on the resolution. Most members will know that the Executive is most reluctant to be concerned with the nomination of candidates. As a rule, this is the constituency's business. Things are abnormal in Solingen. Here, if one may quote words used in the Committee, there is need for temporary protection. No candidate, of course, shall be forced on anyone. Conversations will follow with both sides, but the Executive has the last word."

To me, as to any other Social Democrat who was not concerned in these discussions, events in Solingen were worm-
wood and gall. The quarrel disgusted me so much that when
the word Solingen was mentioned at the Hamburg Conference
I walked out of the hall to have a look round the town.

As I had been since 1896 the Reichstag candidate for Giessen
—an altogether hopeless seat that did not worry me—I had
flatly refused the most flattering proposals from Kassel to
stand for that town. I was not a little surprised, therefore,
when I received a letter from Pfannkuch (24th November,
1897) with the following postscript:

"Just one thing else. Would you not change your mind
about the seat in Solingen? Gerisch and I consider you the
most eligible of those that have been considered. But let
me have your views soon."

At the Hamburg Conference I had already given my answer
to a question from the Executive: "No, you clearly take me
for more of a sport than I really am." Pfannkuch's letter
above I answered in the negative. Then came heart-rending
letters from Gerisch, who appealed to Auer and Bebel. He
pointed out the difficulties of the position and between the
lines let me see, to comfort me, that I was not at all sure of
being accepted by the Solingen people, as the Executive intended to propose six members as selected candidates. "Well,"
said I, "if you recommend six 'old and well-tried members,' then I will be content to take the risk, though only
thirty-two years old, of saying yes. The Solingers will then
make no reflections on me." But it happened otherwise. On
16th December, 1897, I received the following letter from
Gerisch:

"Berlin S.W.
*"*15. 12. 1897.

"DEAR FRIEND SCHEIDEMANN,

"We have just received the news that the Committee appointed to consider the question of candidates, proposed by us, has plumped for you unanimously. The Committee now wishes that you would be good enough to appear here, if possible, next Saturday, the 18th, at the select meeting of the Party members. As many other matters most closely concerned with the settlement of the question of candidates are to be arranged, we should be glad if you would accede to our request. . . . Good luck in your new job."

It was no good to purse up my lips; I had now to whistle. What should I say to my children, my comrades in Giessen? In 1898 the General Election to the Reichstag was to take place. In the middle of December I got tacked on to my Giessen candidature a second one from Solingen, a constituency I could reach only after a four hours' journey. I went off on the day appointed to Solingen, still silently hoping that the meeting to which I was to introduce myself and offer myself as a candidate would turn me down. Yet the Committee of Six, that consisted of three members of the two persuasions, decided unanimously for me, but had not the meeting the right to turn me down amid cheers? I met Gerisch with a worried face in Solingen. "Both parties are wild with each other; the meeting you are to address will be a very stormy one, and perhaps be broken up."

"That's almost what I would like!"

"Don't talk such blasphemy! It's to be hoped it will be all right. Speak as you have never spoken before in your life, then all will be well."

The Committee of Six again declared me to be their unanimous choice. The election meeting at which I was to introduce myself took place one or two weeks later, and in a horrible hall, where there were only benches. The light was miserable. As no extension of time was granted to the landlord, hundreds of working men brought with them in bottles the drinks they considered indispensable. In addition to the strong beer of the Lower Rhine, there was also, as I was assured and could see myself, much more potent liquor.

Gerisch spoke first, and exhorted all to be sensible and united. A long discussion on the agenda followed. Then things got lively. "We will not hear the Hessian comrade the Executive is trying to force upon us."

Gerisch: "We force no candidate upon you. The Executive has to carry out the resolutions of the Party. It has proposed six members for your selection. A Committee with the same number of members has decided for Scheidemann. We know him; give him a hearing and then decide."

"No, no, Schumacher is our man."

From the other side, "What a faithless gang!"

Here and there in the meantime they came to fisticuffs. After another speech by Gerisch, I got up suddenly on the platform; I did not know what came over me, and I started to speak. To my great surprise, quiet immediately followed, and it seemed to me to be getting more and more quiet. I talked about the political situation, and showed how possible it was to alter it for the benefit of the working-class population, the first condition being naturally the determination of the class-conscious worker.

There was a lot of sparring; finally, I was chosen by a big majority as the Social Democratic candidate for the Solingen division. Up to the elections I had work to do which no one would envy: three days on propaganda work in Upper Hesse, three days in the Solingen division; on railway journeys —fourth class, of course—I wrote up my paper; one day a week I kept free to tidy up things after a fashion in the office. The arrangements made in Solingen were not kept. Not long before the election Schumacher came forward again as a candidate, and a certain seat, one of the oldest in Social Democracy, was lost. At the General Election the voting in the Solingen division was: Scheidemann (Soc.) 6,349, Schumacher (Soc.) 5,411, Sabin (United Liberals) 5,843, Centre 5,449. Before the Second Ballot, where the choice lay between the official Social Democrat and the National Liberal, Schumacher gave the password to his supporters "Choose the Liberal," and so Sabin was elected. The S.P.D. had never suffered a greater humiliation. However, I will lose no time in producing a letter I found from Liebknecht, while looking over some old letters, because it clearly shows that according to Liebknecht's view, which I endorse, all the blame for the Solingen "mess-up" cannot be attributed by any means to Schumacher, as far as he personally was concerned. The member indicated by Liebknecht in his letter by F. (God will have forgiven him by this time) edited the paper that was opposing Schumacher. Here is Liebknecht's letter:

"DEAR COMRADE,

"You are certainly right with regard to the Solingen newspaper. You will have often wondered at my being so friendly and indulgent to Schumacher. You are beginning to understand it. He is a man more sinned against than sinning, and the beginning of things started more than twenty years ago. His thick-headedness exaggerated trifles and made friendly intercourse difficult. The others, however, were no better.

After the Hamburg Conference I got as far as to get Schumacher to retire provided that F. were got rid of. This was promised, but the promise was not kept. There was now nothing to restrain Schumacher any more. Gradually he got into the state we saw him in at the Election—furiously hostile to his friends and lost to his party.

> "Greetings to all and good-bye.
>
> "WILHELM LIEBKNECHT."

Disgruntled and embittered, Schumacher later on retired to Cologne, where he managed to keep his head above water by writing, with occasional support from the S.P.D. Subsequently he became reconciled with the Party.

Readers will hardly credit the circumstances in which the election in Solingen was conducted. The Executive had exhorted me to be very careful to avoid being drawn into the struggle between brother and brother. This was achieved. William Liebknecht and Bebel spoke for me, Auer undertook to write the most important manifesto. Both sides were like Kilkenny cats. At one meeting, with Liebknecht and me as referees, Schumacher appeared in response to Liebknecht's special invitation. Liebknecht, who had been on good terms with him, tackled him heavily but in quite a brotherly way. Apparently Schumacher, who was moreover a good speaker, had come to his senses—he didn't dare to contradict old Liebknecht in any hostile spirit. Next day he again began his campaign against the candidate "from outside."

During the months preceding the election I had got to know many very fine men in the Solingen division. Since that time ties of close friendship have attached me to the place. However, I declined at first to be nominated again for the election of 1903, but finally yielded because I could do my propaganda work better from Offenbach. At the June election in 1903 I was elected at the first ballot. The voting was: for the Social Democrat, 17,225; Centre, 6,457; United Liberals, 5,767; Christian Socialist, 648; spoilt votes, a few hundred.

I became very well known in the Solingen division in course of time; quarrels were getting less acute. It was accounted to me for righteousness that I had succeeded in keeping aloof from Party strife, and both sides had greater confidence in me. In addition, some speeches of mine in the Reichstag and a few successful efforts that I made in Berlin in the interests of trade in Solingen won for me more and more the sympathies of the townspeople. My position in the constituency was becoming better and more stable. When the Reichstag was dissolved in the winter of 1906 I was again elected on the first ballot at the new election in January, 1907, though a hot fight preceded it, in which the United Liberals ran Dr. Robert Brunhuber, a smart young editor of the *Kolnische Zeitung,* an excellent speaker and well-informed man, with whom I was on a personal friendly footing. Often of an evening, after very violent battles with our tongues, we would sit down quietly together over a glass of beer. On social-political questions he always tried to be the length of his nose in front of me in his speeches. We opposed each other tooth and nail in all questions relating to the Army, Navy and Colonial policy. At the "Jingo" elections of 1907 the nation was deeply stirred; especially the Liberals, under the leadership of Dernburg, then Minister for the Colonies, whom the Conservatives contemptuously alluded to as "His Excellency Koofmich," made stupendous efforts. Colonial and armament questions played naturally an important part in Solingen. I shall always remember one debate with Brunhuber in one of the bigger villages in the lower part of the Solingen division—either in Leichlingen or Opladen. He had extolled with extraordinary enthusiasm the Colonial policy, and referred to the possibilities of trade with Africa for Solingen industry, and asked whether it was a thing of no importance to knife-manufacturers and knife-grinders. Thereupon I said: "No, it certainly is important. But where are niggers to put their pocket knives? They don't wear trousers." It was impossible to continue the argument. The meeting broke up in fits of laughter following my words. The "knife-grinders" plumped for me.

Result of the poll: Social Democrats, 19,589; Liberals, 10,833; Centre, 7,992; spoilt votes, a few hundred. Dr. Brunhuber, the candidate I had defeated, went off soon after the election on a voyage round the world, and was cruelly murdered by the natives in the Himalaya district.

In course of time I got thoroughly at home in the Solingen division, so much so that every Tom, Dick and Harry knew me, to use a common expression. The election in 1912, in which we had to settle our account with the "Black-blue" Block, was a walk-over for the S.P.D. On the polling day at the General Election 44,245 votes were recorded; of those I received 24,571, the Liberals 10,201, the Centre 8,239.

On the whole of the outside sheet of the *Bergische Arbeiterstimme* (11th January, 1912) a few lines were printed in enormous type that described very well the situation then existing in the S.P.D. They ran thus:

"Whom are we voting for? . . . Scheidemann! He has worked with success in the Reichstag. The Liberal *Kreisäntelligenzblatt* that had absolutely nothing to say in favour of its own candidate, except a short, fatuous puff, emphatically stated for the first time (5th January, 1912):

" 'On the Liberal side it has never been disputed, but generously acknowledged, that Scheidemann has always zealously espoused the interests of his constituency.'

"Every elector who desires the interests of the Solingen division to be represented with energy, skill and success, must vote for our candidate."

This outburst in the *Bergische Arbeiterstimme* found many imitators. As the Solingen editor Dittmann was canvassing in Remschied, and had his hands full with electioneering there and starting a political weekly paper for his district, I was able to work to my heart's content and with great pleasure, on the *Bergische Arbeiterstimme*. I had introduced Ebert, then canvassing in the neighbouring constituency of Elberfeld-Barmen, to his voters at a huge motley gathering. He took special pleasure in the outburst in the *Bergische Arbeiterstimme,* and asked me, as he had, to his painful surprise, to fight hard to win his seat at the Second Ballot, to put a little more life into the Elberfeld paper. It was only possible to do so to a very modest extent, as the editors of the paper were so rooted to principles that any innovation, even if this only concerned a general "stir up" of the journal, was regarded as a betrayal of principles. The district Elberfeld-Barmen was so circumscribed that Ebert felt quite depressed at holding meetings day after day at which only a small number of the same people appeared: in Elberfeld men from Barmen, in Barmen men from Elberfeld. He made no secret of the uncomfortable feeling that oppresses every speaker of having to say the same thing over and over again every evening.

My First Impressions in the Reichstag

Eighty-one men strong, we Socialists marched into the Reichstag on 3rd December after the elections in June, 1903. A feeling of heavy responsibility came over me when I took part for the first time in a Party committee meeting on the top floor, Room 20. The furniture of the room had been taken from the former Conference Hall of the old Federal Council. The armchair in which Singer was sitting was formerly Bismarck's seat. Next to Singer sat Bebel, and then came all the champions, some of whom I knew personally from old Party Congress days, and all the others by name and from the reports of their speeches in the Reichstag. . . . The list of colleagues of those days, whom death has called away, is a long one. Singer and Bebel welcomed the new-comers and gave them all sorts of hints; senior colleagues showed us the numerous halls and antechambers. The House was only well filled on the first days of the session, and then became emptier and emptier, and finally only a small group of regular *habitués* were visible. Out of 397 members not more than 150 at the most were regularly in the House, so there was plenty of room to work in. The bad attendance was due to the members not being paid. The privilege of sitting in the Imperial Parliament, with its universal, free, direct and secret franchise, should be entirely reserved, in the opinion of the "powers that be," for those who could afford to live in Berlin without any special allowances. The Prussian Diet, with its pitiable Three Class franchise, was pretty safe from having paupers elected to it. In consequence, its members, who were to a great extent magistrates, Government officials and big industrials, received 15 marks a day. In the Reichstag, as aforesaid, no one got a farthing. The Social Democratic

Party therefore had to give their members, if they were to come to Berlin at all, fixed allowances from the Party chest. These allowances were very small, and amounted to from 3 to 7 marks a day, according to the member's income. With this, members of the Social Democratic Party had to be content. Those who had to rent a room in Berlin received a small rent allowance every month. To spare the Party chest as much as possible, the Party treasurer, Hein Meister, had to see to it that no member who was not indispensable should ever come to Berlin at all. Any member who had been in Berlin for more than three or four days in the week for any reason whatsoever had to pick a big bone with Hein before he received his daily allowances. Payment was made on Friday afternoons, generally in what is now the Zeppelin Room. Hein Meister, who wore an eyeglass and spoke with a stammer, though he could talk freely enough when required, had at the time one of the stingiest of colleagues sitting alongside him. The two spat like cats at anyone who claimed more than a three-days' allowance, as if he were asking for a huge amount. While Hein's assistant, Frederick Brühne of Frankfurt, an honest fellow, long employed at the job, cross-examined the member demanding his dole and got the receipts duly signed, Hein himself, growling perpetually, would stick a long stocking-needle with a long thread attached through the receipts. Pay day was invariably a great rag, for everybody knew that though Hein and his assistant were the best fellows in the world, they would be terribly keen on saving the chest any and every expense. If a member got his allowance for four days in the week and had not been summoned for an important division, he was told off in these words: "Well, don't let me see you again for four weeks; if you do, you won't get a copper." The non-payment of members had the most shocking effects. Count Posadowsky, then Secretary of State for the Home Department, had often to attend and protest in the Reichstag for three weeks running before his salary was paid him.

The House had never been competent to pass resolutions, and only when we Social Democrats took the members of the Government most seriously to task, did we force a division without threatening to raise the question of competence.

The other Parties suffered just as much under these conditions; they too only whipped up their members by urgent telegrams for important divisions. In the Committees this non-payment of members was likewise very unpleasant. The whole of the Parliamentary business was transacted in each Committee. A few specially appointed members did everything, while the herd in the true sense of the word were "voting sheep" who were summoned by wire when wanted. For eight years, till I was elected on the Executive, in 1911, I did all the political work of all the papers I managed. As the journalistic work of the Social Democratic organs then was—without wireless, telephones and correspondence bureaux—everything went swimmingly. Instead of being forced to be at the newspaper's publishing offices in the morning to read the Berlin evening papers that had come in overnight, the whole MS. was ready for the printer.

The Reichstag that had been elected on 16th June—the first of the twentieth century, as President von Ballestrem once said—assembled for the first time on 3rd December, 1903. We young bloods often sat on hot bricks at the full sitting when a debate did not go as we expected or wished. At any ordinary meeting we should have jumped up and asked to speak. Here only special speakers appointed by the Sections spoke. The President determined the order in which they should speak. Strict discipline prevailed in the Reichstag. The worst of calumnies against our Party could not be refuted at once. Everything was done in strict order. The President was Count von Ballestrem (Centre), an extraordinarily firm and clever man with lots of humour. To be able to say anything personal was an art that many members never learnt. I kept my ears open like a sporting dog, so as not to get off the rails should I ever happen to excite attention.

At the twenty-seventh sitting of the new Reichstag, 8th November, 1904, I delivered my maiden speech. Another speech I had carefully prepared I could only deliver half an hour later in the High Court of Parliament. I therefore spoke twice at the same sitting, and, much to the surprise of the House, had excited some attention by my first speech. I can justly say, as we say in Berlin: "Unaccustomed as I am . . ." This speech came about in the following way. The sitting had opened with a debate on the agenda, in which Bebel took part and over which he lost his temper. As everything went differently from what he expected—*e.g.* prescribed subjects being shelved and others brought forward for which no speaker had been announced by the Section, Bebel said to me, sitting by chance beside him, "This is about the limit; we haven't even announced one speaker to the Ministry of Health; usually a full dozen come forward." I asked him diffidently if he wanted me "to let drive"; I had, I said, investigated the question of well-founded complaints about the stench from the Wupper, and though not really prepared could talk on the question. "If you are sure of your ground, get up." At the same moment Paasche, a member of the Reichstag, was called upon to speak. He was not in the hall, and lo and behold, I was standing on the rostrum, having had barely time to snatch from my drawer an envelope containing cuttings and official papers. The President then announced, "Scheide-mann, member of the Reichstag."

From My Maiden Speech

Ha, a maiden speech! Most of the members were curious; many were even eager to embarrass a man speaking for the first time with interruptions. Nothing of the sort happened to me; I had at once the ear of the House. I referred to petitions protesting against the foulness of rivers. Real relief could only be obtained by an Act of Parliament. To get such powers was certainly a difficult business, for by Article 65 of the Transport Bill (Civil Legislation) the waterways were withdrawn expressly from the Reichstag and handed over to the Board of Agriculture. But I thought, "Where there's a will, there's a way." I gave two examples of the necessity for finding such a way—one from the division I had the honour to represent, that concerned the Wupper, and a second from my home in Offenbach, that concerned the Main. Dr. Wolf, the Prussian technical inspector, had already reported most unfavourably on the Wupper in 1885. "He calculated that the tiny Wupper brings down 150 tons of mud, etc., a day, and that these 150 tons of mud are the cause of a huge stench and poison the whole neighbourhood; that they flood the banks, thereby damaging the fields, and are a very grave nuisance to the public. I think you gentlemen on the Right should take up the question, as land cultivation is injured. When these masses of filth come over the banks tillage is an impossibility. The health of the district is also imperilled—that is obvious, if a river brings down such quantities of foul matter. Dr. Wolf proved eighteen years ago that, owing to the fouling of the river and the stench, in Elberfeld alone compared with other towns 12.8 per cent. of deaths were due to infectious disease, whereas in Düsseldorf and Cologne on the Rhine the death rate was less by a half. Dr. Wolf said: 'I will only allude to the dangers to which the inhabitants of the lower and middle Wupper would be exposed in case of an outbreak of cholera. The bed of the Wupper, with its filth, impregnated with dung and other animal excrescences, is just the right sub-soil for the spreading and development of the plague. My view is that steps must be at once taken to abate the nuisance.'

"Eighteen years have gone by, and nothing has been done. The Wupper, a fine German river, formerly abounding with fish, has had none for many years. Water rats are now the only living things in it. When you approach the fine uplands of the Wupper near Solingen and adjoining Müngsten, where German engineering skill has constructed the fine Müngsten bridge over the Wupper, and see what our technical skill can do and produce, and how it can correct the apparent ugliness of Nature, your heart leaps with joy, but a painful impression is at once created when you see the black, inky waters of the river flowing under this fine structure. The same technical skill, the same industry that improved Nature in such a striking way, has also spoilt the beauties of Nature. That should make us think; it should not be possible for industry to destroy our beautiful countryside in this way."

I answered interruptions by saying: "The Wupper below Solingen is so black, as a matter of fact, that if you were to duck a National Liberal in it you would be able to pull him out as a member of the Centre."

At first this disparaging remark in a maiden speech seemed to the House something they had never heard before, but the tension was relieved by a roar of laughter, and I was soon able to resume my speech to an attentive audience.

Count Posadowsky rose immediately afterwards to say that here was a question that was becoming every day more important in view of the progress industry was making. He mentioned what had happened and must happen in this field, and ended with these words: "I am resolved to give this matter my earnest attention and insist on a gradual improvement of present conditions." The members of the Section were satisfied with my maiden speech, and congratulated me. In course of a remarkable sitting, Rettich, a Conservative member, seized the opportunity of touching on the Meat Inspection Act and ventilating a question that I had thoroughly studied in all its phases and should have discussed in my maiden speech. In agreement with Bebel, I forthwith got on my legs again and spoke—I am sorry to say—for an hour and a half on this uncommonly important food question. Later I frequently discussed it in "Supply" and in interpolations by members of the Section; my object was to prove that many of the Public Health regulations were only a blind, and their chief concern was to stop the importation of cattle and meat and other food products, as far as possible, so that foreign competition, so inconvenient to cattle dealers and farmers, might be arrested in order that these fellows might force up prices whenever they liked.

Questions on agriculture and cattle-breeding were for years my special province. My five years' experience in Giessen came in quite handy, as I had had there to study these subjects pretty thoroughly. Without this knowledge I could never have faced the small country farmer. Great amusement was caused in the Section, when the Foot and Mouth Bill was discussed, on my volunteering to act as its spokesman. My colleague, Stücklen, likewise volunteered out of friendship for me. We two worked very hard in Committee, and sometimes caused diversion on our own hook. And we had fine opportunities, as in Committee every sort of animal disease was discussed. I remember with great pleasure a debate on the itch. According to experts, especially those from the Public Health office, it seemed well-nigh impossible to combat this devilish disease. I asked, with the solemnest face in the world, whether any special treatment of the microbe had been attempted, as whole nations were affected by it.

We were a sporting lot on Committees, in spite of lively disagreements. The gentlemen on the Right got very angry, certainly, when, according to the last section of the Act, it was stated that the export regulations had to be made by the Provincial Governments. Stücklen and I, with very earnest faces, suggested that the export regulations should be formulated by the Federal Government, which should introduce as soon as possible a universal equal, direct and secret franchise bill. Unfortunately, our effort—it was naturally no formal proposal—to drag in the Prussian method of voting via the Foot and Mouth Disease Act was unsuccessful.

Instances of the Methods of Agrarian Agitation

I had once more to confirm an interpolation on the scarcity of meat. From reports to hand from the Prussian Factory Inspectors, I described the distress of the working classes (11th December, 1906), and took a firm stand against the ridiculous statements made in the Agricultural Conservative Press on the utter worthlessness of foreign agricultural produce and cattle-breeding. One example may show the nature of these assertions and my own attitude. Danish salt beef was described as being especially injurious. The *Deutsche Tageszeitung* wrote about Holland in a similar strain. The Dutch peasants and retailers were buying margarine in vast quantities, and the German rustic was so stupid as to purchase this manufactured stuff to save a few coppers, instead of sticking to pure German butter. I said, "Anyone who has any sense of truth and fairness must feel very uncomfortable reading these senseless remarks and this scandalous abuse of the foreigner."

It has been widely stated that foreign cheese is bad and adulterated. To that I say: It is probable adulteration does occur abroad in butter and cheese. But woe betide us if it is put about abroad that a single instance is the usual thing in Germany. What will you say if we, like the *Deutsche Zeitung,* talk of our German Junkers, whose milk (of course by accident) is watered, and blackguard them all as swindlers? Such gentlemen move in very high circles. *A propos* of butter, I will quote the evidence of an Anti-Semite paper, that all is by no means well with butter production in Germany. It writes about a member of the Reichstag elected by the butter-making district of Hesse, the Schwalm, and who should surely know his constituents. He is alleged to have stated that his peasants are as faithful as dogs, but as filthy as swine. I am discreet enough not to mention names. Whoever is interested in the story can read it in the Anti-Semite *Hessische Rundschau,* August 19th, 1918, under the headline: "How Herr von Liebermann Appreciates his Electors."

The kindly reader will readily admit that the sections on Customs duties, cheese and butter adulteration, chicken and foot-and-mouth disease in themselves are not exactly entertaining. Owing, however, to the frequency of these debates, there was always a danger of the House quickly emptying directly a deputy showed signs of renewing the debate on any sort of cattle plague. It was universally acknowledged that I had always treated this dreary subject in such a way that it could be listened to with interest. Old Träger, who was well disposed towards me, regularly sat down near me on one of the so-called reporters' benches as soon as I mounted the rostrum—he was hard of hearing, but, "I wouldn't miss any of the malicious remarks you make to a much-suffering community." As a rule the speeches in the Reichstag were and are so dry and feeble, and almost always so stupid, that one can understand the indifference with which they were received. The invariably selfish policy of these stricken agriculturists in the Reichstag was bad enough. With brutal ruthlessness these lords and masters marched forward. Once when the National Liberals had been a little obstreperous—that is to say, did not dance to the tune of the Landlords' Union— Dr. Dietrich Hahn of the Land League leaders reminded the National Liberals at a public sitting of the account-book of the Landlords' Union, in which was written what had been paid in electioneering costs for the National Liberals.

I can here say nothing further about my efforts in the Reichstag with regard to agriculture and social-political questions. Some quotations, however, shall be given from my political speeches, because they throw a vivid light on the good old days of the Empire.

The Imperial Officials in the Good Old Time

Superior and subordinate officials of the Post Office in Kassel had laid their complaints before me, asking me to take up their cause with a view to getting an inquiry instituted. Zubeil, a member of the Reichstag, had received a similar request. Here can be read the shorthand report of my speech: "Like my friend Zubeil, I have received a protest from a choral society of minor Post Office officials; it is made, as he has said, in the interests of these poor devils, and to-day I got a note from the Executive of the Post and Telegraph Union in which the minor officials state that the contents of the complaint sent by me to Herr Kraetke have excited lively indignation among them. In this note are the words:

" 'The statement made by you we utterly repudiate and shall continue to do so till you can prove the opposite, *i.e.* by giving us the names of the minor officials concerned.'

"This note is a proof of the abominable dependence under which minor officials suffer. But in my reply I spoke not only of minor, but also of major officials. I am therefore expecting the note of protest from the major officials in the course of the next few days. I am to give names. If I should give a single name, I should be unworthy of remaining a member of the Reichstag for a single day. If I should give a single name I should be just as contemptible a fellow as are those who abuse their authority and dictate their views to underlings. I will close with a question to the gentlemen of the Post Office. I will ask if they are at length ashamed of their system of oppression in the offices of the Post Office administration."

Former Treatment of Soldiers

In a speech on 30th August, 1908, I brought up for discussion the treatment of soldiers by their superiors, supported by well-ascertained facts. The men, after an exhausting day, were blackguarded by their officers as pigs, swine, sheep, louts, ragamuffins, cowards, blind idiots, etc. I took up their cause, and concluded thus: "I am of opinion that a man who is invested with the authority of a German officer, against whom the men are absolutely defenceless, and who requires from them the most abject obedience—I mean that expressions like louts, cowardly curs, etc., must recoil on the head of the officer using them to completely defenceless people."

Lieut.-General von Arnim, as the representative of the War Office, had to admit the truth of my words, it is true, but tried to defend the behaviour of the officers. Naturally! Officers in the good old days were demigods, and whoever complained of any one of them was at once accused of having insulted the Corps of Officers—a fellow without a country, on the right road to betray his Fatherland.

Opening Speeches in the Reichstag

In the old days the opening speech was the most important duty that could be laid upon a member. The opening speeches were always, and are still in most cases, delivered by the Presidents of the various Parties, as by this it is made plain that he is speaking for the Party. As long as Bebel, William Liebknecht, Singer and von Vollmar were in the prime of life it went without saying that they would deliver these important speeches. The weakest of the great four as a speaker was Singer.

Since his death the Party has never had so skilful a President as Singer, and everyone who has ever seen this man as President at a Social Democratic Conference will acknowledge that a better and more influential President could hardly be imagined. In the Reichstag, Singer passed as the best judge of the order of business. In every discussion on the agenda he opened proceedings. His ruling on disputed points was regarded as the right one by friend and foe. This is by no means saying that his opinion was always decisive. Far from it; in the Reichstag much more depended on the will of the majority than on the fairness of his ruling. Apart from other means of proof, it can be strikingly confirmed by the decisions of the former Committee of Inquiry that considered the validity of disputed elections. It is, moreover, one of the most humiliating chapters in the often-ridiculed history of the German Reichstag.

As a Parliamentary orator, Singer was not particularly conspicuous. Old Liebknecht died in 1900; von Vollmar, whose health got worse and worse, was in the end completely confined to his bed or wheel chair, and it was extremely rarely that he came to Berlin. Bebel and Singer were ailing. The Section, however, could command some notably gifted colleagues, such as Dr. Ludwig Frank and Dr. David, to name only two. Landsberg did not then belong to the Reichstag. But both Frank and David were, as Revisionists, eyed with too much suspicion by Bebel and Singer for them ever to be entrusted with an opening speech. On the Radical side Ledebour would have been considered, had Bebel or Singer thought him more reliable. Ledebour who occasionally, when he spoke without preparation, was really brilliant, was a complete failure when he was set down to speak. He could not prepare a speech. He was too diffuse every time, tied himself up with minor matters and left important questions out altogether. Bebel always judged Ledebour harshly, and especially reproached him for his lack of industry. I take the most charitable view of Bebel's crushing condemnation. His opinion, however, was confirmed by every colleague who had ever worked with Ledebour, either on the Berlin *Vorwärts* or on the *Sächsische Arbeiter Zeitung* in Dresden. When he turned up at the office he was always late. He had been prevented from coming strictly on time either by rain or snow, heat or cold. The experiences we had with him on the Executive of the Section thoroughly supported this opinion. He was never punctual at any meeting, and always demanded that we should begin the discussion all over again for his benefit. Quite as natural as our refusal was his fury at our high-handedness. Not only did he come late to the Section, but wherever he went, even on most important business. He even came late on 9th November, 1918, and his intimate friends, in fact, reproached him for having slept through the Revolution. We called him, because of his lack of punctuality, "Mr. Too-Late." Ledebour was never considered by Bebel or Singer the right man to open a debate, although he had at the time a downright uncanny influence with the Section as leader of the Radical half. I shall say a few words on the subject, because they will explain much that was unsatisfactory in those days.

Separate Meetings of the Two Halves of the Section

The Social Democratic Section numbered forty-three members in 1907. One half of it was Radical, the other Revisionist. Both parts held separate meetings before the Section assembled. At these irregular sittings the two halves settled who of the Section should speak on the various questions, what motions should be brought forward, accepted or rejected, and who should be told off to speak on especial points in the agenda at the plenary sitting of the House. Both halves naturally tried to keep their meetings a secret. The whole situation was extremely uncomfortable for me. I did not, in fact, fit into either, but the stand-offish way in which my Revisionistic colleagues in the Section treated those of the other persuasion annoyed me so intensely that I went over to the Radical camp. It did no harm to the Section, and I can rejoice even to-day at having been able on repeated occasions to stop proposals that seemed to me foolish, and in the end to break up the separate sittings of the Radicals altogether.

That occurred directly I saw that this nonsense was clearly dangerous both to the Section and the Party.

As not more than thirty-four or thirty-five of the forty-three members of the Section could be in Berlin, the majority of those who could carry a motion in the Section numbered eighteen or nineteen. As also the separate sittings were never attended by all members either of the Right or Left, the motions to be brought before the Section were sometimes settled at the separate meetings by quite a small number of members. This must be made quite clear in order to show the utter worthlessness, from a practical standpoint, of these separate meetings of the Section. Let us say that out of twenty members of each group nine or ten were present; then six of these had virtually the decision in their hands, for the majority naturally decided not only in and for the Section, but the decision of the majority then taken was binding on all members attached to the group. The Radical half was dominated by Ledebour. But Ledebour did not hunt round for four or six supporters in the Section beforehand to get a majority, but buttonholed in the Reichstag this or that member whose support he made sure of; in other words, this man was supreme in the Section for a long time, as the great men, Bebel and Singer, though not officially, were on the Radical side. Neither of them ever attended the meetings of the group, but both were always informed of what occurred.

Imperial Foreign Policy

The younger readers' understanding of the political pre-war situation, the Great War, the collapse and the Revolution, may be considerably advanced by a reference to a discussion that took place in the Reichstag on 11th November, 1908. This discussion clarifies the situation under the ex-Kaiser,

William II., to such an extent that further comment is unnecessary. All classes of the community at that time regarded foreign politics as "taboo." It was regarded by ordinary members of Parliament as if it were a secret science, something that had to be left on trust to responsible statesmen. At the same time the work of responsible statesmen often consisted in repairing the damage that the Emperor had done by his irresponsible remarks. In November, 1908, no less than five different questions were asked, all bearing on the same subject. The text of these questions by the Conservative members, the Party most loyal to the Kaiser, is given here.

"Is the Imperial Chancellor prepared to give further information concerning the facts that have been published from H.M. the Emperor's conversations in the English *Sun?*"

Of the numberless random talks indulged in by the Kaiser on every unsuitable occasion, there was just one that had been published by the London *Daily Telegraph,* in which four points in the main were discussed:

1. The German Emperor had declared to an English statesman that he, the Emperor, was England's candid friend—in opposition to the majority of the German people.

2. The German Emperor had related how he, in December, 1899, sent to his grandmother, the Queen of England, a plan of campaign against the Boers, drawn out by himself and approved by his General Staff, and that this plan agreed mainly with the actual plan carried out by Lord Roberts, that led to the defeat of the Boers.

3. The German Emperor had asserted that in 1899 France and Russia approached him with a proposal for forcing England to end the war with the Boers, and humbling her in the dust—and that he prevented the carrying out of this plan.

4. The German Emperor had requested the English to

hold themselves in readiness to protect mutual interests in the Pacific against Japan and China with the united Anglo-German fleets.

A piteous howl rose from the papers of the Right. The Conservative *Reichsbote* said that such a severe blow had been struck at German policy as had never been struck before. The *Rheinisch-Westfälische Zeitung,* the organ of the great Industrialists, said, among other things:

"It will most deeply wound the soul of the German people that its Emperor worked out the plan of campaign through which the Boers, a brave and kindred nation, have been destroyed. . . ."

The whole Press struck the same note. Prince Bülow, then the Imperial Chancellor, asked to resign. This is how things stood when the above questions came up for discussion. To save space I will only quote two speakers who sat on the extreme Right, and therefore were most closely associated with the Emperor.

Von Heydebrand (Conservative) said:

"One will not correctly account for the excitement by merely connecting it with recent events and appearances. One must quite frankly speak one's mind, that here is a sea of trouble and misgiving, and one may also safely say of bad feeling, that has been accumulating for years in circles whose loyalty to the Emperor and Empire no one has ever doubted."

Liebermann von Sonnenberg (Anti-Semite):

"What the honourable member Singer has said will be endorsed in many points. . . . Every word I must say here to-day against the All Highest gives me, as a loyal supporter of the Monarchy, not only mental, but literally physical pain; trust in the people has fallen to zero."

And the Imperial Chancellor said:

"The view that the publication of these conversations has not produced the effect desired by H.M. the Emperor in England, but has caused deep unrest and painful regret in our own country, will induce the Emperor—I have been convinced of it during these difficult days—to observe even in private conversations that reserve that is indispensable alike to the interests of a united policy and the authority of the Crown. Should it not be so, neither I nor any of my successors would be able to bear the responsibility."

Prince Bülow did not go; the Emperor did not dismiss him, but hated him from now on intensely. The National Parties had not the courage to draw the necessary conclusions and muzzle the Emperor by making pertinent alterations in the Constitution, and so things went on.

Quotations from My Opening Speeches

On Bebel's proposal, I was unanimously chosen by the Section to deliver the opening speech. Not before 5th December, 1908, could I speak my mind for the first time. I will quote but little, and only such passages as will make it obvious how the Section stood with regard to definite questions—especially to military ones.

". . . I miss one item in the accounts. Herr Dernburg has stated there are great diamond fields to be found in our colonies that are far richer than anyone in this world has ever dreamt of. Where are your diamonds and pearls, Mr. Secretary?

"I revert to the word economy. The best economy is a good foreign policy. A small and less powerful state can play a considerable part in the concert of nations with a good foreign policy. A small state with a good foreign policy will be enabled to win for itself a favourable position in the markets of the world, but a bad foreign policy never will. A bad foreign policy will entail sacrifice after sacrifice, without gaining anything. It will be ready to sacrifice blood and treasure over and over again without doing any good to the State, and, on the other hand, will embroil the State in the greatest difficulties. . . .

"Being under the impression that our foreign policy in recent years has been bad, one has hit upon the absurd idea in so-called patriotic circles that we can better our position by war. At the Pan-German Congress it was said: 'What does not get into the head, must get into the legs'—so to speak, therefore, a policy of legs. I beg to decline such a policy. But let somebody tell me what we shall gain by such a policy. One says that successful wars are the outcome of good diplomacy. But I think that those who juggle with war ideas should remember above all a quotation that generals are no better than diplomats, who are at work at the same time. I think, gentlemen, this should give those who are continually spreading war ideas something to think about. . . .

". . . A diplomacy that at one time appeals to the sharp sword, at another speaks of powder that must be kept dry, a diplomacy from which foreign countries must conclude that it is ready to lead out to slaughter hundreds of thousands any day, is bad, very bad. It must lead this way, as the honourable member, Bassermann, pointed out at the end of his speech, when he spoke of the constant new grouping of the Powers, although he forgot the chief thing, which is this, that the German Empire is sitting all alone on the insulator in this new grouping of the Powers."

I then discussed the wide field of foreign policy, as well as the Morocco affair, so painfully settled, and the repeated friction with France and England. The honourable member

Bassermann was surprised at Lord Roberts bringing in a Bill in the House of Lords for a standing army. Are such proceedings on the part of English politicians not ultimately intelligible to anyone who has followed our nation's policy?

"By every German ship that we lay down and by every speech made when she is launched, the power and influence of England—not Germany—are increased. The honourable member Bassermann has also spoken of Italy and Austria; he alluded to the Triple Alliance, quoted words from the Italian Chamber of Deputies and stated as the most material fact that Italy would stick to the Triple Alliance. I should have liked him to quote what Giolitti said—surely a well-known man—that after the expiration of the Triple Alliance one would be forced to seek a close union with Russia, France and England. Austria is, so to speak, the last of the Mohicans among our allies."

I then said something about the employment of secret agents by the police, recalled all the promises, made and broken, of social reform, and then mentioned some incidents at home of the grossest kind. Here are some examples:

Kimpell, a Kassel schoolmaster, had been a Progressive candidate for the Reichstag, but was not elected at the General Election. He was asked before the Second Ballot whom he was going to vote for. His answer was that he would not vote either for the Anti-Semite or the Social Democrat. He was in consequence fined 90 marks. At a Progressive meeting Dr. Theodore Barth made it clear that in the circumstances every Progressive should vote for the Social Democrat at the Second Ballot. Brandau, a schoolmaster, at this meeting was fined 60 marks because he had not called him to order.

I touched on the franchise question at the end, and insisted that serious steps should at last be taken. And then I gave good advice. . . . "You cannot treat the workers, who are conscious of their responsibility to the State, in the senseless way you have done before, but must at last allow them equal rights both in the Empire, province and municipality. How is it to be explained that Prince Bülow can go on sitting as Chancellor and remaining in office? He has recently stated in this House in the debate on the Kaiser's interview: 'Gentlemen, take care that no catastrophe follows on this misfortune.' What does that mean? Prince Bülow is the Chancellor of misfortune, the unlucky Chancellor, and you, gentlemen, stick to him because you fear the next man will be a Chancellor of disaster."

I stated in this speech, six years before the outbreak of war, many things that, although ridiculed at the time, proved later, unfortunately, to be the awful truth: "(1) In war army leaders are no better than diplomatists. (2) Germany, owing to her foreign policy, will be isolated and sit, so to speak, on the insulator. (3) Italy will approach France and England. (4) If Prince Bülow is a Chancellor of misfortune, will not the next be the Chancellor of ruin?"

In the course of my opening speech, as per the shorthand report, a representative from the War Office fainted on the Ministerial bench. In the course of a former opening speech by Bebel everyone knows that Bülow had a slight heart attack, which Court officials definitely called "shamming." Both gentlemen soon recovered; it was therefore no special crime if people did joke about a "judgment" on Cabinet Ministers occasionally in the Reichstag restaurant. Once more there was talk about Bülow's mishap during Bebel's speech. I joined in the conversation, and, turning to Bebel, who seemed to be in a particularly good humour, said, "Well, friend Bebel, you had been making opening speeches for twenty years before you laid out Bülow. I had scarcely been speaking for twenty minutes before a Cabinet Minister was on his back!"

On 30th March, 1909, the Reichstag rejected a Social Democratic resolution in which we desired the Chancellor to take the necessary steps for bringing about an international agreement of the Powers on a joint understanding on the limitation of armaments and the right of capture at sea. I returned next day to this subject. "You have created the impression abroad, where the peculiar character of the Reichstag is not known, that you are opposed on principle to any agreement with regard to these matters. . . . When Ledebour proposed the Social Democratic resolution the day before yesterday, the S.D. Section in the Reichstag sent to the Labour Party in the English House of Commons the following telegram:

" 'The Social Democratic Party in the German Reichstag is bringing forward a motion on an international limitation of armaments and the abolition of the right of capture at sea. In the hope that English and German Socialists will have success on their side in the promotion of peace, the S.D. Party sends to the English Labour Party a brotherly greeting.'

"That this telegram was received with full approval by our brethren in England is proved by the reply which arrived the same day from the English House of Commons and ran as follows:

" 'The British Labour Party is in hearty agreement with you and your efforts to promote an international agreement that will stop expenditure on competitive shipbuilding and abolish the right of capture.

" 'With the best wishes for your success and fraternal greetings from the Labour Party.

"HENDERSON.' "

Then I went on to say:

"I am convinced the agreement on the naval programme will come about because it must come about, unless there is war, and if you put the question to yourselves, the answer is comparatively easy. We only want to realize how the Powers are grouping themselves and what inexhaustible resources Great Britain has throughout the whole world, and that hardly a German ship can sail the seas unless England approves. Things are in any case so serious that it should surely have been expedient for the majority of the Reichstag to have taken a different view.

". . . Our Government seems disinclined to make any concessions, but it should not forget that it is putting itself in the falsest possible position, not only as regards France and England, but also as regards all foreign countries.

"Germany's strength does not depend upon the number of extra dreadnoughts she can build, but on quite different things. Gentlemen, you want a strong Germany that foreign countries can trust, you want a land of culture and peace, then make a Germany that is strong through the freedom and the independence of her people. That is the Germany we want. Make a Germany that is strong in the things I have mentioned, and in secure and lasting friendship with her neighbours, and before all others with England and France."

157

From the Chancellor of Misfortune to the Chancellor of Doom

At the sitting of the Reichstag (10th December, 1909) I protested against the enormous sums that were asked for on behalf of the Army, Navy and the Colonies:

"The effect of the navy fever is pernicious in three ways: in Home affairs through the agitation of the Navy League that has provoked the greatest ill-feeling in South Germany; in financial affairs through exorbitant expenditure; in foreign policy through the mistrust that our warlike preparations have aroused. In the latter England sees a menace that binds her steadfastly to France. On the other hand, it is utterly impossible, even by a considerable increase in taxation, to build a Navy that can be a match for the ·combined fleets of England and France."

Then, turning to the new Chancellor—Prince Bülow had meanwhile been superseded by Bethmann-Hollweg—I said he would be got rid of the moment he did not do what the real rulers of Germany, the Prussian Junkers, demanded of him.

Then I reverted to the election promises of the King of Prussia, and mentioned how the Junkers maintained that a king need not keep his word, and that the Church papers on the Conservative side had defended this view. "Any attempt to violate the promises made in a speech from the Throne was an outrage."

Then I went on: "There were people not belonging to our Party unfortunately—at any rate not yet—who thought every day the Chancellor would make some statement and defend himself stoutly against the roguery imputed to him and say, 'My King and I have nothing to do with the roguery such as those over there demand.' The Chancellor has wrapped himself up in silence. To avoid any misunderstanding, I should like to ask you not to assume that I have implicit confidence in the promise of a King. I know Prussian history sufficiently well to know that breach of faith forms part of the highest traditions of the ruling Prussian House."

International Distribution of Capital

In the middle of March lively debates took place in the Reichstag about the Mannesmann operations in Morocco. Bebel wished to deal with them himself, but felt too ill to do so and asked me to speak. I take only a few sentences from the shorthand report:

". . . A more energetic policy is demanded. You heard that before to-day from Herr Stresemann. I think it is a case of once bitten, twice shy. If, as against the wise diplomacy of foreign countries, the diplomacy of 'twirled moustache ends' had done any good, we might have won a brilliant success. The exact opposite has been achieved: we have suffered a deplorable defeat from the diplomacy of the mailed fist. . . .

". . . One can use foreign policy in the interests of the dynasty, one can use it in the interests of the Junkers, and one can use it in the interests of the working classes. But it is all nonsense to try to convey the impression that one can use it for the benefit of everybody. . . . My duty, I think, is to be frank and I now declare that the whole of the National German Press has been 'got at' and the German people lied to over the Mannesmann affair. It has been said in the House that the general outlook is bright and the economic situation likewise, and though there were no clouds to be seen anywhere, the *Hannoversche Courier* wrote the maddest stuff that has ever been written over this business, as far as I have been able to follow it: that 'right does not cease to be right if it has four million bayonets to back it up.'"

I described at length what was at stake. The Sultan Abdul Asis was "ruling" in Morocco. He had quarrelled with his brother Muley Hafid and so made war upon him. They were a worthy pair, and could say, as they do in Berlin, "We haven't any money" (*Keen Geld hamm'r ooch!*). They borrowed from everywhere as long as they could, made war against each other again, and granted concessions for working the mines. The Emperor stupidly got involved in the Morocco trouble, went to Tangiers and made one of his speeches that was responsible for much bad feeling. Then came the Algeciras Treaty that was ratified by the Powers concerned, who fixed the terms under which concessions could only be granted. Contrary to the terms of the Treaty, the Sultan, after borrowing money from Mannesmann Brothers, granted them valuable secret concessions. They were the "vested rights" for the sake of which Germany was finally to be forced into war.

"A law that only two people knew of, that had not been published or even made known to our Government—this so-called law is the basis of the legal claims of Mannesmann Brothers!"

Now let us suppose that the matter is reversed—that instead of Messrs. Mannesmann Brothers, a Frenchman or Spaniard or Portuguese had succeeded in bamboozling the Sultan into making a secret legal agreement with either of them, I should have liked to hear the outcry they would have made in Germany.

In the course of my speech I demonstrated the international distribution of capital, an interesting example of wheels within wheels in the capitalist groups that has been far too little considered:

"Gentlemen, the economic threads that spread beyond the frontier are increasingly more tightly drawn, and it is really amazing to what extent German capital is employed in France and French capital in Germany. It is a characteristic sign of the times, showing how capital is internationally distributed. In the German group (Mannesmann) Frenchmen and, as far as I know, Portuguese and other nationals are concerned and the 'Union des mines marocaines' contains the names of the Krupps, Gelsenkirchs and the German Emperor. Against this internationalization of exploitation the workers stake the internationalization of the proletariate."

I spoke a word of warning about competitive armaments, and demanded the cultivation of friendly relations with France and England. At the time no man in the street in Germany knew that the Government of Great Britain had three times offered an alliance to the German Empire about the beginning of the twentieth century, and that this had been turned down by the Emperor and Prince Bülow through subservience to Russia.

The Future Belongs to the League of Nations

An Army Bill was once again on the "tapis." On 9th December, 1910, I was the spokesman for the Section.

"Gentlemen, we won't argue the question as to whether we could renounce entirely defensive measures against Russia. But I will stress this fact all the more, that neither in the West nor on the other side of the North Sea can we see a possible enemy. We in Germany and our friends in France and England have firmly made up our minds to prevent the disaster which a war in Europe would mean for the whole of the civilized world. No matter how hard the fight we have to fight on this field, the future surely belongs to the league of the German, French and English nations, and we pledge our honour to work on with this in view."

The Prussian-German Broken China Box

In the same speech (extracts from which have just been given) I talked about Home affairs in the Empire:

"The many promises that have been made in Prussia and Germany to the people as a whole, to individual groups and professions, are like the most brittle china; but the policy you follow is one huge broken china box full of broken promises and bad faith. . . . From the tiny broken crocks on the top in the big box of your Majority Government I will take one thing more, and that is your promise, made in November, 1908, with regard to personal government. That promise was given us here in this place, and was recently discussed long and loudly; now it is said that no promise should have been given us; from this, therefore, it is obvious that a promise was given that was not kept.

"I have only taken out of the chest a few trifles lying on the top. If we were to put our hands down further we should find a whole heap of broken crocks from the Royal Earthenware Factory, all adorned with the noble Prussian coat of arms. As they are only fragments, a big rent goes right across the body and wings of the noble eagle; the only parts intact are its claws and its large Prussian beak.

"If we burrow deeper into the crockery chest of the Majority Government we become convinced that vandals or Bonn Corps students must have been at work here. What has happened to the Royal promise of electoral reform given on October 20th, 1908? What has become of the reform of the franchise promised by the Chancellor, von Bethmann-Hollweg? It has been miserably smashed to pieces by the hands of the Junkers—a fate, moreover, that it richly deserved. It was not intended to please any mortal being who wanted an honest deal with the people. A sigh of relief went through all classes of the German people when the wretched farce of election reform came to an end and the curtain was rung down. One will have to hunt a long time for an instance of such refined perfidy and political incapacity as was dis-closed by the Election Reform Bill. . . . The whole farce is inscribed in indelible letters in German history, and those who have burnt their fingers over this Bill will never lose the scars."

The Fighting Methods of Reaction

In the same speech followed a searching criticism of ir-regularities at the polls and the administration of justice. Then it went on as follows:

"Do not wonder if the last traces of confidence have dis-appeared in consequence of these legal abuses. The *Kreuz-zeitung,* the organ of the gentlemen on the Right, recently said, 'We need special legislation of an extreme kind.' Herr von Heydebrand replied somewhere to that: 'No, we need no special legislation; we only need to tighten up Common Law.' Then the *Reichsbote* up and said, 'We want a *coup d'état.* We can "shut down" Social Democracy by an order from the police, for S.D.'s are outside the law.' This is the policy that you on the Right have been lately pursuing—a policy of downright ruthlessness in its worst imaginable form. I can only say you make no impression upon us by this means. You only prove to us by your speeches and newspapers how dangerous you would be if you only could, as you would like to be. What a lot this gang has forgotten, without learning anything fresh. With lies and deceit, by encouraging men to break their word and the law, the gang behind the *Kreuzzeitung* has been fighting with all conceivable means for years. . . ."

Then I touched on the vicious practice of generalizing:

"If a worker has played the fool, one can't say Social Democracy is responsible for that. What would be your answer if we said that all Conservative editors were asses because Freiherr von Stumm was in the habit of calling the editors of the *Post* asses? And if we were to pass a few general remarks on the editors of the *Kreuzzeitung,* Gödsche and Freiherr von Hammerstein, how badly they would fare and all those on whose behalf Freiherr von Hammerstein has opened his mouth and used his pen. When was your *Kreuzzeitung* most moral and God-fearing? When did it do most for the monarchy and for patriotism? When the late Court Chaplain Stoecker wrote the well-known 'Holocaust' letter, in which it was set out, with underhand devilish cunning, how Bismarck could be entrapped. It was the time when your greatest and best leader, your best speaker and your best writer was chief editor on the *Kreuzzeitung;* it was the time when a convict was at your head. We don't generalize, gentlemen —far from it; we don't draw general conclusions from individual backslidings, as you do. But I will appeal to your sense of decency, as I cannot appeal to your intelligence."

For World's Peace

It is not a particularly pleasant task to criticize foreign policy, because every Social Democrat who presumes to do so always runs the risk of being marked down as a spy and a traitor to his country. I said this much on 30th March, 1911, in the Reichstag, and then added:

"I will again state from this place that we Socialists feel ourselves in brotherly solidarity with the working classes of all countries, and regard war as crime and lunacy. I will go further, and say that the class-conscious worker throughout the world knows only one common enemy—Capitalism, which exasperates a nation and drives it on to murder.

"We Social Democrats are proud of being the first to spread the idea of peace propaganda among the masses. It was a great feat on the part of the International Workers' Congress Meeting in Paris in 1889 to fix 1st May as the day of protest against armaments and of a fine demonstration in favour of peace. The 1st May has proved to be a great day for civilization. Whatever happens among the bourgeois, whatever number of addresses and speeches they may make, what will these mean when compared with the fact that millions of men will come together on the same day in every civilized country in the world to protest in common against preparations for war and launch a unanimous cry for peace and disarmament?

". . . I know that a foreign policy, such as we Socialists consider right, can only be pursued if the working classes have won the upper hand, and by presupposing that Europe and, first and foremost, Germany herself is democratized. The man who opposes this will be answerable for the dangers of war that arise from the competition of Capitalism. I should like to say most definitely that Capitalism alone and its champions will have to bear the responsibility, and we shall saddle the majority in this House with this responsibility if they oppose the peace efforts of International Socialism."

Prussia the German Siberia?

In a speech on Home policy I said in the Reichstag on 17th May, 1912:

"There can be no doubt that we are living in a changing world. Old principalities and powers are wobbling, new forces arise, and new aspirations make themselves heard. The thankless task of supporting what is shaky, of sustaining what is sinking, of persuading corpses that there is still life in them has been set before Herr von Bethmann-Hollweg. Unmaintainable and doomed to perish is the system of personal government that is directly opposed to feelings and desires of the entire people, who expect this House to secure for itself a position corresponding to its authority, and if necessary to fight for it.

". . . Certain remarks by the Kaiser have got abroad about scrapping the Constitution of Alsace-Lorraine and incorporating the country with Prussia. The threat of incorporating Alsace-Lorraine with Prussia we take to be a very grave confession of weakness on the part of the 'powers that be,' and the penalty for disloyalty the heaviest ever inflicted on any State—it is tantamount to penal servitude for life, or to degradation to the lowest category of German society—the Prussian category. [The Right raged and cursed and left the House, along with the Chancellor, at the head of all the members of the Federal Council.] We must most emphatically protest against a personage who is no factor in our Constitution announcing measures by his own authority, without even asking whether the parties concerned—*i.e.* the Reichstag or the Federal Council—without which the thing cannot be done, are agreed to carry out the threat. We mean to put an end to the ominous incidents I have related. No retreat in Alsace-

Lorraine! Advance on Prussia! This is our watchword.

"We accuse you of impeding in an irresponsible fashion the great work of reconciliation between Germany and France —a cause which we have worked for and will continue to work for with a will, to the blessing of both nations and all Europe. In spite of all the vexations that confront us, we will fight on with the same determination as hitherto, and the day will come when the German and the Frenchman will shake each other's hand in friendship and trust. This will be a day that will bring new and happier days. This will be the day of victory, for we shall be convinced that we are serving the true interests of the German Fatherland by opposing this Army Bill. Whatever may be its fate, we will fight for the great and splendid ideals of peace and freedom from the Belt to the Pyrenees. The work of Germany and France, one and all united in the work for freedom and civilization!"

The Last Speech before the War

In the course of latter pre-War years the war danger had been again and again alluded to; the fight against militarism had been conducted in the bitterest way, peace between the nations demanded, and on 5th April, 1914, an opportunity occurred for showing up the police administration in Prussia. I said, among other things:

"I have to-day to complain of the magistrates in a great part of the Empire in that they do not keep to the law, and when applying it, act arbitrarily, illegally and against the interests of the working classes of our people. Many instances were quoted, among others one from Königsberg. A school breaking-up party was given to the children. This breaking-up party was forbidden on the ground that it was a political meet-

167

ing, and dissolved. Now listen to what the row was all about. The organizer was twice placed under arrest, forcibly dragged off the platform and locked up for hours without any reason being given. . . . The youngsters were twice expelled with cuffs and kicks. A girl of twenty was taken into custody on the terrible charge that she was only eighteen or less than eighteen and hauled off to the police station.

"Gentlemen, I should regard it as a grave dereliction of duty if I did not tell you what was going on at this juvenile entertainment thus broken up by the brutality of the police. Here is a copy of the programme that I will now read out to you. It is an innocent document intended for the entertainment of lower class children—and to show up the police. Permit me to read it.

SCHOOL BREAKING-UP CONCERT

1. Organ Prelude. 2. Recitation "To the Young" (Frederick Hebbel). 3. The Vorwärts Glee Club. (a) A hymn with organ accompaniment, "Ernest, Duke of Saxony"; (b) "March wind" (Angerer); (c) "Broken Troth" (Fr. Silcher). 4. Commemoration Address. 5. Piano Solos. 6. Organ Solo, "Andante" (Mendelssohn). 7. Baritone Solos (Schubert). 8. Recitation, "The Weekly Sermon" (Gottfried Keller). 9. Piano Solos. 10. Selections, (a) Uthmann, (b) Chorus of the Priests from the Magic Flute (Mozart).

"Any man of any understanding must feel glad that the youth of the poorer classes are brought up to enjoy in this way an artistic treat. But the police arrived, behaved like brutes and broke up the party. It forbade compositions by Liszt, Mozart, Schumann, Schubert and poems by Hebbel and Keller—proofs positive of a political meeting. I will say no more. The thing speaks for itself, as well as the fact that in Düsseldorf a lecture intended for juveniles on the Evils of Intemperance was forbidden. In Lichtenberg a lecture on the 'Breeding and Development of Silkworms' was likewise forbidden. This, too, was a political meeting!"

VIII

THE PRESIDENCY OF THE REICHSTAG

THE "devotion to principle," even among outstanding
Social Democratic Party leaders, was formerly sometimes rather grotesque, as it strikes us to-day. On the
hundredth birthday of William Liebknecht I reminded his
friends how bitterly the Old Man (everybody in the Party
called him so) complained that he was not considered a thorough-going Radical. To prove his thorough-going Radical-
ism, that was disputed in Berlin, and his absolute devotion
to principle, he definitely declared he had taken a decided
stand against the Social Democratic Section taking any part
in the councils of the Senior Committee. Such an attitude
would only be regarded to-day as a jest. But it is quite unfair to jest at Liebknecht. It should always be realized how
the Seniors and Elders of our Party were sometimes treated
in the past, not only by the police, the Government and the
Law Courts, but also in public and by political opponents.
Our leaders at certain times were treated generally as fellows
of the basest sort. The comic-song writer would sing of Bebel,
"Whether you say Bebel or Babel (*Pöbel*) is all one to me."
It was a long time before the Progressives, the fathers of our
Democrats to-day, gradually understood that Social Democrats
were not topers, spongers (once a sponger always a sponger)
or budding jail-birds. Eugene Richter did some very dirty
work here. An attitude like Liebknecht's was not intelligible
to Social Democrats, who, like myself, had been through
many years of the Socialist Law as active members of the

170

Party. Younger workers can form hardly any conception of the hatred animating our brother outlaws against middle-class society. Yet the Senior Committee was just as harmless in old Liebknecht's time as it is to-day. Its only actual duty was to see that the President and the Party leaders agreed on the best possible method of despatching business, when the meetings should begin, what the day off should be and the time limit for speeches, etc. Liebknecht declined to have any sort of dealings with the bourgeois parties. Far more important was the attitude for the Radical leaders to the question as to whether the Party should take part in elections to the Town Council and Prussian Diet. In both cases, at any rate in Prussia, the Three Class method of voting was considered. It was a long time before the policy of abstention at the municipal elections was abandoned, and a still longer time before permission was granted to vote at the elections for the Prussian Diet. Liebknecht was very strongly opposed to the latter, and took the view that "the Diet, along with its miserable franchise, should be allowed to stew in its own juice."

The reader must be reminded of these differences, that have been settled long ago, because otherwise he will hardly understand the vexed question as to whether the S.D. Party should put in a claim for representation for the Presidency of the Reichstag, and whether, should the question be answered in the affirmative, the member appointed to be the sacrificial lamb should attend all the so-called Court functions. In the Press and at Party conferences there had been some lively discussions on these questions.

The question as to whether the Social Democratic Party should press their claim to be represented for the Presidency became acute after the Party's brilliant successes at the elections in January, 1912. According to Parliamentary usage the strong-

est Party had a claim to the office of President, though in practice it was often ignored. The S.D. Party, with its 110 seats,
was by far the strongest Party in the Reichstag, and could
with full right demand the Presidency. But it was decided
only to claim the office of the first Vice-President, because then,
is was thought, the question of "Court duties" would not arise,
for in the laws and regulations the President, and never the
Presidency, was mentioned. Along with other matters this
cropped up—that the "Black-blue" Block, which had suffered
such a bad defeat at the elections, must be excluded from the
Presidency. It could have been easily managed if the National
Liberals had agreed to promise faithfully to vote for a Social
Democrat as first Vice-President, after the Social Democrats
had voted for a National Liberal as President. The Progressives were to nominate the second Vice-President. There was
not the slightest difference about this.

This plan, so Dr. Franz Mehring wrote at the time in the
Neue Zeit, was made without the "wobblers" in the National
Liberal camp, who badly wanted the "Black-blue" minority to
be represented in the Presidential chair. The question of the
Presidency, which one must certainly not over-estimate, acquired thereby a great political importance. Should the National Liberal flirtation with the defeated members of the
Block begin on the first day of the new Reichstag, the worst
was to be feared for the future, and the S.D. Party had most
urgent reasons for avoiding the slightest contact with these
miserable intriguers. It had declared itself ready to vote for
a National Liberal President if the National Liberals handed
over to the S.D.'s the office of the first Vice-President. But it
naturally had to get a good guarantee that this assurance would
be fulfilled; there must be not the slightest chance of a Conservative or a whole-hogger of a profiteer being elected as the

first Vice-President instead of its own candidate, after it had brought about the election of a National Liberal President. And as the National Liberals declined to commit themselves to a binding undertaking, it was quite natural for the S.D. Section to act on their own in the election of the President and to nominate their own candidate, Bebel.

There the reader has in a nutshell all he requires to know to be able to understand the situation. Mehring, who could find plenty of faults in everything the Executive or Section did or failed to do, was in full accord this time with the S.D. Section. The Section was naturally quite clear on this—that the consequence of its action might be the election of a "Black-blue" President, and, as a matter of fact, this is what happened. However unpleasant this possibility might be, it was nothing compared to the terrible censure the S.D. Section would incur from everybody if they let themselves be tricked by the National Liberals. It was at last high time to put a stop to the out-of-date and perfidious tactics of the Liberals, who were paving the road for reaction by deserting wholesale their own principles, and then making Social Democracy responsible for the victory of reaction, because it would not stoop to intrigue. A "Black-blue" President was certainly an unpleasant thing, but, comparatively speaking, a much lesser evil than if Social Democracy had let itself be led by the nose from the start by National Liberals, as National Liberals had been so often led by Bismarck.

The risk of electing a Social Democrat to the Presidency of the Reichstag was described in the National Liberal and Conservative Press as an impossible monstrosity. Bebel was in great excitement over the choice of a suitable candidate. As I learnt later, he had been in communication with Richard Fischer, a member of the Reichstag and a personal friend of his, with the object of getting his advice. One morning a sitting of the members of the Executive and the committee of the Section was called to discuss the question of who was to be brought forward as a candidate for the Presidency. To my mild surprise, Richard Fischer proposed me, Bebel seconded, and no other name was mentioned. As the Section unanimously concurred, I was once more a candidate.

Three Short Sittings of the Reichstag

I

The new Reichstag was opened on Friday, 9th February, 1912, under the Presidency of the humorous ex-President Albert Träger. The elections for the Presidency were begun. At the election of the President for which we now brought Bebel forward after the National Liberal fiasco, three ballots were necessary. At the first ballot the votes given were: Dr. Spahn, 185; Bebel, 110; Prince von Schönaich-Carolath, 88; Dr. Paasche, 1; Heine-Desau, 1. None of the gentlemen had therefore an absolute majority and all five selected candidates, according to the order of the day, had to be put up again.

Ex-President Träger: "The first nomination begins with the letter C. . . ."

Three hundred and eighty-eight votes were given. The absolute majority, with 385 valid voting papers, was 193. Result: Spahn, 186; Bebel, 114; Prince von Schönaich-Carolath, 85. A second ballot had to be taken. Only the two gentlemen who had polled the most votes were concerned, Dr. Spahn and Bebel. The first nomination began with the letter D. Three hundred and eighty-four votes were given, thirteen of which were spoilt. Of the 371 valid votes Dr. Spahn

Zur Erinnerung an den 9. Februar 1912,

den denkwürdigen „Ehrentag" der national-
liberalen Fraktion des Reichstages, an dem sie
einem roten Genossen die Ehre der Wahl zum
ersten Vizepräsidenten zuteil werden ließ.

TO THE MEMORY OF FEBRUARY 9, 1912

*The memorable "Day of Honor" of
the national liberal faction of the
Reichstag, at which a Red member
was honoured with the election of
first Vice-President*

Caricature by an unknown artist

had 196 and Bebel 175. Dr. Spahn accepted election and took the chair.

Then we proceeded to elect the first Vice-President. The first nomination began with the letter E. The result was: 386 votes were given. Absolute majority, 183. Scheidemann, 188; Dietrich, 174; Dr. Paasche, 3. Scheidemann, member of the Reichstag, is hereby elected.

Dr. Paasche was then elected second Vice-President with 274 votes.

In the Conservative Press a dead set was made against the Social Democratic Vice-President that surpassed anything previously known. The National Liberals, who were "responsible for the election," were almost as bitterly attacked. The reader will see the effects of this outburst in the two official reports here given

II

"On Tuesday, 13th February, 1912, the sitting was opened by the first Vice-President Scheidemann. He said, 'I have allowed three days' leave of absence each to Messrs. Bartling and Heine-Dessau. On account of illness, Prince Salm, member of the Reichstag, has applied for fourteen days extension of leave. Dr. Freiherr von Hertling, member of the Reichstag, has resigned his seat in the Reichstag owing to his appointment as Secretary of State in the Bavarian Government. The necessary steps for a by-election have been already taken. The following message has been received from Dr. Spahn:

" 'Berlin,
" '12th February, 1912.
" 'I beg to inform the President of the Reichstag that I resign my office as President.—SPAHN.' "

III

"*Wednesday, 14th February,* 1912.—Vice-President Scheidemann opened the sitting. He said, 'Dr. Paasche, member of
the Reichstag, has addressed the following communication to
the President of same:

"'*Berlin,*
"'*14th February,* 1912.

"'I beg to inform the President of the Reichstag that I
hereby resign my office as second Vice-President.—D.
PAASCHE.'

"I propose to the House that we should proceed to elect
to-day a second Vice-President to fill this vacancy directly
after the election of the President. This is not permissible
if any member objects. There is no objection. We will
therefore proceed to elect a second Vice-President after the
election of the President. First item on the agenda is the election of the President. The first nomination begins with the
letter H. . . . The result of the election is as follows: 374 votes
recorded, 174 of which are blank; 200 valid voting papers remain. The absolute majority is 101. Result: Kämpf, member
of the Reichstag, 195 votes. . . . Hereby Kämpf, member of
the Reichstag, is elected President. Kämpf accepts office. As
second Vice-President, Dove, member of the Reichstag, has
been elected."

It was a pleasure to read the Berlin morning papers on
15th February, 1912. The joy in the columns of the *Vorwärts*
over the election of a member of the Democratic Party was
counterbalanced by the depression of the papers on the Conservative side.

The *Deutsche Zeitung* (Conservative) was absolutely speech-less with astonishment. It tried to influence the Centre. It could not be expected that the Centre would depart from its decision to take no part in the Presidential election in any circumstances should a Social Democrat be elected.

This paper of the Country Conservative Party printed directly underneath its comments the following telegram: "Privy Councillor von Bötinger, a member of the House of Peers, sends this telegram from Elberfeld: 'According to what I have just heard that a large number of the National Liberal Party voted for the Social Democratic candidate at to-day's election for the President of the Reichstag, I am thereby forced to sever my connection with the National Liberal Party.' "

The warnings of the Conservative Block addressed to Spahn were quickly crowned with success. For three days "big Peter" wrestled with himself and God, and then in terror fled from the presence of the Red Vice-President. Only Paasche was unwilling to announce his withdrawal. He assured me quite angrily during these days that he did not see the remotest reason for retiring from the Presidency. Paasche and I had known each other since 1888. Prior to exchanging his professorship at Marburg for one at Charlottenburg we lived close to each other for years, and often conversed after being introduced at a meeting. In spite of political differences we were on quite good terms. Paasche in the sad but comic days of the Presidential election had spoken abusively to me of his Party friend and rival, Prince von Schönaich-Carloath, a very honest and inoffensive individual. He was firmly convinced that he would have to retire definitely from the Presidency; had he thought there was even the remotest chance of being re-elected he would have immediately sent in his resignation in loyalty to his principles, and not fought with him-

self and his Party two days longer than Spahn had done
before intimating his wish to retire on 14th February.

Some very amusing "posers" appeared in the Press before
and after the sitting over which I presided on 13th February.
If the abominable Democrat, this traducer of the Hohenzollerns, should be really elected, would he go to Court? How
far was he committed to fulfil his Court duties? Had the
S.D. Section made up its mind on the question? What was
his own attitude?

Ah! what a worrying time the gentlemen on the Right
had! It was really delightful to see in what different tones
they gave vent to their woes. My Party, in agreement with
me, had declared its readiness to fulfil all duties that were con-
stitutionally connected with the office of a Vice-President,
and no more. There was nothing in black and white about
any Court duties, either in the Constitution or in the rules
of the House.

It would have been the easiest job in the world to have
elected Prince von Schönaich-Carolath as first President at
the final election on 8th March, if the National Liberals had
not been appalled at the courage they had showed on 9th
February in voting for me. Fearful of runaways like
Bötinger, who had hitherto provided the funds of the National Liberal treasury, but dreading also the grandees east
of the Elbe controlling the Prussian Government, the disciples
of Bassermann would have rather sacrificed the Presidency
than have dared to vote again for a Social Democrat.

In these days Bebel was extraordinarily excited, and on
13th February his nerves had obviously gone. He was living at the time in the Schöneberger Hauptstrasse, about twenty
minutes from my house, in Steglitz. On the day in question
he sent for me twice after the House adjourned to impress

it again upon me that I was in no circumstance to let myself be pushed out of the Chair. He was convinced the Opposition would leave no stone unturned to make me so thoroughly sick of my job that perhaps I might throw it up in a fit of anger. It was quite an unnecessary anxiety, as it was obvious that without the consent of my friends and colleagues I should do nothing on my own hook in such a difficult matter. At one of our talks Bebel touched on the subject of dress. "Have you a frock-coat?" He uttered a sigh of relief on my telling him with a laugh that I had. For Bebel, the Reichstag was a truly great and significant thing. This was not only to be seen in casual remarks and conversation, but in the whole of his attitude to Parliament, even in his clothes. I cannot recollect ever having seen Bebel in anything but a frock-coat, whereas I recollect perfectly his falling foul of a Social Democratic member who had lit up a pipe in the small lobby on the Left side of the House. "The Reichstag is not a village pub." I have no doubts at all that Bebel would have loudly protested against the new practice of turning up here in mountaineering costume—knickerbockers and garters, not to mention pea-green and black shirts.

For Bebel the Reichstag was, in fact, the "High Court of Parliament," which he only entered in his Sunday best, because the people should send here its best man—at any rate those who enjoyed its confidence and would represent its interests.

One should not enter a house of this sort, according to Bebel, as one enters a tavern. I will give you from these days a striking instance of the solemn, earnest way in which Bebel approached anything connected with the Reichstag. For the time being I was the only President in the House during the incidents I have mentioned. Before the sitting began on 13th

February, the Social Democratic Section held a meeting which I naturally attended. The probable course of business in the House was discussed. When I got up to speak (I had been sitting in a dimly lighted corner of the room), Bebel, who had not noticed me, jumped up in great surprise and asked me to leave the meeting! He said that it was customary in the Reichstag for the President to sever his connection with his Party, to show that he was above Party. As I was at the time the only President there, I had to leave the meeting. In no case should we offend against the Parliamentary tradition. Amid the hearty laughter of the Section I had to withdraw.

"The Capable President"

All circles opposed to the Social Democrats seem to have thought at that time that a Socialist was bound to come to grief directly he became President. There is scarcely any other explanation for the rather fulsome chorus of praise from the Press of every political opinion that greeted my very modest efforts in the Chair. Reports of the meetings presided over by me read so comically that a reproduction of some of the Press comments may be justified.

The *Berliner Tageblatt* said:

"Scheidemann is no different from any 'gentleman' President, and one sees that he discharges his functions with extraordinary skill, calm and business knowledge. Herr Scheidemann, in a very quiet, clear voice, as if he had been years in the Chair, opens the sitting. Even the Right must admit that the 'Comrade' one hears with interest does his job very well."

The *Frankfurter Zeitung:*

"Some papers call it a historic moment, but we must acknowledge that Herr Scheidemann, the Social Democrats' first Vice-President, did his work well—as if that had ever been doubted. . . . A slim gentleman, with a sharply cut head, whom you might take for a writer or painter, took his seat in the Chair, as to the manner born."

The Berlin *Morgenpost* wrote quite enthusiastically:

"Everything passed off excellently. Philip Scheidemann, the duly elected first Vice-President of the German Reichstag, overcame the difficulties of quite a peculiar position. The short sitting was long enough for the first Social Democratic President to display a really brilliant capacity for the art of chairmanship."

The opinion of the organs of the Centre was somewhat the same.

The *Magdeburger Zeitung* spoke of a historic moment:

"Scheidemann rises with dignity, puts his waistcoat straight, catches hold of the bell and declares the opening of the sitting. His strong voice is heard in the farthest corners of the hall and every one of his words can be heard. He announces, as if it were self-evident, that *he* has given the two members, Prince zu Salm and Bartling, leave of absence, and that Freiherr von Hertling has resigned his seat."

The *Germania,* the organ of the Centre, spoke also of a historic moment:

"In a loud voice the S.D. President announced the measures he had already taken."

The *Tägliche Rundschau,* the paper of the Evangelical clergy, was completely beside itself.

"As if he had been born to high office, he takes the place of Count Schwerin. This historian of the Hohenzollern family does not do his work badly. Our Ministers have bent their necks under the Red yoke."

Even the extremist organs of the Right find words of recognition, but—they could not change their skins.

The *Schlesische Nachrichten* alluded to the spread of unrest in the country, that concerned all Parties, militant or non-militant, Evangelicals or Orthodox Catholics. It remarked:

"Such an ornamental President of the Reichstag has never been seen in the Chair as Comrade Scheidemann; any stranger would assume that a multi-millionaire sat in the Presidential Chair. Extremely well dressed, a cut-away waistcoat, a faultless tie—in short, a perfect model for the best tailor in Berlin."

But then it let drive about the wild traducers of the Hohenzollerns! Enough said!

I Am Not Going to See the Kaiser

Up to 8th March fresh attacks on me were daily occurrences. My reply to a pertinent question by Messrs. Kämpf and Dove, that they were not to be deterred in any way, owing to me, from asking the Emperor to receive them for the purpose of informing him personally about the new constitution of the Reichstag, was decisive for my final removal from the Presidency; and I added that I would not ask the Kaiser for anything—least of all for an audience. It may seem absurd to-day that Social Democrats were tripped up over these trifles. But I ask you to remember what I previously said on the former position of the Party in regard to the Town Council and Diet elections. One can only appreciate rightly the conduct of Parties and individuals if one takes oneself back to times when such sins of commission and omission, that seem incomprehensible to-day, did occur. My refusal to go to see the Kaiser led to fresh and violent protests in the Press. It was clear that my election would not in any circumstances be confirmed at the final ballot. Messrs. Kämpf and Dove had requested the Emperor to receive them. But the Emperor had sent word to say that while thanking them for their laudable intention, he was prevented from receiving them. He cared nothing for the two old gentlemen, as people said in jest at the time; he wanted only to receive them in company with their uncouth comrade.

Herr von Bethmann-Hollweg made use of the snub at the time to intimidate the bourgeois parties. He wished to point out to them that they would no longer be received by the Emperor should they again presume to elect a Social Democrat.

My Farewell Greeting (C as in Camel)

The day of reckoning, 8th March, had come meanwhile. The Reichstag and its Presidency could definitely be relieved of its Social Democratic Vice-President. Much preparatory work of a serio-comic character had been done before that day came, verbally, in writing and in caricature. Whatever this horrible revolutionary had ever said against Capitalism, the Junkers, against the Hohenzollerns in general and William II. in particular, against competitive armaments and war, every call to order that had descended on his "bald pate" —every mortal thing, in fact, was dragged in; the smallest chip of wood, the tiniest splinter was acceptable for the funeral pyre on which the heretic was to be burnt.

Now the day was at hand, the day on which the previous election was to be ratified—four weeks after the first.

Everything went quite smoothly on 8th March. Kämpf became President. Paasche, with Kämpf as presiding officer, was elected first Vice-President, Dove the second. One hundred and fifty-five votes from Social Democrats and Progressives were recorded for me. I had to preside at Kämpf's election. Right up to the last every attempt was made by the gentlemen on the Right to trip me up; up to the bitter end I was to have difficulties. Here is one of the best jests made by those who, according to the Bible, shall see God. When the President calls out the first letter of the candidate's name—A, B or C—a storm of shouting breaks out from "the poor in spirit." "What A? No, it's K. Or C? Or D? Or E?" All this was intended to make me lose my temper and put me off my game. These attempts and the shouting did not come off, however. What I said could be heard clearly and distinctly in every corner of the House, "The name begins with a C." The members and the strangers in the crowded galleries yelled with delight for minutes together on my answering the idiotic shouts from the Right—"What, A?" "What, H?"—clearly and with good temper as I bade farewell to the Presidential Chair: "No, C as in Camel." [1]

[1] The German word *Kamel* means idiot.

IX

INTERNATIONAL WORK FOR PEACE

FROM extracts from speeches in the Reichstag given in this book, the reader will clearly see with what resolution the Social Democratic Party tackled the question of competitive armaments, that in their opinion led only to war; at the same time it should not be forgotten that all S.D. speakers thoroughly agreed to that in principle. German Social Democracy has always adopted a hostile attitude to militarism in general and to the German Empire under William in particular, but has never been opposed to the doctrine of self-defence, as has been so repeatedly alleged. A whole Party cannot be held responsible for misinterpretations arising from remarks ruthlessly torn from their context, or from the tone of a disgruntled individual, any more than the Conservative Party or its successor, the German National Party, can be held responsible for the actions of its outstanding leader, Freiherr von Hammerstein.

The best and surest protection that can be offered to our Fatherland against attack is what the Social Democrat demanded in his Party programme—universal training for self-defence; a citizen army instead of a standing army; the deciding of peace and war by the People's representatives; and the settlement of international disputes by arbitration. No other German political Party has demanded such an extensive national training in case of war for self-defence. These demands have been ridiculed and rejected partly as Utopian, partly as "smuggish," with a stupid reference to 1848. In the third and fourth years of the War, *i.e.* in the hours of our greatest need, young men were hauled off for compulsory service; they were drilled in a way for a few weeks and then sent to the front and the trenches. Had the Social Democratic military programme been adopted we should have had millions more men at our disposal in 1914 had war then come, and what that would have meant at the beginning is too obvious for words. Another reproach to Social Democracy our opponents thought especially serious was that the English Socialists were first and last Englishmen, the French Socialists were first and last Frenchmen, and we German Socialists were first just International Socialists, fellows without a country, and last, if at all, only Germans. The reproach is as old as the Socialist movement; in France the same reproach is cast at our comrades living there, in England against Social Democrats, as in Germany against us. In England and France we are singled out as patriotic model fellows compared with our comrades living there without a country. How senseless all these reproaches are can best be seen from the resolutions of International Congresses, and also from the conduct of our comrades in the Parliaments of France, England, Belgium and all other lands, in as far as these are democratically represented. The singling out of French and German Socialists provokes downright ridicule among all who know anything of International Socialism. In 1914 the tragic side for both parties lay in the fact that both were ready to do all in their power to stop war, and each was convinced that their country had been outrageously attacked, and no one could leave his Fatherland in the lurch in the hour of need.

But we must not anticipate situations that are to be discussed later; only we must mention what French and German Socialists did in common in the three years before the War to oppose war.

At the elections to the Reichstag in 1912 it was proved that more than every third voter had voted Social Democratic in Germany. In other words, Germany would soon have a Social Democratic majority. This would mean, so people thought at home and abroad, that personal government, which was universally regarded as a permanent war danger, was over. Men were calculating on democratic reform. The working class in Germany were undoubtedly too sanguine, but in France it was definitely assumed that the sword of Damocles would be removed, though all risk of war could not be regarded as eliminated.

Election Celebrations in Paris

As our French comrades' election victories had been celebrated by us as our own, the French in 1912 felt a genuine desire, after our really sweeping victories, to celebrate ours publicly in the eyes of everybody as theirs—as a victory for International Social Democracy. Their congratulations to the German Social Democrats were coupled with the request to send a German comrade to Paris, so that he might speak at a great demonstration of our united intention of seeking and ensuring peace before all things. The Executive deputed me to go to Paris. An inspiring demonstration, animated with the best intentions of making peace secure, breathing brotherly love and sincere friendship, took place in Paris on 30th March, 1912, in the Salle Wagram. The *Humanité* reported this important meeting next morning under this headline: "Six thousand people welcome with enthusiasm the promises of peace." I described the growth of German Social Democracy, the increase of members of the movement, and the increased circulation of the *Vorwärts*—the paper then counted 170,000 subscribers —and then expressed the hope that our combined efforts to secure peace would be successful. "Nous luttons ensemble— we fight together, side by side. When German solidarity and discipline mate with French 'go' and enthusiasm, then unconquerable strength will be given us." The *Humanité* in its report spoke of a great and continuous ovation, which was renewed when Jean Jaurès came forward to speak.

Then a scene was enacted that will for ever be remembered by all present. Jaurès embraced me and literally danced me round the stage, overjoyed, as he said, at my having struck a note he had long wanted to hear and whose sound he had scarcely dared to expect. He told me this before the applause had died down and before he began his speech. Our French comrades had at the time hard struggles with the Anarchist Syndicalists. Only a few weeks had passed since shots had been fired in the same hall at a Socialist meeting. Jaurès reminded us of that when he called upon me to speak. He fervently wished the German speaker would tell them what unity could do. Without knowing what Jaurès meant precisely, I succeeded in striking the right note. Jaurès spoke passionately, with an emphasis I had never heard before in any speaker. During his speech he kept on turning to me, sitting at the table with the Executive, rather than to the meeting itself. At one time his words were like a whisper, as if he were pleading and entreating like a lover to his mistress; at another his voice was like a mighty wind, sweeping everything away that stood in its course.

Continuous cheering followed his speech. While the applause thundered through the hall, he led me to the footlights and embraced me again. This Paris celebration of a German victory to which international importance was attached, was a peace demonstration of enormous significance.

New Peace Demonstrations

The times were over when the good old townsman on his walk on Easter Sunday could find nothing better to talk about than war and rumours of war, for far away in Turkey nations were fighting each other. When the news came that war had broken out in the Balkans in 1912, no European could have gone to bed free from worry. Despite the peace demonstrations of International Social Democracy Europe was like a powder flask. If the tiniest spark from the Balkans got into it the most awful explosion would follow. International Social Democracy quickly got to work to mobilize all European nations against war. In all Western countries thousands of meetings were held and myriads of tracts circulated. In every capital demonstrations were held at which well-known speakers of the International orated. In Germany Frenchmen spoke, in France Germans. Dr. Louis Frank spoke in London; Molkenbuhr in Amsterdam; Dr. Renner of Vienna and O'Grady of London spoke in Berlin. Jean Jaurès was forbidden to speak in Berlin. I was allowed to speak freely in Paris. To my great joy, I was once again with Jaurès, Edward Vaillant, Jules Guesde, the old Paris Communard, Engelbert Pernerstorffer of Vienna and MacDonald of London.

The meetings were everywhere brilliantly successful. The demonstration in Paris was one of the biggest I ever attended. The masses were invited to St. Gervais near Paris, and appeared in their tens of thousands. The *Humanité* the next day printed across its front page: "Tens of thousands of demonstrators against war." Underneath it printed in the largest type a sentence from my speech: "Nous ne voulons pas tirer sur vous," which clearly means to say, "We won't fire on you, because we are working together for peace." No, we won't fire on you; on the contrary, we will shake you by the hand, for we welcome you as friends and fellow combatants, who have one common enemy—International Capitalism. The sense of my speech was so clear that the war-mongers in Berlin could not do anything. Their "creatures" caught hold of one of their most favourite devices—they lied! They simply made out of "Nous ne voulons pas tirer sur vous," "Nous ne tirerons pas sur vous." It naturally cost them nothing to construe this into downright treason: You German Social Democrats refuse to shoot Frenchmen, even if they attack you.

In the Reichstag there was a heated debate. Although I proved it to be a Nationalistic lie up to the hilt, it was later on frequently made use of.

The Congress in Bâle

The Peace demonstration in the European capitals doubtless made a great impression on the war-mongers, who existed, and unfortunately still exist, in all countries. Every demonstration was surpassed by the International Congress that was summoned to Bâle for 24th November, 1912, through the International Socialist Bureau, and was opened, to the horror of all Philistines, by Blocher, the Swiss Prime Minister. The following resolution was passed unanimously in Bâle:

"In view of the threat of the outbreak of war, all workers and their Parliamentary representatives in the countries concerned, with the support of the united effort of the International Bureau, are to do their very utmost to hinder the outbreak of war by every conceivable means, which change according to the intensity of class warfare and the general political situation. Should war break out, it is their duty to end it in the quickest way possible and strive with all their might to utilize the economic and political crisis, caused by war, to rouse the people and hasten the abolition of capitalistic class tyranny."

The resolutions of the International Congresses at Stuttgart and Copenhagen were similarly worded.

Should soldiers of any country have taken offence at the Socialist demonstrations, Socialists should try to enlist their sympathies by referring to the havoc of war in the Balkans, at the same time pointing out the ever-present risk of war, the insufficient numbers of fighting men and their faulty equipment. In Germany there was a new Army Bill; in France the Army was to be strengthened by prolonging the period of service; in England extra ships were being built owing to Germany's warlike naval preparations; and so the "war propeller" revolves *ad infinitum*. The short extracts from speeches in the Reichstag contained in this book will make the Social Democratic policy quite clear against the lunatic armament policy. The dangers of military complications were greatest in France and Germany. For this reason Socialists of these two countries intended to declare to the whole world that they were absolutely determined to resist war at all costs.

Conferences in Berne and Bâle

The Franco-German Entente Conferences came to be held in Switzerland owing to the suggestion of Comrades Stampfer and Ludwig Frank. The French comrades agreed at once. The matter was so arranged that an Entente Conference was summoned by the Swiss Party representatives of every per-

GROUP PICTURE TAKEN AT THE MEETING OF THE
GERMAN-FRENCH INTERPARLIAMENTARY COMMISSION
AT BALE, NOVEMBER 24, 1912

*(1) Dietz, (2) Marcel Sembat, (5) Haase-Königs-
berg, (6) Scheidemann, (7) Ledebour,
(11) Jaurès, (14) Ludwig Haas*

suasion for Whitsuntide, 1913, to which members of Parliament from all Parties in France and Germany were to be invited. The object of the conferences was this: the promotion of friendly relations between France and Germany. One hundred and fifty-six French and German deputies took part: eighty-three came from France, and included several ex-Ministers, whereas only six members of Parliament came from Germany, four of whom belonged to the People's Party and two were Alsatians. The small number of M.P.'s from Germany is proof positive that Liberalism, except for a small section, had gone over completely to Imperialism. The result of the Conference was in every way satisfactory and encouraging. The conversion of such a mixed body of Parliamentarians to the definite cause of peace, as well as the unqualified recognition of the principle of arbitration, as had been required in our Social Democratic programme, were cheering facts. A permanent Franco-German Committee was established. One resolution, unanimously adopted, was as follows:

"The first Conference of German and French members of Parliament, assembled in Berne on 11th May, 1913, is most strongly opposed to the contemptible victimization practised wholesale by Chauvinists, and their illegal activities that threaten to sap the sound sense and love of the population for their country on both sides of the frontier.

"It knows, and declares it a fact, that both nations by enormous majorities desire peace—the first condition of all progress. . . . It invites its members to use their influence with the Governments of the Great Powers to bring about a reduction of outlay on both the Army and Navy. The Conference warmly supports the proposal of Mr. Bryan, Secretary of State in the U.S.A., with regard to Courts of Arbitration. It demands accordingly that disagreements arising between both countries that cannot be settled by diplomatic means shall be referred to the Arbitration Tribunal at The Hague. . . .

"It is convinced that a *rapprochement* beween Germany and France will facilitate the understanding between the two Great Powers and provide thereby a basis for a lasting peace . . ."

The S.D. Sections of the Chamber of Deputies and the Reichstag, as well as the Executives of German and French Social Democracy, before discussing the agenda made a joint declaration in which the fundamental position of the International Proletariate was defined, and the words at the end were these:

"The French and German Social Democrats most warmly welcome the meeting of the Conference in Berne, and express the wish that through it the knowledge of the homogeneousness of two civilized nations may be advanced far beyond the circle of the working classes for the benefit of mankind."

The Social Democrats of France and Germany were not going to rest content with these professions of peace. They arranged for a pamphlet to be signed by both against war, printed on one sheet in French and German, and to be circulated on the same day throughout France and Germany. The pamphlet was entitled, "Against the Folly of War." In the text were the following words:

"The French and German Social Democrats protest with one mind and one voice against the ceaseless war preparations that exhaust nations, force them to neglect their most important moral obligations, increase mutual distrust, and instead of assuring peace, provoke conflicts that lead to disaster with wholesale misery and destruction in their strain. It is the ruling classes in both countries that artificially accentuate national differences, instead of resisting them, fan mutual animosity, and lead nations away from their civilizing efforts and their struggle for freedom at home.

"To secure peace, the independence of nations, and the progress of democracy in every part of the two states, Social Democracy demands that all disputes between peoples should be settled by arbitration, and considers decisions forced by war barbaric and disgraceful to mankind.

"It demands, further, the abolition of the standing army that is always a constant threat to nations, and the introduction in its place of a defence force on a democratic basis only to be employed to defend the country.

"The same outcry against war and the same condemnation of an armed peace is echoed in both countries. Under the flag of the International, that postulates the freedom and independence of every nation, the German and French Socialists should continue the fight against never-satisfied militarism and against devastating war, and for a mutual understanding and a lasting peace among nations."

On the French side this polemical declaration was signed by Jean Jaurès, Pierre Renaudel, Camélinat, Albert Thomas, Sembat, Vaillant and all the Socialist deputies of the Chamber; for German democracy by Bebel, Braun, Ebert, Haase, Molkenbuhr, Müller, Scheidemann and the whole S.D. Committee of the Reichstag.

The Berne Conference, which made a prolonged impression, was followed in the summer of 1914 by the Conference at Bâle. Of the better known Socialists from France and Germany nearly all were present who had been at Berne. One was grievously missed, August Bebel, whom death had called hence in the meanwhile. He said good-bye in Berne with his speech for peace. "We represent truth, justice, humanity, peace and the well-being of nations, and trust that wider and wider circles even of those who still stand opposite us scoffing will one day adopt our ideas." What had been resolved upon in Berne was confirmed in Bâle. The bond between all friends of peace on this and that side of Vosges seemed drawn tighter than before.

X

FROM PEACEFUL MOUNTAINS INTO BLOODY WAR

I HAVE always been sincerely sorry for Party politicians who are only interested in politics and in absolutely nothing else. I have certainly been from my earliest days a hard-boiled Party man. It would be intolerable to me if I could not see first thing in the morning from the papers what was going on in the world and the Party. But I have never understood how a man can have no interest in life beyond politics—a very narrow circle of friends, always confined to the same tiny clique, never going to a public-house, a theatre or a concert, completely indifferent to any form of sport. What sort of fellows are they? What does such a man know of the world he pretends to improve? Perhaps politicians consider themselves ideal people to live with. I have never been overkeen on any form of exercise, but I protest once and for all against what people are likely to say of me after my death—that I was a model youth in the eyes of lazy sticklers for principle and a revolutionary crank on drink and tobacco.

Cranks who get pains in the stomach when they see people drinking beer, or go off into hysterics when a working man offers them a drink, have never impressed me. When, as a political suckling, I tried to drink in the milk of the Marx theories—a hard job at most times, and rarely a soother—I was well-nigh in despair. Such clever men as Marx and his friend Engels are not to be met twice in this vale of tears! Then I read one day that Marx not only regularly borrowed money from his friend Engels, being desperately hard up, but that both at least once got properly drunk in London, and from pure bravado started smashing gas lamps. Then I breathed again, and set to work with renewed vigour on "Capital" and "Anti-Dühring." Now I knew these two Professors of Socialism weren't merely dry bones.

I pardon in advance all those who are much better, wiser and more typical than I am, and who will judge me superciliously after enjoying what is written above. What they have done without on earth may they receive in Heaven. May they then give me freely of their bounty, so that we may all at least live above according to our "several necessities."

After a hectic time in the welter of politics and donkey's work in the office in 1914, I pinned on my hat the Edelweiss badge of the German-Austrian Alpine Club—I had long been a member of the Munich Section, Oberland—to get a foretaste of Paradise in the mountains. Many a time (nibbling as it were at forbidden fruit) had I spent sleepless nights revelling in the Journal of the Club and mapping out fresh trips on its maps of the Alps. Up to now I had not been able to shout and sing in God's fair world from the summits of the Christallo and the Marmolata, though I had been right across the Dolomites. Ludwing Frank had climbed the Marmolata in 1913, and told me all about it—and nothing should keep me back.

Not far from the Pordoi Pass, on the way to the Bamberg hut, my daughter and I came across Austrian Alpine troops being drilled in mountain warfare. With ice axes or bergstocks to steer them, they sped along on their skis, but had numerous falls, causing much blood to flow, and we had to see it. They mostly suffered from head injuries. Many of the recruits fell down, as they started, on their heads. On reaching the hut at the foot of the Marmolata the whole place reeked of carbolic, like being in a hospital; it was no pleasing odour up in the mountains.

Favoured by the best of weather, our excursions were a great success. Fatigue I made light of, as I did five years later when I climbed the Pic Palü from the Bernina hut without over-exertion.

As our leave was soon up, we went north from Bozen via Innsbrück to spend one more week enjoying Nature and resting on the Bavarian-Tyrolese border in Mittenwald, that had been to me for many years a quiet resting-place from the excitement of troublous days.

We arrived at Mittenwald on 24th July, but restful days were not to be thought of. We could not resist temptation, and on 25th July climbed the West Karwendel peak, which we had done many times in previous years, as well as the Wörner.

What a priceless halt it was, nearly 2,400 metres up under the high cross! For five whole years this beauty spot had been in my thoughts. The view was clear—so clear that the next few days were bound to be bad. Nature had done her best. We saw the whole range in all its majesty and glory: all the big peaks of the Tyrol, especially those of the Otztal and Stubai ranges, more than 3,000 metres high, glistening in their magnificently solemn white raiment, lit up by the golden sun. Far and wide not a soul was to be seen. Peace and silence were around us, a feeling beyond compare.

On returning to Mittenwald I heard of Austria's ultimatum to Serbia. "That means war; it's clear they want war." I rushed out into the street, and met a director from the Special Branch of the War Office whom I knew. He did not worry, did not give war a thought, and said jokingly that the week after next he would be again in command.

No power on earth could have kept me back. I wired to Berlin, gave my daughter the necessary instructions, advised her to follow me as quickly as she could, and started at once for Berlin via Munich. . . .

A few days later millions of men faced each other armed to the teeth. Wholesale slaughter was beginning.

XI

CRITICAL DAYS

A T express speed I had returned to Berlin. Everywhere where a word could be heard the conversation was of war and rumours of war. There was only one topic of conversation—war. The supporters of war seemed to be in a great majority. Were these pugnacious fellows, young and old, bereft of their senses? Were they so ignorant of the horrors of war? I only heard voices advocating peace in the circle of my own Party friends, apart from the few Social Democratic newspapers. Yet the vast majority of the people were opposed to war, without a doubt. Vast crowds of demonstrators paraded "Unter den Linden." Schoolboys and students were there in their thousands; their bearded seniors, with their Iron Crosses of 1870-71 on their breasts, were there too in huge numbers.

Treitschke and Bernhardi (to say nothing of the National Liberal beer-swilling heroes) seemed to have multiplied a thousandfold. Patriotic demonstrations had an intoxicating effect and excited the war-mongers to excess. "A call like the voice of thunder." [1] Cheers! "In triumph we will smite France to the ground." [2] "All hail to thee in victor's crown." [3] Cheers! Hurrah!

The counter-demonstrations immediately organized by the Berlin Social Democrats were imposing, and certainly more

[1] *"Es braust ein Ruf wie Donnerhall!"*
[2] *"Siegreich woll'n wir Frankreich schlagen!"*
[3] *"Heil Dir im Siegerkranz!"*

disciplined than the Jingo processions, but could not outdo the shouts of the fire-eaters. "Good luck to him who cares for truth and right. Stand firmly round the flag." "Long live peace!" "Socialists, close up your ranks." The Socialist International cheer. The patriots were sometimes silenced by the Proletarians; then they came out on top again. This choral contest, "Unter den Linden," went on for days.

"It is the hour we yearned for—our friends know that," so the Pan-German papers shouted, that had for years been shouting for war. The *Post,* conducted by von Stumm, the Independent Conservative leader and big Industrial, had thus moaned in all its columns in 1900, at the fortieth celebration of the Franco-German War: "Another forty years of peace would be a national misfortune for Germany." Now these firebrands saw the seeds they had planted ripening. Perhaps in the heads of many who had been called upon to make every effort to keep the peace Bernhardi's words, that "the preservation of peace can and never shall be the aim of politics," had done mischief. These words are infernally like the secret instructions given by Baron von Holstein to the German delegates to the first Peace Conference at The Hague:

"For the State there is no higher aim than the preservation of its own interests; among the Great Powers these will not necessarily coincide with the maintenance of peace, but rather with the hostile policy of enemies and rivals."

The Executive of the S.P.D. wished in any case to do what it could to ward off the horror. On 28th July, it summoned by telegram a general meeting with the Committee of Control, whose members lived in various parts of the Empire. Though the Executive was badly "hauled" (this is what we called it among ourselves in jest) by the Royal and Imperial (K.K.) representatives, as per usual, we came through the meeting very well. We were speechless wnen we were actually congratulated on our efforts. We had never experienced anything like this. But the meeting did not close without a word of blame. A member of the K.K. complained that "Comrade Ebert, one of the chairmen of the Party, has not even returned from his leave of absence. It will create a painful impression in Leipzig, and must not occur again."

On 28th-29th July, 1914, the International Socialist Bureau met in Brussels. Among those present were Jaurès (France), Troelstra (Holland), Vandervelde (Belgium), Keir Hardie, (England), Marjorie (Italy), Haase, etc. The Bureau took a serious view of the imminence of war, and exhorted the workers in every country to agitate.

For September, 1914, an International Socialist Conference was arranged in Vienna, to be followed by a Social Democratic Congress in Würzburg. Owing to the outbreak of War both congresses were declared off.

Bethmann-Hollweg warned our Press, through his henchman Wahnschaffe, Assistant Secretary of State, a clever and honest man devoted to his master, to be very careful, for if war did come, a "state of siege" (martial law) would be proclaimed, and it would be a very grave matter for the Press.

The Executive within a few days launched a manifesto, sent a circular letter to the Press, and published an "extra special" edition of the *Vorwärts*. We were working at high pressure.

The Executive published the following manifesto on 25th July:

"The territory of the Balkans is streaming with the blood of thousands of slaughtered men; the ruins of devastated towns and sacked villages are smoking; starving men without work are wandering from place to place, and widowed women and orphan children; and the unbridled fury of Aus-trian Imperialism is preparing to bring death and destruction on all Europe. . . . No German soldier's blood must be spilt to gratify the murderous intentions of the Austrian tyrant. Comrades, we call upon you to express at once by mass meetings the unshakable desire of the class-conscious Pro-letariate for peace. . . ."

On the afternoon of 30th July, when we were drafting a manifesto to the Party at an Executive meeting, with Haase as chairman, in my room, a remarkable scene took place. While we were going through the draft sentence by sentence the telephone bell rang. I took up the receiver, and distinctly heard that Comrade Stampfer, who handled almost all the news of the Party Press, desired to let off a pithy article on the standpoint of the Party with regard to the War. He had had a violent argument with Ströbel about the article, but had just sent it in notwithstanding. Everyone listened at-tentively. After hearing the first few sentences Haase jumped up excitedly and protested against Stampfer's article. There was a hasty discussion, during which I had a few words with Stampfer over the telephone. Finally I had to ask him, on behalf of the members of the Executive present, to withdraw the article, because the Executive were drafting a manifesto that might be compromised by Stampfer's article. Stampfer was naturally very angry, for he could rightly assume that most members were practically in agreement with his views. The Executive was formally right, notwithstanding, for at so critical a moment it had to try to prevent its official announce-ments from being anticipated through non-official sources. Dozens of telegrams instructing Stampfer to suppress his article met with no success, and it appeared next day in some papers. It set forth the views of the Party—not only Stampfer's—so clearly and pointedly that I shall reproduce it here as an important Party document.

To Be or Not to Be

"As long as the possibility exists of preserving peace, it is only one's duty to work for peace. At a time like this, however, when a world struggle is on the eve of breaking out—and we know not how far off it is—the task of the German class-conscious Proletariate assumes a different phase.

"Germany will have to fight on two fronts, with an ally whose fighting strength will be concentrated on a different theatre of war—and perhaps, in addition to that, will have to fight England in the North Sea. It is a war compared with which 1870-71 was child's play. The vast majority of the German people have no desire for war. But there is in all Germany no Party, no clique and, we believe, no individual who desires Germany's defeat.

"Defeat would be something unthinkable, something frightful. If war is the most horrible of all horrors, the frightfulness of this war will be intensified by the fact that it will be waged not only by civilized nations. We are sure that our comrades in uniform of all sorts and conditions will abstain from all unnecessary cruelty, but we cannot have this trust in the motley hordes of the Czar, and we will not have our women and children sacrificed to the bestiality of Cossacks.

"There is one thing further to think about. Germany's and Austria's position on the map forces them to fight on two fronts. The Allies cannot concentrate their whole strength on one point, and so will not be able, should they win, to appear as victors all along the same line, as certain irresponsible newspapers are now prophesying in advance. Our enemies, however, can deliver a concentric attack on the central point of Austro-German territory. Germany and Austria cannot inflict so crushing a defeat on their enemies as their enemies can inflict on Germany, if the foe can march forward from all sides in the flush of victory.

"Defeat would be synonymous with collapse, destruction and utter ruin for us all. And all our minds revolt against this possibility. Our Reichstag representatives have repeatedly declared over and over again that Social Democrats will desert their country in the moment of danger to be a base calumny. When the fateful hour strikes, the workers will redeem the promise made on their behalf by their representatives. These fellows without a country will do their duty, and in no way allow themselves to be outdone by 'patriots.' Our Section is faced with the momentous question of voting the War Credits, which must in no wise be made more difficult by argument. One must be content with accepting whatever decision they come to. Whoever knows them will be sure that they do not in the remotest way approve of the War, do not take the slightest responsibility for its outbreak or for severing the ties of the International, which, after the War, will come more prominently to the front. Whoever knows them will surely know that their refusal to approve of war in no wise implies that they refuse to fight—this has become for us all a vital and inexorable duty directly war breaks out. It is obvious that the Section will follow out this policy with staunch determination.

"But we ask our enemies at home to respect the deep moral earnestness with which our Section enters on its heavy task. Whoever dares to assert that the opposition of the Section must mean that Social Democracy repudiates the duty of self-defence, is a liar. And, once again, there is no doubt that

Social Democrats recognize this duty and will carry it out conscientiously.

"Our minds are not conscious of any enthusiasm for war, but shudder at the thought. But when no sacrifice any longer avails to stop the march of fate; when we recollect the unspeakable atrocities Tsarism has inflicted on its own people, and further imagine the myrmidons of this barbaric power entering our own country drunk with victory, then the cry comes to our lips—'Surely not that!'

"On the reverse side of all this horror and devastation is another and more pleasing picture—a free German people that has won its country and defends its Fatherland; a free German people in alliance with the great civilized Powers of the West after a just peace, and our good cause everywhere in the ascendant. Yonder, however, in the east are the smoking ruins of the throne of Czars!"

Simultaneously with Stampfer's article, that appeared only in a few papers, came the manifesto of the United Party Press, which ran as follows:

"Our repeated efforts to preserve peace were unsuccessful. The conditions we lived under proved to be stronger than our brothers' will and our own. So we will now boldly look things in the face whatever may betide. We shall not live through coming events with fatalistic equanimity. We shall be true to our cause and hold together, supported by the imposing importance of our mission. Women especially, whom war will hit and hit hard, have in these dour times the duty to work for Socialism so that this unspeakable misfortune be not repeated and this war be the last. The strict regulations of war-time affect with terrible harshness the Labour movement. Thoughtlessness, useless and misunderstood sacrifice

207

harm not only the individual at a time like this, but also our cause."

The Executive had naturally to use more cautious language than Stampfer, as the Section had not yet met nor had any resolution been passed.

Ebert had been spending some weeks of his leave on the island of Rügen. He could not, and clearly would not, believe in the terrible earnestness of events. In a letter dated 27th July he wrote to the Executive that they could not have a second "Bâle" over again—*i.e.* the last International Socialist Conference. On the other hand, a manifesto by the International Socialistic Bureau seemed to him likely to do good. He did not know that members of the International Socialistic Bureau were already on their way to Brussels. "I earnestly ask you to inform me speedily. Naturally I am quite prepared to return at once. We are very comfortable here. But as things are, one cannot be easy, as I told you." Pastor Felden, in his book on Ebert, reports a conversation between Ebert and his wife, from which it is perfectly clear that Ebert alone of all his colleagues did not return to Berlin, because he thought the outbreak of war impossible. "The ultimatum is a warning gun. The Executive think otherwise. In Berlin they look too much on the black side. I said that in reply to their last letter in which they asked me to return. . . . Frau Ebert was doubtful, he was sure; it's nonsense; there will be no war."

The Ebert family had been for a walk; when they came back they found a telegram urgently begging the Chairman to return. His family had never before seen him in such an excited condition.

The Provocation of the "Local-Anzeiger"

On 30th July a lying special edition of the *Local-Anzeiger* appeared, according to which war was a *fait accompli* and the spark had been thrown into the powder flask. The special edition announced:

"GERMANY'S MOBILIZATION"

"The decision has been made, and made in the sense we had been expecting according to the news received. Emperor William, as we hear, has just ordered the immediate mobilization of the German Army and Navy.

"This step on the part of Germany is the reluctant answer to Russia's threatening war-like preparations, directed, according to the present situation, no less against us than Austria-Hungary."

The contents of this paper were naturally telegraphed throughout the world. It did incalculable mischief, for the *Local-Anzeiger* was "the only German paper the Emperor read unexpurgated," as it has itself advertised hundreds of times. The object of the men behind the *Local-Anzeiger* had been achieved, though they were compelled in the afternoon of the same day to publish the following quite meaningless correction:

"Through a gross irregularity the twelve o'clock supplements of the *Local-Anzeiger* have been distributed with the announcement that Germany has ordered the mobilization of the Army and the Navy. We state that this announcement is untrue."

A few hours after the supplement appeared, Ebert, who had come the night before to Berlin, and Otto Braun, the

Senior Treasurer of our Party, went off to Zürich. This journey, later completely forgotten, or often confused with Ebert's
other trips to Switzerland, soon proved to be an unnecessary
precaution. Among the idiotic plans of the authorities in case
of war was, as we knew, the arrest of the S.P.D. Executive
and other suspicious and unpopular persons. As the Kaiser
from the outbreak of war onwards only recognized people
"who were still Germans," nothing came of the arrest of
"fellows without a country." Every politician will see how
natural it was for us to try to avoid getting the Party leaders'
heads cut off; so we packed them off to Switzerland.

Erzberger as an Extremist

It was no other than Erzberger, the Jingo member of the
Centre, who suggested the idea of arresting the S.D. editors.
In the last days of July, 1914, he published in the *Tag* the
following article:

"The official organ of German Social Democracy in its
Saturday number adds veiled threats, should war break out
over the Vienna-Belgrade conflict. In times of peace one need
not take such too seriously, though they may do much harm
in many excitable heads. Should, however, matters become
serious, as the 'Red Rag' (*Vorwärts*) thinks, there is the will
of the German people to be reckoned with, and a clean sweep
must be made of such dangerous activities at home, and the
orders of a Staff General carried out who a few years ago
issued wise instructions for such cases. Revolutionary colleagues in the Press need have no fears for their lives or health
if they are safely locked up. The conduct of the Social Democratic Press in these days necessitates measures of precaution
being taken; yet it is to be hoped they will not be necessary,

as the original Triple Alliance will settle everything to the satisfaction of Europe."

The Münich *Post,* edited by Dr. Adolf Müller, then German Minister in Switzerland, printed Erzberger's article under a headline, "A Black Desperado." From the above facts, that were confirmed in the Press in 1921, it appears that Ebert, apart from the sitting on 30th July, at which his trip to Switzerland was decided on, was never present at any of the discussions before the War, either in the Executive or the Section of the Reichstag. It is necessary, in the interests of an impartial account, that will be possible only after a few years, to establish this fact, as after Ebert's death many inaccurate statements were made about his proceedings during those critical days in July 1914. For acts and resolutions in which he took no part he cannot, naturally, be held responsible. On July 31st, 1914, a meeting of the joint Executives of the Party and Section took place, at which Haase and Ledebour agitated for the rejection of the War Credits. I was opposed to any definite motion. In any case I made up my mind to consult with more intimate friends, whose view I thought I knew perfectly, before the meeting started. The only definite motion at the meeting was to the effect that Hermann Müller should be sent to Paris via Brussels at once to consult our French colleagues. It would have a great effect in the whole world if identical motions could be brought before the Reichstag and the Chamber of Deputies.

Müller started off the same day, although a "state of war" had been declared. Next morning, 1st August, the news reached us of the murder of our friend Jean Jaurès. We were all dumbfounded by the terrible announcement. I could scarcely accept the duty of drafting a telegram of condolence. I telegraphed to the *Humanité* in Paris:

"Deeply moved we read the terrible news that our Jaurès, both yours and ours, is no longer among the living. No more serious loss could have happened to all of us at this grave time. The German Proletariate bows its head before the genius of this great champion and bitterly deplores that this man can no longer be where he was—a man who fought all his life for an understanding between France and Germany. His work will be unforgettable in the history of International Socialism and human progress."

As we learned after the War, this telegram never reached Paris. On the evening of this black day the awful tension was over that had distracted millions and trillions—whether they were men of peace or war. Mobilization! Here was the cruel truth that banished all doubts; now the wholesale slaughter would begin.

For or Against the War Credits

On 2nd August the Executives of the Party and the Section of the Reichstag met together in the Party committee room. The Reichstag was to meet on 4th August to pass the War Credits—that had been told us officially. Haase and Ledebour advocated their rejection, all the others their adoption. Unanimity was impossible, abstention likewise, for a Party of our strength could not think of abstaining from voting in this critical hour for the Fatherland. At this time I felt Bebel's absence more than ever before; he had such a keen sense for reality. Haase, as the Party leader, dissented—in my opinion, in a most unreasonable way. The wise Fischer became so agitated that his nerves failed him during his speech and he began to cry. Haase and Ledebour were not to be won over; but I had afterwards an impression that they were quite pleased to be in a minority. It was arranged that we should meet again at nine in the office of the *Vorwärts,* and then make a declaration—for or against. No matter who secured the majority, we had to work in common at getting out a statement of some sort. At 5 P.M. David, Fischer, Molken-buhr, Schöplin, Wels, Südekum and I met in Goehre's garden in Zehlendorf, and there drafted a statement, after a discussion of several hours. At 9 P.M. another argument with Haase and Ledebour at the *Vorwärts.* Neither had made a formal statement in writing, but only a few rough notes.

We parted about midnight. I spent a sleepless night. Should we succeed in getting a majority for acceptance in the Section or not? In the course of the day a message from the Chancellor, Bethmann-Hollweg, came to my house, inviting me to talk things over on 3rd August at 12 noon.

On 3rd August the Section met at 10 A.M., received a few reports, and then adjourned till Haase and I returned from our interview with the Chancellor. The following, among others, were present at the interview: the Chancellor Beth-mann-Hollweg, Delbrück, Secretary of State, Wahnschaffe, Under-Secretary, and the following members of the Reichstag: von Westarp, Spahn, Erzberger, Blankenhorn, Prince Schönaich-Carolath, Kämpf, Wiemer, Fischbeck, Schultz-Bronberg, von Morawski, Scheele, Haase and myself. At first we talked quite freely, without sitting down, over the motions to be carried along with the War Credits. The Chancellor then read the speech he made next day in the Reichstag; here and there he put in some more or less confidential remarks. The nearer he got to the end, the more agitated he became; he did not know what to do with his long arms, and sometimes hit the table with both his fists. His voice sounded quite hollow when he said, "My conscience is clear." Kämpf thanked the Chancellor for what he had said, and

213

Bethmann-Hollweg at once asked to withdraw, as he had a great deal to do. Delbrück was then questioned about Italy's attitude; Bethmann-Hollweg had said nothing about it. This well-informed man pretended to know nothing. From Italy we went on to the agenda, and discussed the best way of presenting the draft proposals at the full sitting of the Reichstag. As the gentlemen talked as if the unanimous acceptance of all measures, including the votes of credit, was an absolute certainty, Haase and I reminded them that our Section had not finally made up its mind. Haase, by the tone he adopted in the conversation, would have led no one to suppose that he was not in favour of the credits. That made me angry, because before going down to the House he had declared, right up to the last minute, that he would do his utmost to vote against the Bill. I said this to him on the way from the House to the Restaurant Zollernhof, where we dined together, and his answer was: "I have always maintained that the Section has not yet made its decision." Haase's procedure, quite apart from his acting on principle, angered me immensely. It was agreed that Kämpf should make a short speech after the Chancellor, and announce the welcome fact that the votes of credit would be passed unanimously. Even the members who objected on principle to war had given their assent. Haase swallowed all this, while I referred to the Section's not having yet given its decision, and asked President Kämpf to frame with us his reply in accordance with what the Section should decide. All were agreed to that.

We declined to entertain the request that no one should speak after Kämpf, for our decision, no matter what it might be, must be justified by us in all circumstances. After a rather long discussion we finally arrived at this conclusion: the wording of our statement should be submitted to the other Party leaders at 9 P.M., so that they could make amendments. On that Haase solemnly declared that there was no necessity for it. In no circumstances should our statement be aimed at any party, but should in general terms decline all responsibility for a policy that, in our opinion, might lead to war. In its form it should be suitable and worthy of the occasion.

Müller's Report from Paris

The Section met at once after dinner under my chairmanship. The discussion was extremely bitter, and in the course of it Müller arrived from Paris. Surprised by the declaration of War, he had had considerable trouble in recrossing the frontier. He reported as follows: he had been well and kindly received, as usual, by our French colleagues, but unfortunately no understanding had been reached. Pierre Renaudel had given the clearest statement of the attitude of our French colleagues at the meeting:

"The position of the French and German democrat is not the same. The French Socialists were fully informed of diplomatic proceedings by their Government in due course; in Germany this was not the case. If France, whose people and Government desired peace, were attacked by Germany, their French colleagues would be forced to vote for the War Budget, because measures for self-defence had to be taken by France, if attacked. Thus situated, the French democrat could not abstain from voting. The German democrat was in a different position, if Germany were the aggressor. They could perhaps vote against the War Credits."

After one of the French comrades had stated that Germany would be generally considered guilty for the outbreak of war, Müller replied:

"German Socialists are in the habit of speaking the truth
215

in the most pointed way to their Government. We have latterly reproached our Government most bitterly in the public Press because they did not take sufficient care to inform the country before sending off the ultimatum to Serbia. But this is a thing that cannot be altered, and, as matters now stand, the greatest danger is threatened from Russia. . . . Yet it is the general opinion in all Party circles in Germany that Russia would be the guilty party if it now came to war, and that France is in a position to stop war if she will put the requisite pressure on St. Petersburg for preserving peace."

It was very soon clear to our friend Hermann Müller, in the course of his conversation with the French Socialists, that the French would vote for the War Credits. Identical declarations both in the Reichstag and the Chamber of Deputies were now out of the question. After Müller's report the Reichstag Section continued to discuss the War Credits, with the result that only fourteen members voted against passing the War Credits. That a few members abstained from voting, as was stated later, is absolutely discredited.

XII

IN THE HOUR OF NEED

REFERENCES were made to Lassalle, Engels, Bebel and many others who had declared it a duty to defend their country, by members who had voted for passing the credits. Although Haase, Cohn, Liebknecht, Herzfeld, Ledebour and Lensch (the latter had been before the War the chief editor of the rabid Radical *Leipziger Volkszeitung,* and after the War became the chief editor of the equally rabid National *Deutsche Allgemeine Zeitung*) offered violent opposition, the resolution above mentioned was carried. The opposers' arguments created merely a pitiable impression. Haase was tolerable, Herzfeld ridiculous.

The Section's resolution not only met the situation, but confirmed what I said in a speech in the Reichstag on 9th December, 1910, with the consent of the Section: that we Social Democrats were known to be thoroughly in favour of defending the country, contrary to the lying statements of unscrupulous and contemptible opponents. In the same speech I incidentally advocated a league of nations that should do all it could to bring into line the three great countries of civilization, England, France and Germany, and so make impossible, once and for all, any possibility of dissension. A few colleagues, among them David and Wels, were authorized to draft the declaration to be given in the Reichstag on 4th August. Faults were found here and there by the Section with the draft, but apart from some verbal alterations it remained unchanged. Here is the official text, according to the shorthand reports of the Reichstag:

"We are facing a critical time. The results of Imperialistic policy, by creating a prolonged period of competitive armaments and intensifying national differences, have spread like a tidal wave over Europe. The responsibility for this falls on the supporters of this policy: we refuse to take it. Social Democracy has opposed with all its might this ominous development, and has up to the very last moment worked for the preservation of peace by demonstrations on a huge scale in all countries, acting especially in complete harmony with our French brethren. Our efforts have been in vain. Now we are up against the stern fact of war. The horrors of hostile invasion stare us in the face. To-day we have not to decide between peace and war, but to settle the question of voting the credits necessary for our country's defence. We have now to think of millions of our countrymen who, through no fault of theirs, are involved in this crisis; they are those who will be most heavily hit by the ravages of war. Our fervent hopes will follow our brothers, called to the colours, regardless of their political opinions. We will think of mothers sacrificing their sons, of wives and children deprived of their breadwinners and threatened with the horrors of starvation in addition to their anxiety for their dear ones. Tens of thousands of wounded and crippled fighting men will soon be joining these. We regard it as our imperative duty to stand by them, to lighten their burdens and mitigate this immeasurable disaster.

"In case of a victory for the Russian autocrat, whose hands are stained with the blood of the best of his countrymen, much, if not all, is at stake. It is of paramount importance to prevent this danger and to ensure the position and independence of our own land. We stand by what we have ever maintained: we will not desert our own Fatherland in the hour of peril. Here we are in complete agreement with the International, that has at all times recognized the right of every nation to national independence and self-determination, and we, in complete agreement with the International, condemn all wars of aggression. We demand that, directly our security is won and our enemies are inclined to make peace, the war should end in a peace that will make friendly relations with our neighbours possible. We demand this not only in the interests of international solidarity, that we have always fought for, but also in the interests of the German people. We trust the hard school of war will awaken in new millions of people a horror of war, and win them over to the ideals of Socialism and of peace on earth.

"Guided by these principles, we vote the necessary credits."

At a meeting of the Section at noon on 4th August, at which the text of the declaration was approved, a short but violent argument took place as to who should read the declaration at the plenary sitting of the Reichstag. As Haase, the most downright opponent of the declaration, has often been reproached subsequently for having been ready to read the declaration in the Reichstag, the following remarks must be added to justify his conduct. At the close of the debate Stolten asked who would read the declaration. I replied that, at Haase's request, and with the assent of the Executive of the Section, I was to read it. Every one of Haase's supporters, led by Dittman, rose and shouted that Haase must read the declaration. But the latter flatly refused. No one could expect him to. Further uproar. I declared I had not pressed myself forward or announced my willingness, but had to emphasize the fact, as had been stated in the discussion, that there was no first or second chairman in the Section, but only chairmen with equal powers. This remark was greeted with cheers and counter cheers. "But Haase is at the same time chairman of the Party," they shouted. Oskar Cohn forced his way through the crowd up to the chairman's table and gave Haase a paper on which was written: "On behalf of my Section I am to read the declaration." Many wildly shouted out, "Haase must, Haase must." I called the excited crowd to order, and said I would put it to the vote. "If we unanimously ask Haase to read the declaration, he will accede." I myself voted for Haase, and gathered, as far as I could see (as a matter of fact, I intentionally could not see at all), that it was the unanimous wish that Haase should read the declaration. Haase said he was now ready to read it. Hoch, Herzfeld, Dittmann and David-sohn were jubilant. Before the Section separated, Haase fore-shadowed his resignation in the autumn.

One notable fact must be mentioned. On 4th August, 1914, two meetings of the Reichstag took place. At the first, beginning at three o'clock, Bethmann-Hollweg made his speech in which he mentioned the advance through Belgium. The House then adjourned for an hour. In the interval there was a meeting of the Section, at which Ledebour made a scene, merely because some S.D. members were said to have shouted "Hear, hear," during the Chancellor's speech. Such minor incidents never escaped his notice. At the time we all believed that Germany had been attacked—that the French had poisoned German water supplies and French airmen had dropped bombs on Nuremburg and Fürth. These were only newspaper reports, that later turned out to be mere rumours without exception. We were all convinced that all parties concerned throughout Germany had done their best to prevent war. The Section, at a full-dress debate in the Reichstag, approved of the War Credits demanded *nem. con.;* even Karl Liebknecht voted with the "Ayes," although no one would have thought any worse of him had he abstained, as Kuhnert, Member of the Reichstag did.

At noon on 4th August members of all Parties, except the Social Democrats, were summoned by the Emperor for the opening of Parliament in the Schloss. The story got about that the Kaiser had been misinformed about all Parties being present. The Kaiser, it was said, was so highly delighted that he rushed up to one member, exclaiming, "I am specially glad you are here, Herr Scheidemann." The gentleman in question, whom he had mistaken for the Social Democrat, was a well-known honourable member who, owing to a cold in the head, had a red nose—not because he was fond of a drop! As the Kaiser probably imagined the Social Democrats to be such, from descriptions given him, it came quite natural to him that out of a hundred and fifty people with white noses the Social Democrat should have a red one.

In the evening of this memorable day many friends from the Section had gathered together in the garden of the Weihenstephan on the Schöneberger Ufer. There we heard of England's declaration of war, and there we saw Ludwig Frank for the last time. Graver than all the others, he was absolutely silent, although usually a lively and witty conversationalist. I took him back later to his hotel, close to the Anhalt railway station. We shook hands without saying a word. Next day he joined up voluntarily. On 31st August he travelled from Mannheim to France, four days later he fell in action with a bullet through the head—the precious life of a good patriot was over, and Social Democrats lost one of their very best.

War fever during the first weeks of the War had infected wide circles among the working classes. I recollect one pay day in Radical Steglitz when Konrad Haenisch and Daniel Stücklein were present. It was reported with indignation that in the north and east of Berlin flags had been hung out from the windows up to the third and fourth floors after every report of a victory. In the first weeks everything seemed to be going splendidly with our armies. Russian attacks in East Prussia had been generally anticipated. But when it was announced, in the middle of August, that the French had captured many of our guns near Shirmeck, there was a general drooping of heads. It was soon seen that many of the fire-eaters "boxed up" completely when they heard their food and victuals were to be extensively rationed.

Six Thousand Meetings

Ebert returned to Berlin on the afternoon of 6th August. Otto Braun followed on the 10th. Everybody was naturally very busy on the Executive. We wrote circular letters to the Associations and the Press. We were also present at numberless interviews with Secretaries of State and Privy Councillors about the censorship, rationing and war conditions, and at meetings of every possible kind. Talks at the Executive, ditto with Party Unions, committee of control, select committee, trades unions, later with the clubs, discussions with the Party Reichstag Executive and the Section itself, consultations of the Party leaders, later with the Unions, then negotiations on the Executive of the Reichstag committee and the committee itself, regular discussions in the Select Committee, meetings of the Senior branch, general Reichstag committees and attendance at full sessions, in addition to sittings of the Press Committee of the *Vorwärts,* local and regional committees, etc.

If we reckon the duration of the War to be about 1,500 days, and the number of daily meetings, consultations and conferences (on many days there were more than ten of these) to be four, the result is that every member of the Reichstag Executive was present at about 6,000 meetings of most various kinds during the War. One will appreciate the stupidity of the legal gentry of the "Right" who asked in various lawsuits many years after the War this or that S.D. member whether he heard or said this or that on such and such a day in January or July in such and such a year. It was said in the defence of libellers, criminals and their confederates when they, perhaps with only one thought in their heads, were asked for simple facts only one, two or three years back: "How can you ask a man to remember so long ago whether he was concerned in a murder conspiracy?"

Social Democratic Messengers in Neutral Countries

Heavy duties lay before the responsible Social Democratic authorities at the end of the first month of the War. Events in Belgium, especially the destruction of Louvain, had unexpected results. On 21st August Edward Bernstein rushed, wildly excited, into the Executive meeting with a letter from Comrade Vliegen in Amsterdam. "Vliegen is horror-stricken about the atrocities of the German Army in Belgium. He is obviously judging from lying reports." It was resolved by the Executive to send Südekum to Milan and me to Amsterdam. We despatched to Stockholm William Janson, a Swede, but a strong German sympathizer, who was admirably fitted for this mission. The real object of our sending delegates was to ask our comrades in neutral countries to insure the neutral character of their Press by all possible means. Janson could not do much, because Branting, the leader of the Social Democrats and chief editor of the Stockholm Party Press, was on the side of the Entente. Südekum disappeared completely for some time. One day he came back to Berlin, having done nothing. His reports were later fully confirmed by the course of events. At a sitting of the Executive on 31st July he reported thus: His trip had been unprofitable. The Board of Control were, in his opinion, Syndicalists with no notion of how matters stood in Germany. There was a slight hope of the neutrality of the *Avanti*. But things, he was convinced, would change but little, for Anti-German feeling, as the managers of the paper emphasized with pride, had caused its circulation to rise from 24,000 before the War to 70,000.

General satisfaction was expressed with the result of my mission to Holland. At any rate, I had talks with very intelligent and friendly comrades, but cannot speak of my own performances.

At first my negotiations were complicated owing to my being obliged to get all newspaper articles and announcements translated. In three days I could read Dutch as well as German.

On 27th August a meeting took place in the "Sparbank," attended by thirty to thirty-five members, to hear my complaints and demands. I reported on an article in the *Hamburger Echo* on Dutch neutrality, on Vliegens in the *Het Volk*, on a letter of Vliegens to Bernstein, and, so far as I knew them, on the atrocities and the violation of Belgium's neutrality, commented on the conduct and dissensions in our Section, and requested my colleagues to be fair and strictly neutral to all the Powers, even to Germany. A long discussion ensued, in which the violation of Belgium's neutrality was severely condemned.

Troelstra thus summed up the result of the discussion: "A neutral policy on our part is obviously necessary. We will do our best also to be impartial in all circumstances."

I sent in daily reports by telegrams in code to the Party Executive through the German Consul-General in Amsterdam.

I returned to Berlin on 30th August with the greatest difficulty. There I learnt that all my telegrams had been delivered much too late by the Foreign Office, and that of the letters and wires sent to me not one of them had reached me. Unfortunately!—I had been advised by letter to undertake a further mission.

Various Callers

Of the visits the Executive received in the first weeks of the War one must be mentioned of three Russians, Schenkeli, Stickloff and another. They cross-examined us so boldly and gravely—strict Marxists, apparently, in their opinions—that we all held our tongues, without arranging to do so beforehand, and let Haase talk. He was plainly disgusted with their impertinence, candidly explained the attitude of our Section, to our great satisfaction, with vigour, and defended it splendidly. He referred to the declaration given by him in the name of the Section, which contained every practical reason for voting the War Credits. The three Russians were obviously not over-pleased at Haase's remarks.

About two weeks later, on 14th February, Victor Adler called upon us and took part in a meeting of our Executive in order to report on the situation in Austria. "You in Germany have really and truly freedom of the Press compared with us in Austria." He was pleased with our action, which he said was the only one possible. A Party like ours could not fly in the face of the whole country. Adler made some highly interesting comparisons between the German Empire and Austria. He touched on the position in Serbia and gave the Serbians their due. "But, excuse me, I am not a Serbian." He could not have expressed himself more clearly if he had said: "Excuse me, I am in the first place a German." Haase made no sort of reply to Adler's speech.

Liebknecht—Father and Son

A letter from Troelstra came to hand in the course of these days. Karl Liebknecht had been giving lectures in Holland, and in them had cracked up his own special point of view. Pannekook fell foul of the Party in Germany. Troelstra was very pessimistic; he feared the German and the Dutch Social Democratics would not understand how to make use of the situation; that the Party, both here and there, owing to internal dissension, would not think of taking a strong line as soon as War was over. "I fear," so I wrote in my diary at the same time, "that Troelstra is right. Our crazy dogmatizing fanatics will rather let the Party go to the devil along with all we may win than depart one iota from what they consider their immutable principles. They intend to make more noise."

Reports on Karl Liebknecht's tactics in Holland against the S.P.D. aroused pleasant recollections of what his father did in Holland for the S.P.D. in the 'nineties of the last century. William Liebknecht was in his manner as modest as his son was presumptuous. After a lecturing tour in Holland the "old man"—as he was called by the Party—wrote a few letters about his trip. He described, for instance, how astonished he was to be charged so little for enormous beef-steaks in Holland. Once he had served him such a huge one that he could with the utmost effort only get outside half of it. A witty Dutchman solved the mystery later with great humour. Liebknecht, in company with a Dutch friend, had such a beef-steak put in front of him; he had merely overlooked the fact that, although served on one dish, it was meant for the two of them. The Dutchman, on Liebknecht expressing his satisfaction at its size, did not want to damp his ardour. He refrained from making any explanation, and ordered something else to eat for himself.

The "Vorwärts"

The *Vorwärts,* we saw very quickly, was not up to its work in these critical days. Instead of reporting the Labour demonstrations Unter den Linden as extremely important politically, it simply advertised them by the silly headline, "Jagow's Demonstration." Jagow was at the time Chief Commissioner of Police in Berlin.

Soon meetings of the Executive were frequent; at these we must have appeared, to our extreme regret, very spiteful to many of our Radical colleagues. Such a meeting occurred on 3rd September, 1914. Arthur Stadthagen had signed a memorandum presented to him from the highest military authority, much to the indignation of the editors of the *Vorwärts,* pledging him to see to the "patriotic" policy of the paper. His co-editors were up in arms, and reported the incident to the Executive. Stadthagen defended himself in a pettifogging sort of way. The Executive decided on sending a protest to Delbrück, Secretary of State, in which complaint was made against the demand made to Stadthagen. Wahnschaffe, the Under-Secretary, in answer, excused himself by saying that it was usual for the military authorities to have all records placed before them and signed where evidence in writing was required. This had been done in Stadthagen's case.

Quarrels between the editors and the Executive over the

THE MAKING OF NEW GERMANY

Vorwärts question became more and more frequent. Hugo
Haase had been every evening since the outbreak of War to
the offices of the paper, and through his legal knowledge of
the Censorship had shown how things should invariably be
managed. After the editors (almost all of them later joined
the Independents) had been instructed in the way they should
go, Haase surprised the Executive on 11th September by sug-
gesting that I should from now onwards go each evening to
the editor's office. I firmly but politely declined the offer.
I had already had a terrible row the first evening with all the
editors, with no practical result.

At the same meeting there was a violent dispute between
Wels and Haase. Wels rightly reproached Haase with trying
to create the impression that he was "running the show," and
having repeatedly said so recently: "I've done this, I shall do
that," etc. Haase was naturally very upset. The air was becoming more and more sultry.

The policy of the *Vorwärts* provoked more and more dissatisfaction in Party circles. Hugo Heinemann, one of our
best comrades, respected as an outstanding criminal barrister
by the Bench as well as beloved by the working classes for
being always ready to help them, came to see me one day to
warn me seriously of some of my Radical colleagues. "If only
these fellows would turn their backs on the Party I should be
uncommonly pleased." A few days later there was a scene at a
Party meeting between Ebert and Haase that personal violence
only could have intensified. Ebert had publicly expelled a
pretending Radical through Janson without telling Haase
beforehand.

Disputes over the *Vorwärts* were an everyday occurrence.
The Berlin Press Committee, with the same powers as the
Executive in the affairs of the *Vorwärts*, was completely in the

228

hands of Rosa Luxemburg. To appeal to the K.K., a higher authority in settlement of differences, did not occur to the Executive, as it would have had the same effect as complaining of the devil to his grandmother, *i.e.* to Clara Zetkin.

Fines inflicted by the Censor and the shutting down of the *Vorwärts* occurred repeatedly. While a conference of the Social Democratic Party editors from the Empire was taking place, the *Vorwärts* was once more suppressed. Its editors at the time had no notion what might or might not be written under "a state of siege." I wrote in my diary: "They are gradually seeing that things cannot go on in the same way as before. They offer us this proposal for the future. Däumig shall be invested with absolute powers and shall finally decide whether an article be accepted or not. The Executive, as Senior Censor, shall send one of its members every evening to the office, and he shall decide, if Däumig cannot. I declined the offer of this dubious duty with thanks. . . ."

Däumig, the editor aforesaid, who played a considerable part in extreme revolutionary Labour circles during the first weeks of the War, was a bit of an adventurer. Though well educated, he had enlisted, apparently out of devilment, in the French Foreign Legion, and later, having done his job as a German inspector of wagons-lits, became editor of the *Vorwärts*. Wags, who have fortunately always existed among Social Democrats, put down Däumig's sleepy articles in the paper to the fact that he had previously been connected with sleeping-carriages.

The Censorship—A Disgraceful Business

It must be expressly stated that there were intelligent and educated gentlemen among the officers appointed to the Censorship. I shall always remember a remark of Captain von Vietsch's, who said to me casually, "Employment in the Censorship is a disgraceful trade; if we do it, we only do so in the country's interest." Haase had sent a letter to Wahnschaffe asking him to release the *Vorwärts*. He reported very favourably on the paper. I did not trust this report. The Executive requested Müller to enter the *Vorwärts* as Chief Censor; Müller accepted under certain conditions. "I am glad the hard-working Hermann consents to sacrifice himself, but am convinced he will come to grief and have nothing but worry."

Haase, as a matter of fact, took too rosy a view of things. General von Kessel by no means contemplated letting the *Vorwärts* go scot free. His one condition was that from now on nothing about class hatred or class war should appear in the *Vorwärts*. On account of this unheard-of demand a joint meeting of the Executive and the editors took place. The editors were ready to acquiesce and to publish a statement to this effect: "As our Berlin colleagues and the Executive intend to keep the *Vorwärts* going at all costs, its editors are prepared to accede." We set about them properly. The Executive did not intend to keep the *Vorwärts* going "at all costs," but insisted on knowing quite clearly how the editorship was to be conducted. "Then we will ask Gross-Berlin and take steps to wind it up." In such crises Ebert was splendidly ruthless.

On the afternoon of the same day there was a meeting with the Press Committee and the Gross-Berlin Central Executive. Rosa Luxemburg, true to her principles, spoke against yielding: rather no *Vorwärts* than one that could not say a word about class war for months together. All the others, except Comrade Friedländer, who did not want "Rosa to have it all her own way," as he said afterwards, accepted the conditions of General von Kessel. The latter said he was prepared to set free the *Vorwärts* if the General's letter was printed on the front page of that paper. No more therefore about class war! The Press Committee swallowed this pill as well.

In October, 1914, I wrote in my diary, "The *Vorwärts* is here again, but it has an ugly spot on its forehead that will give a shock to all honest men—the letter of the General in supreme command of the Mark: the letter will be a lasting disgrace to the Army, not to the Party that had to yield to force."

Questions of censorship were set down on the agenda. Day by day we had to champion the cause of this and that paper. Even at meetings with Secretaries of State the clumsy procedure of military censors was talked over. Civilians were absolutely powerless against the military demi-gods that were loosed on literary matters in general, and the Press in particular.

Except for its loyalty to principles, the *Vorwärts* as a paper was more than deplorable. To enable our Berlin colleagues to have a chance of comparing it with other Party papers, I carried a motion on 20th January, 1915, in the Press Committee, that every member of that Committee should have the right of ordering any four Socialist papers he liked. The result was astonishing. A fortnight later, at the meeting on 9th February, it was generally acknowledged that the *Vorwärts,* when compared with the selected provincial papers, was certainly the worst and dullest of the lot. The editors had probably expected some such result, and for this purpose brought with them Comrade Haase to defend them. But Haase also, though in full sympathy with *Vorwärts'* loyalty to principles, had to admit grave editorial deficiencies. Richard Fischer, who always expressed himself in broad Bavarian, gave the most downright verdict: "Obstinate as a pig, but a stickler for principle."

Start a Revolution!

On 14th October, 1914, Ebert and I were to be consulted in a private and confidential conversation with a very capable Privy Councillor, acting on behalf of the highest authority—not the Chancellor's—with a view to our starting a revolt in Finland. We listened attentively, but were not responsive. As the young diplomatist informed us in a tone of comic mystery, "it was a question of throwing out a feeler or of getting information beforehand, and further discussion with influential gentlemen would follow." What was really in the wind? The National Parties in Finland had sent word to say that they had unfortunately no general system of organization throughout the country. Everything depended on the Socialist Party; a minority had been desirous for a long time to break away, and the majority considered the venture too risky. The reason for holding back was that they had their doubts about a German victory. No news reached Finland that shook their belief in Russia's inevitable success. All depended upon their convincing the Finns that Germany had won many victories and would certainly win through in the end. The young man had evidently told his superiors it was likely we should issue some sort of statement, and became more insistent. We wished to know what venturesome policy the authorities had in their minds, did not exactly laugh in his face, but told him that hitherto we had never interfered in the affairs of our brothers in foreign parts. We referred him to our friend Janson, whom we were expecting back every day from Scandinavia. We must first hear his information, that was always reliable, about the position of affairs in the North. The conversation was ended by the arrival of a telegram for the Privy Councillor announcing the sinking of the English cruiser *Hawk* by a German submarine.

Some days later Janson was in Berlin. We naturally talked to him of the situation in Finland. He held out no hopes. My report was considerably abbreviated, although I gave information on 28th October, 1914, of another consultation at the Foreign Office at which Count Pourtalès, the German Ambassador in Russia till the outbreak of War, was present.

According to Janson there was, on the whole, no evidence of the Finns being inclined to revolt. Supporters of such a rising could only be our Social Democratic brothers—that was the general opinion in Finland, and the question was asked what would happen after a successful rising when the War was over. Big Russia would fall upon little Finland and annex it.

The gentlemen "from the Government" made all sorts of suggestions about satisfying the Finns' wishes, *e.g.* by guaranteeing their independence in the peace treaty. One of the gentlemen, the cutest of the lot, thought it his duty to emphasize the fact that one could not go the length of expecting the Finns to envisage a second war with Russia should Russia attack them. After Ebert had maintained that the Finns' attitude was pure common sense, I said quite frankly that it had never been our job to make a row by request. The gentlemen who in their elementary knowledge of Social Democratic principles imagined that revolutions could be brought about, so to speak, by order, made very long faces.

A Trip to the West

Very soon after the outbreak of War complaints from the Army kept coming to hand, till there were piles of them. Our attempts at redress clearly did not come to much. The officers mostly denied that there was any justifiable ground for complaint, and pacified the authorities at home, to whom we had to apply, times out of number. Finally, it was more insistently demanded that competent members of the Party should be sent to the front and the rest billets, to convince themselves on the spot that these complaints were not groundless. Naturally every soldier should be protected from abuse or punishment after answering our questions. As we became more and more insistent, some superior officers organized trips to the front, so that "honourable members" could see for themselves the faultless treatment and rationing of the soldiers. We stipulated that we should not be shown model billets and could ask the soldiers any reasonable questions, but not in the presence of a superior officer. It said much for the authorities in Berlin that they acceded to all our demands. On 17th September, 1915, Dr. David, Ebert, Schöpflin, and I travelled via Frankfurt and Metz to Charleville, where Comrades Dr. Küster, then war correspondent, and Captain von Bunsen received us. Von Bunsen was to conduct us and give or get us all the information we required. He proved himself a very good guide. We saw not only the more important billets, but also struck on less pleasing places, despite vigorous protests from the staffs. The result was that many complaints proved without foundation, for in war everything cannot be done to suit everybody. Most of the complaints, however, proved to be justified, unfortunately. It was almost always the case that, wherever good cause of complaint did not arise, tactless officers and N.C.O.'s unsuitable for their jobs had given offence. We were able in numerous cases to improve matters, as we were later told from the field repeatedly. N.B.—Relief could be obtained in cases of personal ill-treatment, misunderstandings, unfairness in granting leave, etc. As for the commissariat, the number of complaints was greater where the rations were smaller. To be perfectly frank, it must be said generally that many more officers were praised than blamed. But those who were praised were only known and popular in a comparatively small area, whereas anyone against whom real complaint existed was decried far and wide. Officers and N.C.O.'s who were unsportsmanlike to their men and still retained their insolent barrack-square manners were hated, whereas those who were affable and showed their men a good example generally were popular. We came across stirring instances of devotion and loyalty of the men towards their officers.

This trip to the front was really no fun for us; it was simply fulfilling a duty to the soldiers, whose lives we wanted to make less hard as far as we could. That we as civilians were going round among men who were fighting was a depressing fact for us, as it was clear that not everyone was aware of the object of our journey. In Zeebrügge we had to dine in a restaurant that had been commandeered for an officers' club. The words "Officers' Club" were painted on it. On leaving the restaurant, somebody took a photograph of us, that appeared later in a Berlin illustrated paper. This innocent photo, for the reproduction of which we were in no way responsible, roused blazing anger among the Radical Opposition. They published a pamphlet with the title, "Pictures without Words," and reproduced the photo along with a fancy picture of Clara Zetkin behind prison bars. The lady had been locked up for some remark or other in a speech. Naturally the Executive moved heaven and earth to get her released. On 13th October, 1915, our colleague Dietz wired from Stuttgart that he had managed to get her out of prison and would take her

235

with him to Stuttgart. But how had he obtained her release? He had bought it with a 10,000 mark War Bond! It was a fine feat on the part of Comrade Dietz. Someone else should follow his example!

XIII

THE WORRIED CHANCELLOR

I HAD hardly returned from the front to Berlin, when I was earnestly requested, on 29th September, to see the Chancellor. Bassermann, Spahn and von Payer were there. The Chancellor wanted to talk of many things in strict confidence, and we were not to say a word, not even to our colleagues. He alluded to events in the Balkans, especially how we had succeeded in winning Bulgaria over to our side. In August, 1914, a treaty between Bulgaria on the one side and Turkey and Germany had as good as been brought about. Then came the battle of the Marne, and everything had gone awry. The Entente immediately got to work in the Balkans. However, we had succeeded in reopening negotiations with Bulgaria. This had only been made possible by a loan from the Diskontogesellschaft. The amount was about three hundred millions. Everything seemed to be going well. Then came the defeat of the Austrians in the Carpathians, and everything was all wrong again. "Again the Entente and the Central Powers were wrestling for Bulgaria." Eventually we worked it, owing to our military successes. The treaty had been signed and ratified. It was to last five years, and was to be kept a secret from all the Powers. The Chancellor could not give any of its terms. He trusted Roumania would preserve her neutrality. The situation in Greece was obscure. He knew the King was friendly to Germany; on the other hand, the Prime Minister was on the side of the Entente. No one could say how things there would shape. In Russia the Duma seemed to be working harmoniously with the Party of reaction. At all events, the Peace Party could not yet assert itself. The Czar was certainly a weak man, and would probably be inclined to peace if there were strong men in Russia who could win him over. It was a misfortune that Witte was dead. He, the Chancellor, was waiting for the psychological moment to enter upon negotiations for peace, but when would that come? In France everyone was again full of hope, now that the offensive had brought them some success, as we must frankly admit. Incidentally he would like to say that he had had a wire to-day from Headquarters, saying that they were ready for further fighting, but the crisis was considered over. As things stood, we had to make up our minds to another winter campaign. All his hopes of coming earlier to a final peace had been frustrated. England's object evidently was to humble us in the dust at all costs. First and foremost his eye was fixed on Russia and France. In Italy the war fever had died down enormously. Cadorna had refused to give up any troops for France and the Dardanelles. Everything depended on whether we could hold Constantinople. If we could, the war *furore* would cool down and perhaps there was hope of a turn for the better. We were on good terms with Denmark, likewise with Sweden. The Finns were ready to revolt, if they were helped. It was regrettable that America had lent five hundred million dollars to the French and English, but it was by no means as bad as openly quarrelling with America.

We may incidentally remark that the quarrel with America was actually provoked by the renewal of ruthless U-boat attacks—in spite of Bethmann-Hollweg's opposition. Every word Bethmann-Hollweg spoke showed he was terribly anxious. Every sentence was inspired by a deep longing and a strong will for peace. How senseless must the demands for Annexation from the Conservatives and Pan-German National Liberals have seemed to those behind the scenes.

XIV

PAN-GERMAN WAR AIMS

THE more successful our troops were at the beginning of the War—of their defeat on the Marne the people knew nothing—the bolder became the Pan-German paper-strategists, who had been longing for war for many years. Among the most short-sighted Annexationists after the outbreak of war, apart from men who were then Conservatives and afterwards turned German Nationals, were numbered the "honourable members" Bassermann, Stresemann and Erzberger. The latter himself drew up a wild programme of annexation and handed it on to the parties concerned. Bassermann proposed that no inch of ground should be given back that had been watered by the blood of one German soldier.

We must devote more space to Herr Stresemann, as over-enthusiastic friends have tried, and still try, to spread the rumour that he had only one object in life—to reconcile nations and assure the peace of the world. Herr Stresemann's life-work has been very varied. The day on which his policy of reconciliation began came long after the Peace Treaty. It would be futile, even though only interviews are dealt with, to speak plainly of his career without giving data. Still more futile, naturally, is the attempt to describe the policy of Herr Stresemann as not only running in one straight line, but also as directed against Annexations.

Rochus von Rheinbaben, obviously a warm supporter of Stresemann, has written some biographical notes as an introduction to a book published by Carl Reissner in Dresden. He remembers Lloyd George's words: "My greatest enemies are my speeches"; to this he adds a remark, "Compared with his, Stresemann's speeches and essays indicate a consistent line of policy, though in detail determined by circumstances." If words have any sense, they can here only mean that Stresemann has pursued a consistent policy—contrary to Lloyd George—a policy that was naturally influenced by events of the day. There we have a straight line! Herr von Rheinbaben, however, becomes clearer; because the German's love of peace has been so ill rewarded, Stresemann argued that one must get security for Germany in accordance with those possibilities that victory may give. He always spoke, however, plainly against a policy of Annexation. . . . Oh! oh!

What is the good of such nonsense, and why does Stresemann stand it? Nobody will find fault with him—a former Pan-German—whose Jingo policy we have incidentally specified, for having been possessed of the *furor teutonicus* at the start of the War. We will therefore not quote from his speeches of the first year and a half of the War. Stresemann was for years incorrigible, and even to the bitter end of the War fixed his hopes on Courland—where at any rate, so to speak, the annexation plans of our stay-at-home warriors were buried in a common grave.

A bright light is shed on Stresemann's War period by an incident described by the late Conrad Haussmann, a democratic member of the Reichstag, in his book "Schlaglichter" (Frankfurter Societäts-Druckerei, 1924). Haussmann had an interview with Zimmermann, then Secretary of State for Foreign Affairs, one of Stresemann's predecessors:

Zimmermann: "Look here—this Stresemann, I trouble you —I won't waste words, it's abominable. Now he is attacking us, and in December he was shouting with joy over a torpedo incident, because it made war inevitable with America.

"To be sure, Stresemann and his National Liberals pursue the most inconsistent policy imaginable. I have given them a bit of my mind—to be sure, I have—and will inform you if anything special turns up with regard to you."

That Herr Stresemann was awarded the Nobel Peace Prize is not a bad instance of historical irony. As if to prove the more easily the accuracy of this remark and the inaccuracy of his biographer, Rheinbaben, he printed many of his speeches and essays in a very dainty type, under various titles and with different publishers. It is therefore easy to string a few pearls on a thread.

In the speeches we give the date; in the essays the title.

"If a German dares to say that Germany, with its seventy million inhabitants, has the same right, and can create a German Gibraltar, if he wins it by his sword, he has not only to defend himself against German enemies abroad, but also against Philistines at home. I have the confident feeling that English prestige, that is only artificially maintained, will collapse in this world war." (7th June, 1916.) On 19th January, 1917, there was a demonstration in Berlin of a so-called Independent Select Committee, in which there figured as speakers Professor Dietrich Schäfer, a hot-headed Nationalist; Count Westarp, about whom nothing further need be said; Dr. Pfleger of the Centre, who founded in Munich a Society for the Destruction of England; Pastor Traub, the former Radical-Liberal who wrote and spoke blood and thunder in the War; as well as Dr. Stresemann. Of these Herr Stresemann is the only one who interests us, because of the others no one has dared to assert that they were opposed to Annexations. Let us feast on Herr Stresemann's remarks.

He was up against all who referred to the sensible policy of Frederick II. when he made peace at Hubertsburg, and against Bismarck when he made peace at Nicolsburg: "You seem to have forgotten one small point, that it is one thing making peace with your own kith and kin, and another thing making peace with Englishmen and Serbians. Frederick II. moreover wrote the words: 'A war that does not lead to annexations is a war wasted, in my opinion.' We need more land for agriculture. . . .

"Courland is just the spot. But on further considering this matter I should like to recommend that the Select Independent Committee should include in the scope of its peace deliberations the question of how far in the future Roumania's surplus of corn supplies can be secured for Germany and her allies. (*Applause:* Oil.) The same may be said with regard to the Poles and all lands having political, national or economic relations with us. . . . It is sad when we find Germans saying to-day that we must give up insisting on a war-indemnity."

This meeting wound up by passing a resolution in which there were seven clauses, which we need only give in abbreviated form, because they frankly show how the "straightline" (what a horrid word!) policy of Herr Stresemann from Riga to Longwy-Briey, from Calais to Locarno, and from Bukarest to Geneva has run.

1. Rectification of our frontiers in East and West.

2. A wide extension of our agricultural land in the East.

3. The acquisition of enemy territory on the frontier, the products of which (minerals and coal) our people need.

4. The possession of the coast of Flanders, so as to insure free passage for our mercantile marine to the Atlantic and effectively stop a blockade.

5. Political, economic and military control in Belgium and Poland.

6. Colonial possessions, so as to support and insure our dominion and our trade connections overseas.

7. The transference of the bulk of our war costs to the enemy in the form of money payments or by surrender of territory.

The concluding sentences of this resolution read as follows:
"A final peace settlement, through which these indispensable conditions are not absolutely fulfilled, will as a matter of course contain in itself the seeds of a fresh and bloodier war. . . . We only need a peace guaranteeing its permanence by the strength of our power. . . . We are prepared to fight on till we have won it by our victories."

We? *We* were Professor Schäfer, Count Westarp, Dr. Pfleger and Dr. Stresemann. Not one of them has ever fought anywhere except from the platform or the writing desk. They were, however, quite ready to fight where they were till the last drop of blood—naturally—of those who were lying in the trenches.

Such were the men, according to Stresemann's biographer, von Rheinbaben, who had always opposed a policy of Annexation.

Let us listen to what Herr Stresemann has further to say. By his definitely declared policy of Annexation, England had naturally to be laid low. This could only be possible if ruthless U-boat warfare fulfilled what its keenest adherents, to whom Stresemann's party in the first instance belonged, expected from it. Within a few months (the time was definitely fixed) the submarine would make England bow the knee. As a matter of fact—and everyone knew it—the only practical success won by this ruthless form of attack on the sea was that the U.S.A. declared war against us, as everybody thought she would, and thereby brought the War to an end.

"Listen, Yokel!"

The chief hope of all Annexationists was centred in the U-boat. It was evident that Stresemann pinned his whole faith to it, if one reads what far-reaching plans he based upon it in his book, "Michel, horch, der Seewind pfeift" (Listen, peasant, the seawind is whistling).

"Haven't we, with our seventy millions, the same right as England has to rule the world, with her forty-five? Don't we too lie on the North Sea? Don't we plough to-day the seas like the Hansa League of old? Why shouldn't we use a success for our own benefit, as our enemies would probably do if victory was theirs? . . . We are all agreed in the idea that Germany must be 'greater still' for Germany's glory and the peace of the world.

"We want a greater Germany—especially along the coastline. We are not without a coastline, but we have no means of extending it eastwards and westwards in order to hold Cronstadt in check on one side and Dover on the other. . . . Our coastline must be lengthened, therefore; England must be checkmated; she must be deprived of the pleasure of playing her own game again. Have we no right to create a German Gibraltar and make the North Sea again the German Ocean? England has shown us the way. We have in Shakespeare, England's greatest poet, a good guide; it is as if he had prophesied it to us in his verses.

" *'And then to Calais, and to England then,*
Where ne'er from France arrived more happy men.'"

The man who has ideas like these in his head would naturally be angry when others doubted the success of the U-boat. Erzberger, unlike Stresemann, had his eyes gradually opened; he attacked the U-boat blunder tooth and nail, and had drawn attention to the world's tonnage standing at England's disposal according to the statistics of the Admiralty, which Helfferich supported. Stresemann waxed wroth.

"Erzberger is certainly wrong there. That England won't last out is incontrovertible. Her fight to-day against the U-boat is slackening already." (July, 1917.)

Stresemann believed in the success of ruthless attacks by submarines, and in England's collapse; he must have believed it, if his repeated demand for a German Gibraltar was not to be utterly ridiculed. After quoting Goethe and Shakespeare in the support of his plans for annexation, he invoked Napoleon as a witness on.

"Napoleon once compared England with Carthage. Carthage came down from her height; so may England and she shall. On our side stands moral right, and on our side is power to stab her to the heart, if we only understand how to seize the chance." (29th January, 1917.)

Perfectly unintelligible is the hatred—irreconcilable hatred —he has vented against England. In his war book, "Michel, horch," he says, "We all trust that after the War an era of reconciliation with France and Russia will dawn, and that the lapse of years will bring about understanding and peace. But there is one thing no one can expect from the German people—a reconciliation with England. Hate lies too deep; a hate that is morally justified. Nothing in the last few weeks has appealed more to the heart of the people than the poem the Crown Prince of Bavaria issued to his troops—verses, as a weapon of war—the last lines of which ran:

" 'What matter to us the French or the Russ?
Shot against shot, and blow for a cuss,
We fight the good fight with iron and steel
And make it all up anon and awheel.

" 'Thee we will hate for a long time—yes, hate;
Ne'er one jot or tittle our hatred abate;
Hate on the sea and hate on the land,
Hate in our heads and hate in our hand,
Hate of the anvil, and hate of the great,
Hate, that can throttle, of millions of men.
United we love, united we hate,
Hate only we breathe on one single pate—England!' "

If it is beyond our understanding that Herr von Rheinbaben could have quoted the above sentences on Stresemann's policy and his alleged aversion to annexations, it is absolutely baffling that Herr Stresemann did not cut them out, as he must have seen them in proof before the book was published. All attempts to whitewash him, as being a politician who could go straight and to whom all annexations were distasteful, are shattered by the simple fact that his speeches and writings are in print under our noses. However, Monsieur Briand's policy is just as straight, and consequently the two gentlemen work quite well together.

Not without interest, naturally, is Herr Stresemann's reply to the question as to his attitude with regard to the establishment of arbitration courts and a league of nations. At a meeting of the Reichstag on 28th February, 1917, he inveighed against the "dream policy of everlasting peace."

"I have many times thought on the old words of Goethe in *Faust* during these days:

247

" 'Dream ye of peaceful days?
Let him dream them who can.
War's the word that solves the crux,
Victory—that's always the slogan.'

"It was always so, since the world began, and so will it re-main. The fate of nations will not be tied down to the terms of the League of Nations, for these will be torn up directly the vital interests of a big strong Power are at stake." (28th February, 1917.)

Almost a year before he gave vent to much stronger lan-guage against dreamers and idealists. "A lasting peace can only be one that makes us stronger. In this sense the German people is aiming at the security of the German frontiers and their extension. . . . The solution is not by Treaty, but by a display of force in Flanders and elsewhere." (22nd June, 1916.)

Stresemann did not care a snap for the ideals of the League of Nations or for idealists in general. His Annexation policy could not have been brought into line with the views he en-tertained ten years later as German representative to the League. He wanted to annex territory both in the East and West. From the annexed coast of Flanders he intended, how-ever, to hold the mailed fist under the nose of England. By way of a treaty of mutual understanding, no enforced treaty would have been possible, naturally, and therefore a dictated peace appeared ideal to him, such as the Entente ultimately forced upon us.

"If we could conclude a dictated peace, no one of our Party would protest if we did snatch a bit of foreign territory be-cause it was contrary to an agreement among nations."

Capitalists and Their Professors

It would naturally have been of no importance had only a few individuals indulged in these sweeping demands. Behind them, unfortunately, were not only unworldly Professors, but also mighty economic bodies that were all very vocal. They systematized their demands for annexation. Through this arose great difficulties within the S.P.D. that must be discussed. Wherever German Annexations and political ignoramuses were agitating *pro patria,* there were always the Professors ready to help them. The spiteful words of a King of Hanover about racehorses, Professors and gay ladies cannot be quoted exactly, but it may be concisely stated how German Professors, industrial Jingo politicians, "poverty-stricken agriculturists" and narrow-minded wire-pullers, all tried to outdo each other in their insane demands for Annexations. What the Farmers' Unions cried out for (here given briefly) is essentially on the same level with war aims of the Professors.

Silence! German Jingo politicians are now talking to the Imperial Government:

"Your Excellency,

". . . In common with the whole of the German people, all German employers of labour in agriculture and industry, handicrafts and trade have firmly decided to fight on to the last in the life-and-death struggle that has been forced on Germany, regardless of sacrifices, so that Germany may emerge from this conflict with increased strength and with the guarantee of a lasting peace abroad, and also with a guarantee of an assured national economic and cultural development at home. . . .

"The announcement of the *Norddeutsche Allgemeine*

Zeitung that no one capable of judging can think of sacrificing Germany's favourable war position for a premature peace with any one of her enemies, was welcomed with approval. . . . No premature peace therefore, for, from such, no adequate prize for victory can be expected.

"But it must be no half-hearted peace; it must be one that embodies in it all the political advantages we hope to gain by our military successes in every branch of commerce. For it must not be overlooked that all the advantages of our military position should not only guarantee the increase of Germany's power abroad and the safety of our future, but also ensure (and this is equally important) that the willing sacrifices and determination of the German people be utilized for domestic affairs in the coming days of peace. The price of victory must be in due proportion to the loss of hundreds and thousands. What the conditions should be—subject to military success, naturally (and these must be drawn up according to the views of the signatories in order to consolidate Germany's political, military and economic position and enable her to look calmly forward to the future), can be read in the petition given below, dated 10th March of this year and addressed to Your Excellency. The petition ran thus:

" 'The undersigned associations have considered the question of how far the much-discussed topic of obtaining an honourable peace in this war can be carried into effect, be made commensurate with our losses, and ensure a lasting peace. In answer to this question it must be borne in mind that our enemies are always saying that Germany must be destroyed and disappear from among the Great Powers. To thwart these intentions we shall find no security in treaties, which can be trampled on at any time, but in so weakening our enemies, economically and militarily, that peace may be ensured for a considerable time.

"'Coupled with the demand for a Colonial Empire that shall be fully adequate to Germany's many-sided economic interests, the security of our financial and commercial future, and the acquisition of a thoroughly practicable and satisfactory compensation for our war losses, we consider that the chief objective of our struggle, that has been forced upon us, lies in guarantees and a remodelling of the former position of the German Empire in the following directions:

"'Belgium . . . must be placed under our Central Board of Trade for military and economic purposes, as well as for Customs, Banking and Post Office. The railways and waterways must be incorporated in our general transport system. The control and management of the country must be transferred to German hands; the Walloon and the Flemish population, that vastly preponderate, must be separated, and all important economic undertakings and property handed over to German rule in such a way that the inhabitants shall acquire no influence on the political destinies of the German Empire.

"'As to France, and in the same way with regard to England, the acquisition of all coastal territory bordering on Belgium as far as the Somme, and an outlet to the Atlantic Ocean, must be considered a vital question for our future position on the sea. . . . Any further acquisitions, apart from the necessary annexation of the mining districts of Briey, must be decided by military exigencies only. . . . In addition to acquiring the line of the Meuse and the French coast on the Channel, possession of the coal districts of the Departments du Nord and the Pas de Calais, apart from the mining districts of Briey, should be conceded. These acquisitions, after our experiences in Alsace-Lorraine, naturally postulate that the population of the absorbed territory should not be able to exercise political influence on the future of the German Empire, and all present economic resources in these districts, inclusive of smaller and larger holdings, should be transferred to German hands that France should compensate and adopt their owners.

" 'As to the East, this single recommendation should suffice, that the big industrial development to be expected in the West should correspond to one of like magnitude and value in the East. . . .

" 'With respect to granting political rights to the inhabitants of the new territories and the security of German economic influence, what has been said with regard to France should apply. War compensation from Russia would mainly consist of acquisitions of territory.

" 'The want of harbours, right on the Channel, will, as formerly, cramp our trade overseas. An independent Belgium would be England's bridgehead, her *point d'appui* against us. The natural fortress line in France would mean a constant menace to our frontiers. But Russia, if she comes out of the War without loss of territory, would ignore our power and strength, that should hinder her from interfering with our interests, whereas failure to acquire agricultural land on our eastern borders would lessen the possibility of strengthening the defensive power of Germany by an adequate increase of her population.'

"It should be specially noted at the end of this note that the political, military and economic objects the German people should do their best to attain, are most closely connected with each other and cannot be separated."

This note was signed by the chairman of the six following Unions: the Landlords' Union, the German Farmers' Leagues, the Westphalian Farmers' Union, the Central Union of German Manufacturers, the Union of Employers, and the Imperial Middle Classes League.

The Professors played their cards much more adroitly than the magnates of industry and the ever-grousing farmers, under the lead of the country nobility and the middle classes. The Professors naturally made their demands on a scientific basis. Here is an example in a sentence from their paragraph on War Compensation:

"Should we be in a position to levy a War Compensation on England, no payment in cash could be great enough. . . . The purse is the most sensitive part in the anatomy of this 'nation of shopkeepers.' She must be, before all else, hit in her money bags, should we have the chance."

From a political standpoint nothing more stupid could ever have been imagined. "Should we be in a position, no payment in cash would be too great." When we hatch the eggs, then! When we win the first prize in a sweepstake——! This extraordinary note was signed, among others, by Frederick Meinecke, Professor of History at Berlin; Hermann Oncken, Professor of History at Heidelberg; Hermann Schumacher, Professor of Political Economy; Reinhardt Seeberg, Professor of Theology; and Frederick Schäfer, Professor of History at Berlin. Audacious to excess was its appeal to the people and public opinion. Public opinion, it said, was in full agreement with the demands of the magnates of industry and the Professors! We will not waste words about that. We have only to refer to the way in which our enemies made use of it, and what untold harm it did to the German people. One is tempted to say that the dictated peace at Versailles in its chief clauses was drafted to suit the demands of the German Annexationists, who had longed for a dictated peace.

Rumour has attributed to them many qualities they never possessed and acts they never did, while others are dismissed as inferior beings—one has only to think of Erzberger. It seems to be my duty with regard to this to take every opportunity to destroy legend and get at the truth. Lloyd George's quip, that his speeches were his worst enemies, applies more to Stresemann, the worst chatterer in Europe, than to him. Owing to his being a well-read man, he is able to revel in quotations, and produces them wholesale in every speech. But he does not appear to have heard of one saying, "Silence is silver." Yet a quotation from the Bible exactly applies to him, that "there is more joy in Heaven over one sinner who repenteth, than over ninety-nine just persons" who have never stumbled. We will rejoice over his fundamental conversion, but his friends should cease describing him as he is not and never was. The Stresemann who wished to rule in Courland, Poland and Belgium, who wished to annex the coast of Flanders and howled for a German Gibraltar, who preached everlasting hatred against England, yearned for a dictated peace and rejected every idea of a league of nations, was a different man from the Stresemann who won the Nobel Peace Prize ten years later, as the friend of national reconciliation and the League of Nations. We congratulate him and ourselves on his change for the better.

XV

FIGHTS IN THE S.P.D.

THE more audaciously these demands, against which we Social Democrats at once distinctly protested, were advanced by the Annexationists, the stronger became the opposition to them in the Social Democratic Party. While the majority of the S.P.D. took the view that they could not refuse the War Credits, because demands had been made by short-sighted people of which the Government disapproved, the minority's view was that no extra War Credits could now be sanctioned, for it was obvious that war in self-defence had long ago developed into war of aggression. Not only had general meetings of the Party become the battle-ground of faction, especially in Berlin and Leipzig, but also the sittings of the Executive, the Select Committee and the Party meetings in the Reichstag. At first discussions were more or less trivial "leg-pulling" and were conducted in a sporting spirit, but very soon this harmless banter degenerated into violent opposition and personal abuse. Ultimately practical discussion was out of the question, and the leaders of the Party and their following in the Reichstag were attacked in the bitterest way. It could be clearly seen that former quarrels about Party tactics had left their sting behind.

Revolutionary tactics, advocated by Rosa Luxemburg, Clara Zetkin, Karl Liebknecht and others, were rejected by the Party conferences. This had bitterly offended the supporters of Russian methods, which were quite unsuitable for Germany.

The fight at the Party Conference in Jena in 1913 is described elsewhere. The Reds thought their chance had come at the outbreak of war. I was horrified when Heinrich Schulz, later Secretary of State for the Home Office, told me of an interview he had had with Rosa Luxemburg a few days before the outbreak. Both were prominent persons on the Educational Committee of the S.P.D., the former as director and teacher in the Party school belonging to my department in the Executive, the latter as a mistress. When all Germany, during the last days of July, 1914, was in a fever of excitement, quivering in hope and fear lest peace might or might not be preserved, Heinrich Schulz, finding himself alone with Rosa Luxemburg in a classroom, said, in a worried way: "It's to be hoped that war won't come." To that Rosa Luxemburg replied across the table: "I hope it will." She, I take it, fancied it would bring about a revolution throughout the world.

A meeting of the Select Committee took place on 27th September. Haase was in the chair, as Ebert now only attended rarely. On this occasion, however, Ebert was reporting on the condition of the Party, and said: "As to the attitude of the Party Press, it was clearly seen in the first days of the War that a number of papers had imbibed the war fever. In our circular letter of 11th August we wrote against it; afterwards things improved."

A few remarks throwing interesting light on the spirit of the Party from within may be given here.

Mehrfeld (Cologne) said: "A comrade, well known to me, was in a hospital at Cologne with both eyes put out, and afterwards died. In Belgium our regular troops are unpopular, but the Territorials (*Landsturm*) are liked. We should try, by co-operating with the International, to get exact information on things going on there."

A few facts from Comrade Keil illustrated the policy of the Opposition: "In Stuttgart the conduct of the Section has been criticized in a way that throws the gloomiest light on the state of things prevailing in the Party. After the outbreak of war confidential meetings were summoned and the policy of the Section was discussed. The whole Section, including even the supporters of the War Credits, were denounced as rascals and blackguards, who for forty years had deceived the Party."

Fleissner (Dresden), belonging to the Opposition Party, demanded that we should not surrender what we had been maintaining by our arms for forty-four years, but went on to say: "We desire Germany to win. We shall forget later on that Social Democracy did its bit. The war-mongers will then say Germany was saved by being prepared."

In the course of the debate Haase stated that the Party Executive was unanimous on the question of Annexations and was opposed to them. "Special circumstances prevented the Section from saying anything about violating neutrality at the time. Twenty-four hours later we were sorry no one had raised this question before. The declaration had been previously settled and thoroughly discussed in all its details. It so happened that one sentence had been altered as a matter of form in the declaration on the day the Reichstag met, so that England should not form wrong conclusions from this declaration. In the interval no one proposed that anything should be said about the breach of neutrality."

Hilferding remarked: "We are not only concerned with the policy of the Section; it seems to be a fact that the opinion of the people supported the Section when it voted the Credits. The remarks against Czardom coincided with the feeling of the masses."

A few sentences from Ebert's concluding words must be given: ". . . Contrary to expectation, Hilferding tried to enter into the question of the origin of the War. I did not touch on the question this morning, because we have more urgent and important business on hand. His speech contained nothing very new. His view that Imperialism in all countries is the *ultima ratio,* we have often heard before, but this is not the crux. It is simply a question of knowing what happened in the time immediately preceding the outbreak of war. At this time Germany was undoubtedly threatened and forced, on the ground of self-preservation, to defend herself. We have not allowed ourselves to be led away by popular opinion. But the declaration of war just showed how rightly we acted. The Russian hordes, already mobilized, proved that Russia had been preparing for war for months. On the question of Annexations I agree entirely with what Haase has said. We were all along against an Annexation policy. But the present is not the time to take strong action against the policy of Annexation. The French are still in Alsace, and the Russians are only just out of East Prussia, and are trying to attack on another side. We warned the Press most distinctly by our circular letter. We are all agreed that treaties of neutrality should be observed."

The course of the discussion made it evident that more grievous difficulties were in front of us as a Party.

As an instance of war fever, referred to by Ebert, may be quoted the *Wahre Jakob,* a paper that circulated in hundreds of thousands of copies. In its first number after the outbreak of war it produced a picture with these words underneath: "Now, children, up and at them! A good thrashing is the only thing!" The picture represented German working men, armed with flails, going for French, English, and Russians, hiding under straw. The Executive tried to hold up this number. It was the number dedicated to the fiftieth anniversary of Lassalle's death, and, in addition to a portrait of Lassalle, contained a photograph of Jean Jaurès, who had been murdered by a French Nationalist. A poem on Jaurès and also a manifesto were not only wholly free from possible incitements to slaughter, but also expressed a profound desire for peace and freedom quite after the style of the dear dead man:

"With this oath on our lips we dip the Red Flag over thy grave."

Things were a great deal worse at the January meetings of the Select Committee, 1915, than at the September one. Liebknecht meanwhile had started his independent action, and therefore ignored the resolutions of the Section. Ebert reported thus on 13th January, 1915, to the Select Committee: "The French Social Democratic Party are to-day in full sail on the tide of Chauvinism. Even Viviani's speech in the Chamber, couched in terms of demagogic revenge, defended the Party. Vaillant is trying in the *Humanité* to outrival the Chauvinistic tirades of Pichon and Clemenceau. The Party Press has printed an effusion from one of Vaillant's articles in the *Humanité*:

"'Vaillant protests in the *Humanité* against a premature peace, and declares war to the knife an imperative duty. Public opinion is amazed at the delay in appealing to Japan, and will soon lose its temper. France has no interests in Eastern Asia to be compared with her own in France and Alsace, and the Belgians have their own country to consider. The complete defeat of Germany means salvation for France and freedom for the world. To effect the immediate intervention of Japan by all means in our power is the desire of the nation and the duty of the Government.'"

In Italy the Executive of the Italian Social Democrats had been obliged to remove the fire-eater Mussolini from the chief editorship of the paper of the Centre. The official organ of the Swiss Party, the Berne *Tagwacht,* advertises its International brotherly love by daily cursing the German party in the foulest and bitterest language.

In spite of this, the situation was quite clear for the S.P.D.: "We remain loyal to our Fatherland till the enemy is ready to make peace."

Again Haase's point of view was quite different:

"I most deeply deplore Vaillant's action. But even here a similar tone is adopted, and if it spreads will do us grievous harm with the International. We hear people talking about 'sticking it out' till the enemy lies prone on the ground. We must notice that Vaillant invariably preaches only the annihilation of Prussian militarism, and never the subjection of the Prussian people. People here talked like this about the War meaning the shattering of Russian Czardom. . . . We must not condemn the English working man because he takes up his country's cause. 'God Save the King' in the *Daily Citizen* is answered by the cry for organizing Boy Scout societies in Germany, which would espouse the cause of Emperor and Empire."

It was the same old contention between us and Haase. He would complain of us because we did not refuse to grant our own country the means for a war in self-defence, while he was doing his best to excuse or even defend the worst forms of Chauvinism among foreign Socialists.

Leinert, Hermann, Müller and Severing rounded badly on Haase, while Dissmann, Dr. Hilferding, Louise Zietz and Fleissener rushed to his assistance. At Ebert's request, I put my name down on the list of speakers, in order to relieve him from winding up the discussion that in the ordinary course would not last for hours.

I pointed out that Haase, as a clever lawyer, could plead for others at any moment, and had done so with extraordinary volubility on behalf of the English, the French and the *Vorwärts*.

"Volubility is not synonymous with truth. Haase made great play with 'ifs' and 'buts' to defend others—'what should we have done, etc.' It is essential to judge of our actions by the situation in which we are placed, and not by what we should have done had such and such been the case. Haase has even drawn a parallel between the alliance of the Russians with Prussia in 1813 and that of the Russians and the French in 1914. If the alliance was no disgrace for Prussia at that time, it is no disgrace to the French at this time. This seems to me a remarkable argument. The French simply do not come into the picture, but the French Socialists who talked of their 'brave allies' the Russians, as marching with resolute steps to Berlin—to fight for freedom. . . . What the Section had to say to justify itself is pertinently stated in the declaration: 'In the hour of danger, etc.' Latterly one has been taken to task for using the word 'Fatherland.' You can read in the *Labour Leader* Rosa Luxemburg's remark about that miserable word 'Fatherland. I do not want two distinct kinds of argument on our side, one patriotic before, and another unpatriotic after the Elections. According to me, these comrades must behave as democrats, and support the unity of the Party in the interests of the proletariate. Woe unto us if we flay each other as soon as we are free again to act, instead of pressing on all together and manfully to those big tasks that await us after the War. Only if we stand together can the days of 1813 and 1870 return; there is no other way."

Ebert condemned Haase's pet idea of contrasting the policy of French and English Socialists with our own. Our own Socialists do not behave in this way, but the Pan-Germans do. As there was some talk about a fresh peace movement, Ebert declared concisely: "A peace movement has no sense unless it is taken up by all the Parties in the nations now warring against each other. In the first place, French and English must abandon their previous negative attitude."

Tempers Get Worse and Worse

From meeting to meeting the irritation grew worse and worse. Haase, Bernstein and Kautsky had launched their thunderbolt against the Party with the title, "The Command of the Hour," after the Berlin *Tagwacht* had raged against the Party, and the wildest anonymous broadsides were fired off wholesale against the policy of the S.P.D.

At the Imperial Conference in September, 1916, a debate took place of the greatest importance. This Conference, a substitute for a Party Congress, the summoning of which was regarded as impossible, was held in the hall of the chief Select Committee in the Reichstag. It was so splendidly attended from all parts of the Reich that the largest of the committee rooms in the House could hardly seat them. The atmosphere from the very start was electric. Johannes Timm, a member of the K.K. branch of the S.P.D., a most sensible, temperate and popular colleague, was so angered during Ebert's speech by Stadthagen's interruptions that he jumped up and hit Stadthagen in the face.

The methods of the Opposition Party employed at that time will be vividly illustrated by a memorandum sent to Ebert and myself before we delivered our speeches at the Conference: "Shorthand reports of the speeches are being circulated to individual speakers for inspection and possible alteration, with the request that all corrections should be sent back by return of post."

All corrected copies were speedily returned except by Haase. This eventually turned up after repeated applications. At the same time arrived Haase's speech, already printed as a broad-sheet. This had been circulated all over the Empire. Then the Executive determined to print Ebert's speech and mine.

Ebert at the Conference had spoken of the work of the Executive in the War, after I had spoken about the policy of the Party. Ebert on this occasion inveighed against strikes, and, naturally, against unprincipled individuals encouraging strikes. Something more will be said about this in a later chapter. I should only like to recall two passages. I had referred to the unanimity with which nearly all my colleagues had voted supplies at the outbreak of War for self-defence.

"Were these all fools who did not know what they were doing? Or were they traitors who had sold their convictions for thirty pieces of silver? No, they were honest Socialists who were doing their bit towards helping materially their own people in distress. They no longer asked how it had all come about; they saw the great danger and entered the breach; they acted according as their convictions told them to act and as the entire German people desired them at the time to act. If on 4th August, 1914, the people themselves, instead of Parliament, had voted, how think you the voting would have gone? If the question had been, 'Do you vote for war or for peace?' the whole of the German people would have voted for peace. It is only common sense; then for the first time those who thought otherwise would have seen what a miserable handful they were in the Empire. Aye, even had the Reichstag had to vote for either war or peace, think you there would have been any dissenting voice in the S.D. Section? The whole Section would have voted for peace. But things were not like this. The War was there—a terrible, indisputable fact, no more to be kept from the world— and now the question arose whether Russia with her allies would win or be thrown back. How do you think the people would have voted if the question of War Credits had been referred to the popular vote? The well-tried members in our Party and the Unions, the visitors at our meetings, in whose ears all our complaints against Russia echoed—they would have been the first at the polling booths. In a chorus of Ayes the few No's would not have been audible. The senseless principles that anyone can be insensible to the fate of his country can only be entertained by political outsiders and unworldly prophets. But such a principle cannot be entertained by one Party that is already a big bit of the German people, and intends to become the whole of the German people. Such a Party cannot deny the fundamental duty of self-defence, or it will not be able to remain what it is; it will never be able to become what it intends to be."

Another passage, directed specially against Opposition talk about Annexations, ran as follows:

"Just as the critics over-estimate the effect of throwing out the War Credits, so do you under-estimate the danger in which we are. This danger is thought too little of in wide circles inside the Opposition; they think we are out of the wood already. This is, however, not the case. We are now in the third year of the War, and we are living in awful danger. When the War was barely three weeks old, one of the

CARICATURE OF SCHEIDEMANN BY OSKAR GARVENS

CARICATURE OF SCHEIDEMANN BY MAJOR

best speakers on the Opposition side, now a member of the Labour Union, said:

" 'It is most certainly a vital question for Germany that she survive this War. Belgium, France and England have little to fear for their internal development from a German victory. For Germany, however, her social, economic and moral development, should she succumb to the coalition of these lands with the help of autocratic Russia, would be postponed for decades, if not for a whole generation. What this would mean for German Labour and the Labour Movement, we need not discuss.'

"Comrade Edward Bernstein wrote thus on 25th August, 1914. If the danger was then so great as Bernstein said, I will say that the danger then was a mere trifle to what it is to-day. . . .

"Should Germany meet with defeat such as our enemies have intended for us, then, comrades, we should very soon notice how very much this concerns us. Our land would suffer terribly, its economic progress would be arrested and crushing taxation laid upon us. What would then happen to Socialism? What good would a just redistribution of wealth do for us in a land whose people would have to deliver the greater part of its goods not to capitalists at home, but to conquerors abroad? For two years we have been standing on the edge of a precipice, and not a man among us can fathom its depth."

A New Survey after the War

However senseless the policy of the Imperial Government towards the Labour movement had been up to the outbreak of war, every effort was now being made to show how conciliatory it could be. "I no longer recognize any Party."

That things could not go on as they had up to 1914 was now recognized by the advisers of their most gracious Emperor, King, and Overlord, who had up to then so totally misinterpreted the signs of the times. At a meeting summoned by Delbrück, Secretary of State, Haase and I represented the S.P.D. Delbrück referred to the coming meeting of the Reichstag on 2nd December at which War Credits were to be voted, though no discussion was to be allowed in any circumstances. To give the Reichstag an opportunity of airing its views on the Bill, the Government would submit to it. Delbrück thought it expedient, with the assent of President Kämpf, to form a Committee of the Reichstag. His idea was that this Committee, like the Committee on the drafting of the Budget, would be able to discuss the Bill and arrive at an agreement as to how it should be passed at the plenary session. It must be made possible to pass the Bill as it stood at one sitting. That could be done if there were no debate. And a debate would do us untold harm, especially abroad. In the discussion it was pointed out by nearly all members that Delbrück's proposal would settle various differences in Committee. Grievances, however, were audible from all sides. The Conservatives complained that, while the Social Democrats enjoyed full liberty, they, the Conservatives, were immediately hauled over the coals if they said a word against Social Democracy. We naturally protested strongly against these absolutely untrue statements. We agreed that a discussion in the Reichstag would be inevitable, because there was no possibility of criticism elsewhere, neither at meetings nor in the Press, and that a feeling of injustice was now rife.

Each Section then gave vent to its grievances, and the Secretary of State became more and more uneasy. Seyda, the Pole, referred to the conduct of his countrymen in this

War. All charges against them had fallen to the ground. Whether his Section would abstain from discussing the Bill would entirely depend upon how they intended to treat the Poles after the War. Groeber referred to the treatment of the Jesuits. Delbrück kept on imploring more earnestly: "For God's sake don't bring that up now!" He thought it was obvious that after the War some revision and reform in Home policy would have to be initiated.

I emphasized, in spite of Haase's muttered dissent, the importance of revision and reform, now announced for the first time, and asked Delbrück whether some public assurance could be given on the point, for that perhaps might be, and could be of great consequence. Delbrück replied: "I have made my statement, with the Chancellor's consent, but have up to now not received his authorization to make it public."

With regard to "revision and reform" another meeting with Delbrück must be mentioned, that took place on 26th February, 1915, *i.e.* more than three months later. A War Credit of ten milliards was then asked for. The S.D. Section was represented by its three chairmen, Haase, Molkenbuhr and myself. At this meeting Haase proposed the repeal of Section 153 of the Trades' Union Act, a demand that had been supported for years by the Trades Unions. As Delbrück made objections, I asked, "Yes, but how about the Franchise Bill, above all?" "To introduce any legislation on that in war-time is quite impossible," replied Delbrück; "in the first place, we have not staff enough to draft a Bill, and secondly, it is very doubtful policy to introduce highly contentious matters in war-time, when we want peace among our citizens." I replied that considerable difficulties would doubtless arise, but wider legislative reforms could be drafted according to plan, at any rate. Delbrück answered, "That is almost more risky than the Bill itself. What can the Government announce if it is uncertain of special details and if it knows that violent controversies will occur? Bülow had a very unhappy time over the Finance Bill as well as over the Franchise." Wahnschaffe chimed in: "The present Imperial Chancellor is far too prudent a man to announce any legislation the details of which he does not know exactly."

I wrote in my diary as follows in connection with this meeting: "In the first place, there is no prospect of reform, and never likely to be. I anticipated it. It comes to this: we are to get no reward for having voted the War Credits. I have had no illusions—it is just this: we have to fight when we are told, and fight ruthlessly moreover. It will be easier, on the strength of our conduct in the War, to get after the War what was impossible before."

High Treason

Meetings with Government officials followed hard upon one another, now social-political questions were on the "tapis," now corn and potato prices. On 10th October, 1914, Richter, the Under-Secretary of State, told us that the maximum price for Magnum Bonums must be fixed at from 2.75 to 3.05 marks, and that he had actually to smuggle to get the common necessities of life. The prices of smuggled potatoes were enormous. While fixing prices the urgent need became apparent of combatting the danger of corn going out of the country, where a good market could be got and higher prices obtained. Owing to the great difference in the prices obtained, it was not possible, in spite of the strictest Customs regulations and a sharp lookout on the frontier, to stop completely the corn leakage across the border.

A letter from the well-known ex-Member of the Reichstag,

von Oldenburg-Januschau, to the then Home Secretary, von Loebell, must not be omitted. Here it is:

"YOUR EXCELLENCY. DEAR FRITZ,

"About to return to my job in Poland, I thank God I shall be free of all these rows about foodstuffs and with civilian officials. It is now really unbearable in the country with these constantly changing regulations. I am going to let five hundred acres go out of cultivation, and lots of others are doing the same, because the uncertainty of the crops and the fixed prices are far more than I can stand. Potato prices are now comparatively reasonable; half the pork will get rotten in the brine casks. Disaffection in the country is rife and will break out seriously after the War; in addition to that, confidence in the Supreme Command of the Army is dwindling; confidence in the Supreme Civil Administration went long ago.—You know that. Finis."

The letter was written and sent off on 15th April, 1915. It was about the time when the English blockade was playing "old Harry" with us. How many of the Junkers let their lands lie fallow because compulsory cultivation went against their grain! The War might be lost and the Fatherland destroyed for all they cared. The Junker must be first and foremost!

These words give a fairly clear idea of what profits were made among certain classes even at the expense of the vital interests of the fighting, bleeding, starving people. These German "traitors" must be sought in the ranks of the ruling landowners, who let their lands go out of cultivation because the instructions of the authorities did not suit them and because prices were too low. The worst treachery naturally was the export of German foodstuffs because a higher price could be got abroad. Brill of Kassel, the German National, sent in a note to a military authority, which was confirmed by a Court of Law (dated 21st July, 1916), to this effect:

". . . The landlords are consistently and with impunity opposing every official regulation, though these are the very people who are doing splendidly out of the War. . . ."

Much more important is what the peasant leader, Dr. Heim, said in the *Fränkische Bäuer*, 1916, No. 11:

"Unfortunately, from the reports I have received from un-prejudiced sources, I must state that there are certain farmers who, exploiting to the full the bad times and the distress caused by War, are asking enormous prices for their goods. They are only, I suppose, isolated instances, but their conduct is doing harm to the whole farming class now and in the future. . . . These never-satisfied people bring incalculable disgrace upon their brother farmers. If potatoes, the food of the poorest of the poor, are made an article for profiteering, it is a downright scandal, and I will go as far as to say that such growers and landowners who make huge profits from their potatoes are a disgrace to the whole farming class."

And why were the people and the Army so completely worn out? Because for years they had had to starve!

It would be thoroughly wrong to speak only of agricul-tural offenders in this connection, for the manufacturer has also known how to fleece his own countrymen. In one special case the Prussian War Office appointed a commission of in-quiry during the War to investigate the methods of a South German business. Its findings were really startling, but no action was taken against the firm. Here are a few sentences taken from the official report:

"Findings of the Commission.—The munitions firm con-cerned made a net profit of 15 million marks over what they

declared to be their annual profit (81 million against 96 million). Errors were partly due to the chronic mistakes of those giving the contracts; this has caused an advance in prices everywhere, resulting in great hardship generally to the German people. If this business had confined itself to Government contracts and aimed at higher prices, this system would have been legitimate in view of rising costs of material and wages, the contingent risks of war and expenditure involved in restoring machinery, etc., intended for war purposes, back to peace purposes.

"The system was illegitimate in so far as profits were made far in excess of ordinary trade profits, and were derived from the country in critical times which the tax-paying citizen has ultimately to pay for.

"The border line between honest and dishonest dealings, *i.e.* moderate and immoderate profit, is a debatable point as long as the materials supplied are of good quality."

That the firm in question was not aware, or at any rate not fully aware, that its profits were derived from the country stricken by war was unanimously acknowledged by the Commission. In this matter the firm was not an isolated instance, but only a typical example of a great number of munition factories, and the Commission was of opinion that it would be unfair to punish and condemn this particular firm when a great number of others were doing the same thing owing to the War, as well as private individuals.

Ergo: in spite of exploiting a starving people, which means the decay of their power of resistance, and incidentally aiding and abetting enemy interests, the company in question, after a thorough inquiry, was found to be a typical instance of the majority of German munition industries.

Fresh Difficulties

After an official interview, with Richter, Under-Secretary of State, in the chair, I had a private interview with Lewald, then Assistant Secretary. I told him that things would not pass off peaceably in the Reichstag on 2nd December if we appeared before the Section empty-handed. The unemployment dole—whether it was paid directly by the Empire or by local authorities with State assistance—was the minimum that could be offered. Lewald had a certain sympathy with the difficulties of the Section, and promised to see Delbrück next morning, who had not yet come back from his wife's funeral. In the course of the interview it was clear that Lewald had an excellent knowledge of the inner working of the Section.

I asked him, in a further conversation, to try to mitigate the strictness of the Censorship and abolish the "state of siege" for Home affairs. Lewald at the time took a very gloomy view of the military outlook, and thought that the "state of siege" could not possibly be abolished.

Meanwhile a newspaper row had broken out in Stuttgart. The Radical editor, Crispien, had been superseded by William Keil. Haase made a great stir about it. Ebert and Braun had to go to Stuttgart to see what was wrong. The organ of the General Committee of Trades Unions attacked the *Vorwärts,* especially Stadthagen. A meeting at Lichtenberg resulted, at which Stadthagen most violently attacked the Executive. Otto Braun, who was present, got so excited in course of his reply to Stadthagen that he collapsed from an attack of nerves. At the Executive and Party meetings unpleasant scenes were continually occurring. On 21st November, shortly before the new session of the Reichstag, the Section held a meeting. I advocated the necessity of passing a further War Credit; Haase opposed.

The Chancellor on Our Enemies

Von Bethmann-Hollweg invited Haase, Molkenbuhr and myself to another conversation on 21st November, 1914. He gave us first an abstract of the speech he was to make next day in the Reichstag. On my remarking that all three of us were pleasantly surprised at his confidence in the course of the War and its result, he became speechless with amazement, and gradually said this: "We have under-estimated all our enemies. We have over-estimated Austria. The Russian Commissariat are excellent, likewise their equipment. Their mobilization was a surprisingly good bit of work. The only difficulties they have are with munitions and the officers. Their supplies of men are absolutely inexhaustible. The French are better on the offensive than we imagined, and we knew, of course, they were brilliant in defence. Joffre's leadership is quite excellent. A surprise for us, too, is the performance of the English. No one anticipated they would be able to send fresh troops every day across the Channel. The English, moreover, in France are "top dog" completely, both in politics and war. We were also not prepared for the stout resistance of the Belgians. The position is so different from what we expected that we gladly accepted help from the Turks. One cannot see what effect Turkish intervention will bring about; in any case, peace negotiations will be terribly complicated owing to it."

The Chancellor then wanted to know whether we intended to vote for the War Credits, in agreement with the other Parties in the Reichstag, and whether we would bring forward any wishes we might have before the Charity Committee (which had replaced the Household Select Committee). We enlightened him on these points. Our Section, we said, has said neither yes nor no. In no case would the new Credit Bill be approved without explanations. We were bound to say many things and to declare publicly that we were always prepared for a peace by agreement. Bethmann got more and more nervy, and begged us, literally wringing his hands, not to insist on any explanation and to say nothing about peace. Every word from us would be made use of abroad and be interpreted to Germany's discredit. We flatly contradicted him. He replied, "Do you imagine I would not make peace to-morrow were it possible with either France or Russia? But we dare not talk of peace now; otherwise they will say, 'Look, they are ready, let's fight it out.' The exact contrary of what we intended will come about. It is hard luck that Jaurès is dead and Caillaux dismissed. We had said in our declaration on 4th August what we considered necessary, and need not repeat what we have already said."

We replied that we would duly report to the Section what had been told us. Bethmann told us incidentally that he had not gathered from his conversations with Frenchmen, of whom he knew none, any impression of hatred against Germany. He had noticed no trace of revengeful feeling among the population on the walks he took from Headquarters, and was convinced that this talk of vengeance only came from people who made the Alsace-Lorraine question a kind of springboard for their political propaganda.

The Fight for a Declaration on the War Credits

By the Executive of the Section it was decided to press for an explanation on 2nd December. Three drafts were finally prepared, one each by Haase, Hoch and Heine. In Heine's clever draft occurred some sentences that had to be struck out; this gave us no end of trouble. They were impossible at the present juncture, but they testified to the bitter feeling of even the moderate men, arising from the mode of handling the "state of siege." There was a hot fight for the declaration of 2nd December in the Executive of the Section, in the Section itself, at conferences with Wahnschaffe and Zimmermann, with Bethmann and Delbrück, and finally at a meeting of the chairmen of all Parties called by Delbrück. The latter was held in the small hall of the Diet in the Reichstag. Haase, Molkenbuhr and I from our Section were invited. Delbrück and Kämpf were downright broken-hearted about our declaration, which we had given them at their request in its final form. Every sentence was microscopically examined. Haase was the only one of us who spoke for the declaration as it stood. Molkenbuhr and I, who were prepared to make some concessions in view of the crisis, held our tongues. Wahnschaffe and others told us afterwards we might have been more vocal. At the Executive meeting of the Section the fun began again after Haase's report on the meeting, with Delbrück in the chair. I proposed some alterations. Haase jumped up and said, "This means a split. I'm against that. We are not going to let ourselves be dictated to as to what we shall say and what not." I said that was nonsense. We could and must say what was not right from our point of view in spite of what other Parties said; in the present situation we should say no more than we could be answerable for to ourselves, our comrades in the trenches and the whole country. David got up to support me. Ledebour backed Haase. Ebert tried to mediate. Then I was called out from the meeting. Wahnschaffe was expecting me in a very excited condition. "What do you say to you and Haase going to see the

Chancellor to-night?" I declined flatly, as it was absolutely useless. I was perfectly sure of what I had to do, and Haase wasn't to be won over. The Section was to decide definitely the next day. Wahnschaffe replied, "I don't want this interview with the Chancellor on your account, but on Haase's. Don't under-estimate certain qualities in the Chancellor. There is such a lot depending on it, for your comrades in the field as well. If you're agreeable I'll ask Haase in a few minutes to go with you at once to the palace." I replied, "Yes, I'm quite willing."

A quarter of an hour later Haase and I went with Bethmann. I won't say how Haase stormed in this interview. It was long past ten. Wahnschaffe was with the Chancellor. The latter was in evening dress; round his neck hung a terribly long, thin gold watch-chain. In this get-up he looked very awkward, too lanky, not at all imposing, and too countrified. He sat down in his chair facing the diplomatic table. I had quieted down, but Haase was trembling with excitement in all his limbs. He was all hunched up and really looked awful. Bethmann referred to his speech of the previous Sunday. "I asked you earnestly not to make any statement this time. . . . And now here it is. You can't defend it. You again decline any responsibility for the War—that will be interpreted thus: the Government and all other Parties bear the responsibility. Do you imagine I haven't done all in my power to prevent war?"

A conversation followed that lasted till close on midnight. The Section had been summoned for next morning at nine. I arrived punctually in the room. After a time several groups were talking excitedly in the Section's room. At last Haase came in. I rushed up to him at once, and asked him whether he had made up his mind to a few alterations. "I have naturally," he said, "not had a wink of sleep the whole night, and I couldn't get the thing out of my head. Here," said he, handing me his corrected copy, "are the alterations I propose making." Before I was aware of it, Haase had disappeared in a hurry to a corner of the room where Ledebour was talking excitedly. I immediately ran across to Haase to ask him to make the proposed alterations at once. I had scarcely come near the group when Ledebour addressed me very snappily, "You see we want to have a talk here." I turned angrily to the other members with the words, "If it has got so far that separate groups may discuss matters confidentially among themselves and reach conclusions even in the Section's room, then it had better be stopped." Haase hurried after me, held me by the sleeve and asked me to stay. Other members rushed up and asked what was the matter. I said in a few words that Ledebour was holding a private meeting in the Section's room and had instructed the servants that his "conventicles" were not to be disturbed. Thereupon it was stated by several members that it was a continuation of a special meeting of yesterday. Late in the afternoon about thirty colleagues met in the Section's room for consultation. The heads of the group were Ledebour and Dittmann, others present being Bernstein, Wurm and Emmel. They had discussed what would happen if the majority altered the declaration. Their decision went as far as to say that the minority independently would declare in favour of the first form of the declaration. A further motion to frame a new declaration that should satisfy all that the so-called Radicals demanded found no support.

The Second Declaration of the Section

After order was restored, Haase reported on the discussion and put forward his alterations, which were certainly not un-

important. David and others wanted to debate the passage
about the violation of neutrality. This was rejected. No one
wanted any further discussion. The declaration as it was
finally given in the Reichstag was as follows:

"In connection with the Imperial Chancellor's statements
about Belgium, I declare in the name of my Section that, in
our opinion, the facts which have later become known are
not sufficient to cause us to dissent from the point of view
taken by the Chancellor on 4th August with regard to Luxemburg and Belgium. I beg on behalf of the Section to make
the following declaration. The S.D. Section adheres to the
standpoint of its declaration on 4th August. Up to the last
moment we opposed the War, the reasons for which lie deep
down in opposing economic interests. The frontiers of our
country are still threatened by the enemy. The German people must therefore exert its whole strength for the protection
of the country. The Social Democratic Party therefore votes
the new Credits asked for.

"In gratefuly sympathy we remember all brave sons of the
people who have given their lives and health for us, and all
who, amid unspeakable privations and trials, are serving their
country. On 4th August we, in common with the International, asserted the principle that every nation has the right
to national independence; and it is our unshakable conviction
that a successful development of nations is only possible if
every nation renounces all interference with the integrity and
independence of other countries, and so abstains from sowing
the seed of future wars.

"We adhere therefore to what we said on 4th August: 'We
require, as soon as the object of security has been reached and

our enemies are inclined to peace, that this War should end in a peace that shall make friendship between neighbouring people possible.'

"Social Democracy strongly condemns small but active circles in all countries that, under the cloak of exaggerated patriotism, try to stir up hatred against other nations, and at the same time ignore every consideration for truth and honour. As long as the War goes on we must work untiringly to soften its attendant woes and miseries, to take good care of all those who have lost their health in the campaign, and of all those dependents and relatives of our fighting men in the widest sense, of those who have been driven from their homes by the enemy, by providing work and relief for our comrades out of work, as well as giving all help that is needed to maintain the strength of our people, and, furthermore, by organizing plans for providing our countrymen with food and articles for their daily use. The activities of our Party and the Unions in social schemes of this kind have partially fallen on good ground as far as the Government is concerned; yet our conviction is that still more has to be done everywhere. We expect, however, from the Government of the Empire trust and confidence in our people, who are standing as one man fighting for the threatened Fatherland. The extension of precautionary measures by which the depressing war conditions and the curtailment of constitutional rights, especially of the Press, are still maintained, is by no means justified, and is likely to awake suspicions of the capacity and resolution of the German people. The policy of the Censorship continues unceasingly to produce misunderstandings and economic injury. We ask that we shall be very speedily relieved of these nuisances in the interest of resolute defence and the prestige and welfare of the German Empire."

There was previous to this a lively scene in the Section because Haase again refused to read the declaration. He refused absolutely and definitely, but did read it after all. At his request I got a ticket for the gallery for his wife, because he wanted to go home meanwhile and put on a black coat. At the last minute Haase said he was prepared, after another conversation between von Jagow, Secretary of State, and me, to read the declaration, omitting the sentence about Belgium, which should be worked in more or less as a kind of introduction of a quasi-personal opinion, and then to continue: "However I have, etc."

At this sitting of the Reichstag, Liebknecht, who had voted for the Credits on 4th August, voted against them. His conduct was regretted in an announcement of the Executive as being an offence against Party discipline—a more lenient view was not possible.

New Year 1915

At the first sitting the Executive held in the New Year there were lively doings. As I could get nothing into the *Vorwärts,* I was obliged repeatedly to ask hospitality from the Hamburg and other Party organs when I wanted to say anything. The paper of my division of Solingen was in Dittmann's hands; I had therefore to take refuge in the advertisement columns whenever I had to talk to my constituents. In the New Year's number I got the following lines into the *Bergische Arbeiterstimme:*

"The Best Wishes for the New Year.

"Heavy anxieties press upon us. Excruciating are the sleepless nights when we think of our dear ones in the field. Cruelly does pain rack the hearts of those who have had to sacrifice what they loved most.

"Hats off to those heroes who have fallen for the Fatherland. Stronger than pain and worry must our unbending will be and our unshakable determination. We will not only live through the terrible time with our wits about us and our eyes open; we will also bring to naught the plans of our enemies: we will win!

"And so I wish that all at the change of the year may have strength to conquer trouble and pain. I desire for all the unconquerable will to hold on—right on to victory! . . .

"To our sick and wounded soldiers I wish quick and complete recovery, and to you and your comrades in the trenches, on the sea or on watch in the service of your Fatherland, the best of luck. I press your hand warmly. Hold on! On you depends the fate of our country and the German worker.

"May the New Year bring speedy victory and lasting peace!"

Though even Fleissner, the Radical, as we have stated, wanted to win, and though I had explained at meetings and in the newspapers that the defeat of the Entente would be a brilliant victory for Germany, and though I had been the first, as far as I knew, to advocate a peace by agreement in public, Haase attacked me furiously for my New Year's wishes. When I told him that everyone, whatever he was and whatever the nature of the conflict, whether in social questions, personal disputes or legal questions, must be out to win, should the opposing side be unwilling to come to an understanding, he replied that my wish would certainly be misunderstood and misinterpreted. I admitted that. "Yet even at the risk of being misunderstood," said I, continuing, "I could not retract a single word of my New Year's wishes. I might mention that even an anti-War man like Kautsky thought the desire to win quite natural. In October, 1914, he wrote: 'So long as men are not prepared to make peace, the practical question ceases to be War or Peace—the question is victory or defeat for one's own country.' "

Grievous anxiety about our food supplies came on top of our other difficulties. On 15th January, 1915, a Conference took place at the Home Office on political-economic questions. Bauer, Ebert, Legien, Dr. August Müller and I were invited to attend. We proposed that the maximum prices, an increase in which was demanded by Prof. Eltzbacher, should not be screwed up any further in any circumstances; that all important foodstuffs should be immediately commandeered and a uniform war-bread baked; also that steps should be at once taken in cattle markets and butchers' shops as far as possible against increased profiteering. People were giving very rotten excuses: "One doesn't know yet exactly"; "The question is being considered." But I spoke out plainly, and told the gentlemen to tell Delbrück that he had to think of the impression that would be made if hungry men in despair raided bakers' shops. The gentlemen made long faces and promised to report the matter conscientiously.

Abroad newspaper articles were becoming more and more frequent on the real or alleged proceedings inside the S.P.D. and its whole attitude, that must have given fresh hopes to the enemy. These articles were mostly signed "Homo" (Grumbach) and "Parabellum" (Carl Radek, whose real name was Sobelsohn). The differences within the S.P.D., though serious enough, were grossly exaggerated. The accounts were calculated to give the impression that nine-tenths of the Party were opposed to the Executive. On behalf of the Executive I wrote denying these articles; naturally this did no good, as no one took any notice of them on the other side of the frontier. One day the Chancellor and Wahnschaffe were terribly upset

283

because Sir Edward Grey had sent a wireless telegram to this effect: "It is reported in the *Nieuwe Rotterdamsche Courant* from London that Liebknecht, a member of the Reichstag, told the leaders of the International that, according to him, anti-War feeling was enormously increasing in Germany. Nearly all Parties were of his opinion." To this telegram was added: "To be circulated in France." It was sent from England to Paris (Eiffel Tower) and was intercepted by the Germans. We had to call Liebknecht to order, as the Government did not want to make him a martyr. We naturally brought Liebknecht to book, but he assured us he had made no such statement to the International. Molkenbuhr pointed to the probability of the statement attributed to Liebknecht being a "hash up" of equally damnable contributions to the *Labour Leader*. He may have been correct.

I did my best to counteract this twaddle, at any rate in America, and from there to the other countries. Until every chance of agreement with the U.S.A. had disappeared I wrote every week articles for the New York *Jewish Daily Forward,* which had a circulation of hundreds of thousands. My copy for this paper, printed in Hebrew characters, after being translated, was regularly handed over to the New York *Volkszeitung*. My last article went down with a German U-boat.

At the beginning of February, 1915, we were again requested by the Foreign Office to agitate—this time in St. Petersburg; at any rate, "we might frame a manifesto that could do some good to the German cause in England and France." It is clear how anxious German official circles were to imitate English and French methods. I declined with thanks. Thereupon the official expressed his view of Liebknecht, and told us to kick him out of the Party in our own interests. What fine work he was doing for the enemy Exchequers! Conservatives and Clericals would always hang Liebknecht round our necks, and when work on reform began after the War, would cause considerable trouble. They would point to Liebknecht's tricks as having been done with the consent of the Party. I told the gentleman that I could not talk with him about a member of the Party in this way, though the Party thoroughly disapproved of his actions and had repeatedly opposed him publicly.

Rebellious Women

The greater the food scarcity became, the worse became the scenes and rows within the Party. As an instance of the rancour of the Radicals at this time against the management of the S.P.D., the following incident must be quoted, because it vividly shows up the proceedings of certain revolutionaries. In the big hall of the S.P.D. in the Lindenstrasse, the Select Committee met together to discuss in common with the Executive the food problem, which was growing more and more serious. The report had been entrusted to our friend Otto Braun, then our Head Treasurer, later the Prussian Minister of Agriculture and afterwards Premier. Before he had begun his speech we received the news that a deputation of women were about to ventilate their grievances against the Committee and the Executive. In fact about a hundred women were in the quadrangle. Frau Zietz, evidently one of the organizers, suddenly burst into the room from her office to tell us that a deputation of women wished to consult the Executive and then speak to the Committee. Ebert sent word to the women that we were now unable to interrupt our proceedings—he had just asked Braun to speak. The deputation should confer with the Berlin members of the Committee, and these would tell them what was required of them. Meanwhile Pfannkuch, Bartels and Haase had gone out to face the women.

We could hear a "certain liveliness" going on in the corridor. Suddenly the door was wrenched open and about a dozen women rushed, cursing and swearing, into the room. They at once made for the centre of the room, according to a carefully concerted plan, and shrieked.

Ebert (ringing his bell continuously): "What do you want here."

First Woman: "We are going to speak here."

Ebert: "You are all members?"

Many Women (yelling): "To be sure, and jolly good ones, not like you."

Ebert: "If you are members you must know we have to keep order at our meetings."

Chorus of Women: "Rats! *We* are now going to speak. You've nothing to say!"

Ebert: "I forbid you to speak."

All (meanwhile at least thirty women have forced their way in; a real scrimmage ensues): "You can't stop our mouths! What a feat that would be! Well-fed chaps like you; our stomachs are rumbling with hunger."

Ebert, despite his efforts with the bell, could not quell the women; he therefore adjourned the meeting for an hour, in a high state of excitement. Stairs and corridors were now swarming with females.

The Executive met during the interval to consult on what was to be done. Ebert and Müller opposing, we decided that they could send a deputation with one speaker, and the other women should go to the offices of the Berlin Workers' Training School. The excited women agreed to this, and Eugene Ernst conducted them to the rooms mentioned. One of the women read a speech some stalwart Radical or more capable comrade had written out for her. The reading finished, Ebert said: "Well, we thank you, and will now go on with our business." Thereupon the women once more began to vociferate.

Braun could now go on speaking. He said it was not the women's fault if they agitated in the wrong places. They were the victims of well-known agitators, who for years had been raging against the Party and its responsible officials on every pay-day and in every "rag."

Opposition Opposed

The more active the Opposition was and the more pronounced the suspicions of isolated members of the Opposition became, the keener was naturally our counteracting effort to convince the masses of the absolute necessity of our political action. I had spoken, a few weeks after the begining of the War, on our attitude with regard to it. I found support everywhere. The longer the War lasted, the more extensive did my lecturing tours become. They took me from Königsberg and Breslau, to Karlsruhe and Mannheim, from Kiel via Nuremberg and Fürth to Munich. The greater the distress of our people and Fatherland, the more I realized that we should be lost souls if no opportune agreement could be come to, and the more zealously did I advocate a peace by agreement. I was aware likewise of the widespread misery in Austria, and Bethmann had often talked to me of a similar state of things prevailing in Turkey and Bulgaria. A peace by agreement and a mutual renunciation of annexations and reparations were absolutely vital to our interests, and should be soon declared. The reproach cannot be made against me that I was one of those who later on said that they knew all about it from the start. I can refer especially to my speeches in the Reichstag and the Press reports of my meetings. My oratorical efforts brought me into extreme disfavour. Any dissenting voice was hailed by the Right as high treason: "Shoot him." At one time in the papers it was solemnly stated that I had been bribed by England, convicted of treason and imprisoned. Slanders from the Left, that affected all my friends to almost the same extent, hurt more than abuse from the Right. Social Democrats had become Social Patriots who betrayed the working classes. The S.P.D. were called Scheidemann's men, and my name was to be a byword and reproach for the Party.

I was debarred from going to Solingen, my own constituency, which I represented for many years in the Reichstag, even according to my enemies' admission in their own Press, with energy and skill, and where I, if I may say so, enjoyed great popularity. Dittmann, later the Independent, though an absolute "Jingo" at first, who had on the platform and in his paper stoutly defended the war policy, had altered his opinions. He had, as editor, not only the *Bergische Arbeiterstimme* under his thumb, but was trying to oust its business manager from his job. This old stalwart of the S.P.D. in Solingen wrote me at Easter, 1915, that he had resigned the Chairmanship of the organization because Dittmann's conduct and that of his friends had become past bearing. On the same day Dittmann came to see me in Berlin to give me good advice. I told him the present unfriendly attitude of the Solingen Labour Party to me, according to his statements, was due entirely to him. He made all sorts of protests, and finally asked me to do him the service of releasing his paper; it had been "shut down" for three days. I naturally helped him, and, what is more, with success. At the end of the conversation he asked me, at the request of the members of the Party in Solingen, to address a meeting of supporters, *his* supporters, in the near future and afterwards a general local gathering. I joyfully accepted, but had fully made up my mind to prove, without mincing my words, how unjustly I had been treated up to now and how unfairly my actions had been interpreted.

A few days after this interview Dittmann rang me up from Solingen saying that the Prefect authorized the meeting as a special favour, but there was to be no discussion after my speech. I then refused to speak, because I did not want to speak if my opponents couldn't. A few weeks after, on 27th April, Haase, my fellow chairman, Dittmann's special friend, surprised me by asking me whether I had any objection to his speaking at a meeting at Solingen. I told him he could speak there as far as I was concerned, but made him aware that I had declined to speak at any Solingen meeting if my colleagues were not allowed to do so. My good friends then insisted on my speaking in any case, for Haase would certainly speak. These men could not tolerate the paper and the management being taken out of their hands and Haase allowed to speak against me, when I had declined for good reasons to do so.

On 2nd May I went off to Solingen, after being fully initiated into the policy of the Radicals. I ascertained at a private sitting of the local officials the extent of this bullying. There were about one hundred and fifty people present, many of whom I did not know, but who showed from the commencement a very bitter feeling against me. Speaking for over an hour, I described the policy of the Party and maintained that any other policy was quite impossible. After me the wife of the editor Merkel delivered a well-prepared speech that took more than an hour. "We have no longer a Fatherland. The very word is mere patriotic humbug," etc. "We want peace at any price." This is a fair sample of what she said. Her husband and Frau Wasser spoke in a similar strain, and Dittmann was not appreciably milder. He condemned the policy pursued by the Section, root and branch, though up to March he had been an enthusiastic supporter of it.

I could have no doubts about what the great majority of these officials thought. They had been stirred up by the one-sided views of the *Bergische Arbeiterstimme* against the policy I had defended. Some of the Radical officials went so far as to forbid me to speak at the General Meeting summoned for 3rd May, as discussion was not allowed and they had therefore no opportunity of opposing me. They would have been quite satisfied if only Haase spoke. These are quotations from my notes. "I might have been milder in my remarks, after all this had blown over, in order to offend nobody and protect myself from further attacks. But how can one understand the horrid quarrels that happened later between the workers, if one's own experiences are given in a garbled form?" The General Meeting held the day after the official sitting was open to the public in the "Kaisersaal" in Solingen and crammed to excess. Many thousands, however, were standing outside; more than two thousand were inside, but only a very small number of townsmen among them. My remarks made undoubtedly a deep impression; there was no disturbance, although "ructions" were threatened from Wald. Rapturous applause greeted my speech; I abstained, naturally, from all personal remarks, and spoke to the point.

In the same hall four weeks later Haase spoke to the electors on the hash that had been made of things by the member who had represented the town since 1903. The *Vossiches Zeitung* and the *Vorwärts* reported the meeting under the headline "Haase against Scheidemann." A similar case is not known to me in the history of Social Democracy. N.B.—The S.P.D. was then not rent asunder. Haase and I, as chairmen of the Reichstag Section, were still to the fore in the "united" Party.

The Call of the Hour

Haase, Kautsky and Bernstein published a manifesto in the *Leipziger Volkszeitung* in the latter half of June, 1915, that sharply attacked the policy of their own Party, the S.P.D. Every single colleague without exception told Haase what he thought of him. He tried to justify his conduct by referring to articles I had written. He had done nothing more than that. My articles dictated the policy of the Party, pointed out its necessity; his manifesto condemned this policy. Could there be any wider point of difference? My articles were aimed at showing the hopeless condition of our country and the German people—Haase's called for new political methods, and, above all, the rejection of the War Credits—otherwise. . . . He always pictured the Party in danger. Ah, the Party was dear to us all who had served it from our youth up, but we were all united on one point—that the Party was only a means, intended to achieve the highest state of efficiency, economically and educationally, for our people and Fatherland, and serve in the best way the vast majority of the nation —those who worked with their brains and hands. The Fatherland was the jewel box that it behoved us to guard, protect and take care of—this was the aim of politics as a whole, but the Party was only a means to an end. Haase's outlook was quite distinct from ours; he did not see that his attitude as chairman had become impossible. At a full sitting of the Executive the bomb burst. Our colleagues, Molkenbuhr and Pfannkuch, most of all, in their simple way explained matters to him, relying on their ripe experience. "Ebert treated him brutally," as I wrote in my diary. I held

back as far as I could; the more excited the others became—
especially Müller—the better I could observe Haase. He repeatedly changed colour, hammered on the table, but did not
do what everyone expected of him—he held on!

The Section supported the majority of the Executive, and
agreed on an official reply to Haase and his friends, that was
to be published in the Press. The Select Committee with
twelve dissentients censured Haase.

The feeling against Haase among his colleagues on the
Executive continued to increase because they had got it into
their heads that he was always doing things behind their
backs that he was not justified in doing—much less authorized
to do. We began to understand Hugo Heinemann better,
who had seriously warned us of Haase's procedure. In March,
1915, a telegram from Troelstra for Haase came into our hands.
He was expecting a visit from Haase on 23rd March. That
Troelstra, who was on the friendliest terms with us and justified our attitude to the International on every occasion, should
apply to Haase was wholly out of the question. Haase could
only have applied to Troelstra without informing us. He
pretended to be quite innocent, and announced his intention
of accepting Troelstra's invitation and travelling to Holland.
We cooked his goose by deciding that all members of the
Executive who belonged to the International Socialist Bureau
(I.S.B.) should go to Holland. At the time Ebert, Molkenbuhr and Müller were members.

At a later talk in Holland a question arose about the alleged
willingness of the English Socialists to take part in a conference with the Socialists of the Central Powers. Four weeks
previously a similar report had got about, and was so definitely
stated that Adler and Seitz came from Vienna and took up
their abode in Berlin. In the middle of February Troelstra,

however, wired to everybody, "Conference postponed," but Adler hoped it would only be for a few days, and as he was half-way on the way to The Hague he would stop a little longer. Perhaps . . .

How many were the hopes we entertained of meeting our foreign comrades, and all ended in smoke! Incidentally at this visit that Victor Adler and Seitz paid us in Berlin there was a talk on the subject of Annexations that must be mentioned, as it clearly showed once more the fundamental differences existing between Haase and Adler. Adler was perpetually grasping at straws whenever any wish for peace among English and French Socialists was talked of. He hoped on quite undiscouraged. Perhaps—there might be a chance! I had boldly stated that from all the demonstrations on the other side of the border and abroad I only heard one thing: no peace till Prussian militarism (not a word about French militarism or English navalism) was smashed. In the course of this conversation Haase and Adler and Frau Seitz dropped into my room one after the other, while Seitz and the others were detained with Ebert or Müller in one of the front rooms. The topic of Annexations turned up. Adler thought it right that we should help to detach Poland from Russia, if possible. Haase, who saw even in this an attempt at Annexation, was horrified. "No," he cried, "if you start this game, you will have to go on with it," and he was dead against Annexations. We tried to convince him he was wrong. But he said, "If you depart only a hair's breadth from principle, you're lost." "Well, dear Haase," said Adler, "I must say I can't follow you. If you start this game, you will have to go on with it, it may be true, everywhere else, but—excuse me—not in politics." At an aside from Haase, Adler added, "What has politics to do with logic?" We burst out laughing. Then

Adler went on, "You act first—excuse me—and afterwards you try to prove that you have acted logically or rather, I should say, reasonably." The conversation was ended by a telephone call from the Wilhelmstrasse (Foreign Office) to the effect that in Rome at the opening of the Chamber things had happened that looked ominous.

What Will Italy Do?

As Italy had not entered the War at the start on the side of her allies, Germany and Austria, the possibility of her one day fighting with France against her allies had to be faced. The longer the suspense lasted, the more violent were the accusations of bad faith brought against Italy; yet everybody was clutching at the last straw of hope. On the evening of 3rd March, 1915, there was a secret conversation at the Chancellor's house at which all Parties were represented. Haase, Molkenbuhr, Robert Schmidt and myself were invited as representatives of the S.P.D. There was a remarkable number of Government officials present. The Chancellor, who sat between Kämpf, President of the Reichstag, and Delbrück, Secretary of State, reported on the military situation, and remarked: "I have yet another thing to tell you. Matters between Italy and Austria are nearly settled, but for the Lord's sake keep it to yourselves—if it appeared in the papers everything would go wrong." All agreed; thereupon the Chancellor said good-humouredly, smiting the table with his fist: "Well, gentlemen, I swear I haven't said a word about Italy."

All present heaved a sigh of relief that a load had been lifted off their minds. The Chancellor had spoken so confidently, contrary to his usual caution, that one might be sure that everything was nearly all right. Yet it was to happen otherwise.

The Italian question hung in the balance for months. In May, 1915, there was once more a confidential meeting, where two representatives of all Sections were present. Haase and I from the S.D. Section were invited. The Chancellor referred to Salandra's retirement. Bülow, who had been appointed Ambassador because of his well-known friendly relations with Italy, uttered a warning against any premature optimistic view. In the Senate Giolitti was supported by a big majority. Unfortunately, the Court, the Queen and the Queen Dowager favoured war. The King likewise had been badly influenced by Sonnino. The War Party was uninterruptedly at work. They intended to bring about a collision on the frontier—to get a *casus belli*. Austria had been requested, and had given a promise to give no provocation. The greatest caution was necessary in treating the Italian crisis. Bülow, always a good judge of the importance of the Press, had three times telegraphed to be very careful. There was to be no praise of Giolitti, because his position would thereby be rendered more difficult. A political debate in the Reichstag on the general situation was quite out of the question. He had intended to speak, but had refrained; that naturally applied to all members of the House. Italy must now speak——

The statement was strikingly inadequate. The Chancellor then gave some details on the military position and went on: "Any inclination towards peace is non-existent. However, in certain Russian papers there is evidence of a better state of things, and even the *Daily Mail* has a remarkable article ('The German Star'), and here and there in *The Times* are sensible remarks." At this time the *Lusitania* affair was making a great stir. Then he came back to Italy. "If Italy maintains her neutrality, we may assume it will be a benevolent one towards us. The position of Italy in the Triple Alliance is in the circumstances a very dubious one. Even if Italy should let fly at us we shan't have lost the War. It would be awkward, but nothing is to be feared. The matter would be naturally worse for Austria."

The Chancellor did not please us at all on that evening.

The uncertainty about Italy's decision had a paralyzing effect on the whole of political life. When Hoch, a member of the Reichstag, at a Section Meeting on 17th May, proposed a peace resolution, even Haase, a friend of his early days and a brother undergraduate, condemned such a move as ridiculous at this time in reference to Italy. Nerves were increasingly on edge in all Sections.

On 25th May the news of Italy's declaration of war against Austria came to hand.

On 27th May the Chancellor received the chairmen of all the Sections; from our Section Haase, Molkenbuhr and myself were there.

In consequence of the news I had received in the meantime, I asked Bethmann-Hollweg if it were true that the President of the Swiss Republic had sounded America and the German Government with regard to instituting negotiations for peace, and whether Germany had assented and America had declined because the time was not opportune. The Chancellor's reply was: "All kinds of questions have naturally been asked by various sides in neutral countries, and even among Wilson's friends. Up to now there has been no definite suggestion or proposal made of concrete peace propositions." The way the Chancellor answered me showed pretty plainly that he would have said yes if he could have directly answered my inquiry.

The Chancellor's Yearning for Peace

A notable conversation took place at the Chancellor's after
Italy's declaration of war against Austria. Beside Haase,
Molkenbuhr and myself, Ebert, at my express request, was
at last also invited. He had never previously been asked by
the Chancellor. As usual, I made a few notes on the report
for discussion in the Section, and at my request it was carefully read by my three colleagues to ensure strict accuracy.
We were perfectly clear about the importance of the report;
the Chancellor had not only declared his willingness for peace,
but also said lots of things about his war policy. "Italy coming into the War is a grievous blow, but I hope it will not
be actually dangerous to us. I don't think Italy will send
troops to France and the Dardanelles. Italy has not yet declared war against Turkey; it even seems as if Italy were in
tacit agreement with Turkey. I take it that Italy will employ
her whole strength against Austria. Should she, however, send
three to four hundred thousand troops, as many think probable, through the 'gap' to Upper Alsace, it might prove very
dangerous to us. I am now under the firm impression that
Italy decided in December to join the Triple Entente. I have
been working since July to induce Austria to make certain
concessions to Italy. History tells us that Austria has always
been rather slow in making up her mind. Italy, moreover,
has a poor Press, even in neutral countries. The English,
though they do not say so, think Italy's conduct very 'low
down.' In spite of this, I do not think it right to excite bad
feeling against Italy.

"Italy has not declared war against us, nor have we. We
have broken off diplomatic relations, and told Italy that our
troops will act together with the Austrians. Should the latter

be attacked, the Italians will be up against our troops. In Roumania the news of our victories has made a deeper impression than Italy's declaration of war against Austria. I trust it will be quiet in the Balkans. We must not forget that money plays a great part in the Balkans, even in very high circles. The Entente makes big offers at the cost of others. We cannot compete with them in any way. Not only has the whole of Transylvania been promised to the Roumanians, but also the whole of Banat in Hungary as far as the Theiss.

"By Italy's entry into the War prospects of peace have been thrust into the background, unfortunately. I had previously reckoned on the possibility of our getting peace in July or August. In England and France there is at present no inclination towards peace, though I am following with great attention every tendency in this direction. I have given people in England and France to understand—not by direct means, of course, otherwise I should have been kicked out, but by indirect channels, which are always available—that I am prepared to open negotiations for peace. I still think that Russia will ultimately declare she cannot go on. I know through agents that a certain war weariness is noticeable at Court. They are saying there: 'If only this dreadful War was at an end.' Russia, it is true, signed the treaty on 4th September, 1914—no separate peace, but as there has been some unpleasantness between the Russian and English Governments, it is quite on the cards that Russia will say to England: 'Excuse us, we'll cease dealing with one another and will do our business together through France.'

"A basis for peace is frightfully hard to find. No one in his senses will think of making annexations in Russia, but no statesman can give up the idea of securing our Eastern frontier, for strategical reasons, providing the military situation admits of it. It is intolerable that Thorn, for instance, can be bombarded by long-range guns from Russian territory. Necessary alterations only of a strategic character must be considered in the West. The crux is Belgium. I can only discuss her in a negative way; we must in all circumstances try to prevent Belgium being exploited by England against us, either economically, politically or militarily; I am thinking of a Customs union that should include, I think, a lien on the railways, a uniformity in legislation, and, if we can get it, the substitution of the Code Napoléon by Belgian Common Law (BGB). We dare not let Belgium become dependent on England, as France after the War will be a vassal state of England's. We must not be in a worse position after the War than before it. No one yearns more than I do for a speedy peace."

Though at the beginning of March, after the Chancellor had humorously prophesied that Italy and Austria would soon settle their differences, he had made some dubious remarks about War aims and had talked of guarantees, increased liberty of movement and the possibility of a greater and stronger Germany, the whole speech, with the exception of some words about Belgium and security of frontiers that we should stoutly oppose, was inspired with a frank and deeply felt desire for peace. "No one yearns more than I do for a speedy peace." *C'est le ton, qui fait la musique et—la politique!* He was always afraid he would fall out with the Left or the Right or the Supreme Command, and consequently never satisfied either the Left or the Right or the Supreme Command.

Icy-cold water ran down my spine at that meeting in March, when Bethmann-Hollweg discoursed about a greater Germany. Molkenbuhr and Robert Schmidt felt equally uncomfortable, naturally. Haase, on the other hand, appeared quite pleased that the Chancellor had found a new word for the "war of annexation." On our way home I intimated to Haase that Bethmann-Hollweg, after his previous statements, could not have possibly meant that Germany's position should be strengthened by an increase of territory; it seemed to me to be quite out of court. "If Germany wins this War she would naturally stand higher than before, even if she did not win an extra square inch of territory." Haase dissented strongly. "It has always been unintelligible to me that Bethmann-Hollweg should make such a remark, for it was in flat contradiction to what he had said to us on other occasions—especially at one other conversation in March, 1915." Then Haase and myself were his only visitors. He was very excited, and after listening to the notes I had made for the Section—Haase and I were, naturally, very careful over the report—he said as follows: "In strict confidence—no one else knows a word about it—tiny seeds are shooting up in Russia, seeds from which peace may grow. We should tread them down if we talked of peace. One would interpret it as weakness, and Russia would again become conscious of her strength. The objects demanded by the Pan-Germans are nonsense. I don't think of trying them. Annex Belgium! A country with an entirely strange population speaking a different language. I fancy we can get closer trade relations with Belgium, perhaps a military agreement as well, and if I succeed in fixing to some extent the frontiers of the Vosges, that now run under the ridge, it would be something of great importance; likewise if we could raze Belfort. We have had to incur fearful losses on these frontiers. Haase and I—Haase's statement was made in his presence in the Section before I spoke—declared that these statements had quieted us considerably, or at least dispelled many doubts. Bethmann-Hollweg then talked about being willing to make a separate peace with Russia or France. The thing to do was to smash the Coalition, and in between came the words, "Don't talk of peace." Witte made a few attempts—the Press wrote about them—and Witte was got rid of on the spot.

The Chancellor was at the time in an almost unbearable position. Every word he said about war and peace was carefully noted. Every word of his was condemned as "wishwash" by the Right and by the extreme Left as a desire for annexations. It was evident to me and my intimate friends that Bethmann-Hollweg was really convinced he had done all a man could to prevent war, and was genuinely striving to end it quickly.

XVI

A SPLIT COMING

ON 4th August, 1914, only fourteen members of the Section voted against the War Credits; in December, 1914, on the passing of the second Credit Bill, three more members were added. Owing to agitation in the Party, the number of dissentients in the Section rose, in March, 1915, to twenty-five, in August to thirty-six, and to forty-three in December 1915, out of a total of one hundred and ten. The increase of the Opposition was not due solely to the demands for annexation, but also to many happenings at home. The Press Censorship, managed chiefly by narrow-minded Government clerks, allowed the Right greater elbow-room than the Left. That caused just as much dissatisfaction as the handling of the "state of siege" and the threat of arrest. Food problems, never adequately solved, as well as the unsatisfactory relief for soldiers' wives, in addition to hundreds of complaints about the unjust treatment of soldiers, aggravated matters. It was reported from many places that the officers were fattening in luxury while the soldiers were starving. In granting leave there was much favouritism, etc. Naturally we went into all these complaints and demanded redress. The Government officials we consulted were often genuinely up in arms at our reports, and promised relief. Sometimes they could keep their word, most often not. The worse the time our men got in the trenches, the easier were conditions in the billets. People talked of these "swine in billets."

These facts clearly show that the Opposition had plenty to catch hold of. Many of the Opposition were quite delighted to pose as brave men having the pluck to "go for" the Government and the Supreme Command. Karl Liebknecht, who was obviously steering straight for gaol, might well have said so of himself, but, as with many others, this so-called pluck in defying the Government was only fear of his own followers. It will not be forgotten that one of the later malcontents tried to justify his action in previously voting for the War Credits to his fractious constituents by saying that any member of the Reichstag daring to vote against the Credits on 4th August would not have reached the Brandenburg Gate alive. In the course of this unrest it was interesting to watch the varying effects of leaders not sure of themselves on the masses and of the masses on the leaders. By the various interpretations "made on principle," of "the confusing expression defence of the realm" alone, the Opposition would not have grown so numerous or so active. In the presence of men already wounded and crippled; in the presence of young lads, daily expecting their call to the colours; in the presence of wives, whose husbands were daily on the look-out for the summons or whose husbands were already wounded or were somewhere in the trenches, perhaps long since buried in a common grave—in fact, in the presence of ill-clothed, shivering, starving men, partially or wholly broken in spirit, no particular skill was required to make an impression by representing the essential standpoint that it was a matter of indifference to a German working man to know who was exploiting him. Little was said of the differences between pre-War conditions in Russia and those in Germany, and just as little about the undoubted certainty that after a successful war for Russia and France, things would be no better for the German worker.

The majority of S.P.D. were especially angry because the Opposition asserted, contrary to facts and falsified by experience, that a spirit of revolt in Germany would produce the same spirit in countries warring against us. Socialists in the Entente countries had made no sort of response to any of our peace demonstrations. They made no approaches and abstained from attending the Stockholm Conference. Because of the refusal of passports, their attitude was not completely justified, for—just to ask one question—can one refuse to obey a Government any further that has refused passports to Party leaders because they wish to work for an honourable peace by agreement? How would German Social Democrats have behaved in such circumstances? To ask the question is to answer it. It is by no means a pleasant thing to be reminded of these experiences, but it is necessary to be able to explain the policy of the S.P.D. (the German Independent Socialist Party) in the War. It is one of my bitterest recollections when Bethmann-Hollweg said to Haase, when he and I were discussing with him a proposal of peace, "Herr Haase, can you mention the name of any one French Socialist who is following your example?" Still more painful than Bethmann-Hollweg's words was Haase's complete silence.

In addition to the restless activity of the Liebknecht group, Rosa Luxemburg and Mehring (the publications of the "International," the *Junius-Broschure* and the *Spartacus Letters*), other individuals of the Opposition were working on their own—Julian Borchardt, known in the Party by the name of the "economic" Julian, who was trying to set in motion a group called the International Socialists of Germany. No one of the groups, big or small, attained any great importance till the Communist Party emerged from the Spartacus revolt in 1919. Beside the S.P.D. there was only the U.S.P.D. (the German Independent Socialist Party), led by Haase and Ledebour as a Socialist Working Men's Party. In the War and in the first year after the War it acquired great importance, though it was of no use to the German Labour Movement. When the S.P.D. and U.S.P.D. amalgamated at the Nuremberg Conference in 1922, the Independents as a Party were wiped out, as it turned out, soon enough. The editorial staff and the Secretaries of the former U.S.P.D. joined the united Party, and by far the greater number of the members who had been in revolt for years went further to the Left to the Communists.

The German Opposition Party were able to hold two "Congresses" abroad in the course of the War, the first in Zimmerwald near Berne, the second in the spring of 1916 in Kiental, also situated in the Bernese Oberland. These meetings were attended by forty "delegates" in all, apparently from France, Italy, Serbia, Portugal and Poland. These "delegates" were mostly fugitives from these countries who had been living for a long time in Switzerland as exiles. In Kiental, where they assembled after the meeting in Zimmerwald, there were very lively scenes. At the first meeting they drove away the oldest living Socialist in disgust—Greulich, a man honoured by the whole International. The Spartacist Group turned on the Radek Group from Bremen, and these threw the sons of Spartacus into the gutter. The Spartacists arranged conferences and manifestoes; they wanted to see "deeds," mass actions! This appeared too dangerous to the others, and not appropriate to "actual facts." Karl Liebknecht shortly after got involved in an "actual mess." On 1st May he, although a soldier, yelled out on the Potsdamer Platz in Berlin, "Down with the War! Down with the Government!" The result was (any political tyro might have told him) that he was locked up, and in spite of all our efforts to get him out he was not released. Only in October, 1918, did I succeed in getting him out.

The Split Complete

Ledebour made Haase's life a burden to him. Once at a public sitting of the Reichstag he attacked his colleague in the bitterest way. On my saying to Haase, for whom I still had some personal sympathy: "I wish you luck with a comrade like that; upon my soul, I don't envy you," Haase said, very taken aback, "Well, his temper is the best thing about him." Ledebour and Liebknecht, not to mention many smaller "high-principled" fry, were admirably fitted for spoiling and smashing up everything they did together. They were incapable of producing anything constructive; it wasn't in them. Their chief pleasure in life was talking. Though grieved at Liebknecht's fate—I made his acquaintance when his father brought him as a student to see me at Giessen— no matter how seriously I condemn the cowardly act of his murderers, I cannot, however, rid myself of the conviction that Liebknecht, Rosa Luxemburg and Ledebour did most grievous harm to the German people, and before all else to Socialism, especially in the critical days after the collapse, and brought the Republic into a very serious predicament. A revolutionary working man who had long sympathized with Liebknecht, Emile Barth, who had been appointed a delegate in the revolutionary Government by the Independents, said quite rightly that Ledebour and Liebknecht were the fathers of the Reichswehr (Defence Force).

Owing to disputes in the S.D. Section, it was decided to

form the Social Democratic Working Men's Union, that was to act independently of the S.D. Section (24th March, 1916). The Opposition, who had up to then formed part of the organizing department of the S.D., held a conference at Gotha, and founded the U.S.P. (Independent Socialist Party). The heads of the organization were Haase and Ledebour, their consultant being Carl Kautsky. The historian, Dr. Bergsträsser, in his "History of Political Parties," described them not inappropriately as a group of those who stand between theory and practice.

Wars between nations, as we have learnt to our cost, are terrible; civil wars, as we have likewise experienced, are more cruel; but wars between brothers are the most abominable of all. Such a war had now to be fought out for years in Germany among the working classes.

Within the Veil

From what has been said, it can be clearly seen in what difficult circumstances the work of the S.D. Party and the Reichstag Section was carried on. They were to help, and had to help, naturally, all they could when any cry of distress was raised about the suppression and oppression of the Press, the ill-treatment of soldiers, arrests, and prohibited meetings, and the refusal of leave; about the dearth of potatoes, soup, bread, fat and meat; about the lack of shoes, linen, clothes—in fact, about any lack of anything in the necessities of life.

At countless meetings abusive official reports, to be treated confidentially, were showered upon the authorities responsible for the policy of the Party; the Opposition saw to it that they should get their share of the crossfire of slander and suspicion; complaining dependents of fallen soldiers loudly demanded the release of their relatives who were still fighting. Here a

Party paper had got into financial difficulties; there an editor was writing heresy. There were also rows and worries of other kinds. One day a gang of about fifty excited women raided the offices of the *Vorwärts,* where Hermann Müller did his thankless and unprofitable job, and demanded the blood of the traitor. Müller was badly mauled, and had to go off to the nearest hospital.

At countless smaller gatherings the rod was broken over the backs of the Party managers. Every single member of the Executive was badly heckled in his own constituency. With the threat of the "sack" an impression was made and the change required carried out. One motion, agitated for and passed by hundreds of sectional meetings, was that not one of the majority Socialists in the Reichstag should ever be elected again for any seat.

English and Belgian prisoners were said to have mutinied and were condemned to death. These we saved by protesting. Bad news came from neutral countries because they were showing their sympathy more and more. This and that were wanted in the field. Soldiers were asking us to visit the front once again—though the wish could not be fulfilled—and see for ourselves how badly treated they were by unsuitable officers. Over and over again we opposed any annexation policy. Every reactionary kennel dog was loosed at us. We exhorted the people to "stick it out," as everything was at stake. We were vilified as wretched traitors by the Left. When we beat about the bush at the Chancellor's with, "Won't you speak about peace?" we were answered by, "For God's sake not now." The Opposition increased and our difficulties became worse.

During this awful time it was necessary, before all things, that the leaders of the Party, who were, as a matter of fact, perfectly united on vital questions, should show a united front with no gaps whatever in the ranks. Here we were successful, though we had our differences—differences certainly on minor matters, that could only be explained by the nervousness prevailing more or less in all classes. It would be pitiable cowardice not to add a chapter that is altogether so human that everybody can understand, and only bad-hearted people can misconstrue. All members of the Executive were convinced that Ebert was the wisest of the lot of us. In all Party matters and tactical questions he was our superior. It is quite wrong when well-meaning men, who had not been on close terms with him, said after his death that he was the only man of a restless and nervous crowd who kept his head. The contrary is true. Ebert was, as a temperamental man, easily stirred and more easily hurt. Even in small things he harboured too long a spirit of resentment and dissent that I always deplored. He was also rather quick to anger, and could sometimes be downright unpleasant. Dr. Wirth, who, as Chancellor, knew him well, said in his book, "Ebert and His Time," that he had the excitable blood of a child of the Palatinate. Sometimes his anger became the more pronounced the less reason we thought there was for it. At least, it appeared so to all who were unbiased.

Pastor Felden, a friend of Ebert's, tells some wonderful stories about Ebert's childhood in his book already mentioned. He makes the child Fritz talk and act so wisely that the twelve-year-old Jesus in the Temple could retire into the background.

The War had been raging for months before Ebert, apart from countless talks on social-political and censorship questions, was invited to share in any of the more important political consultations with the Chancellor. Along with Haase, Molkenbuhr and myself, the three chairmen of the Section, Dr.

David, Robert Schmidt, Legien, etc., all of whom had been for many years members of the Reichstag, were invited to these discussions. I had repeatedly told the gentlemen concerned that they should most certainly invite Ebert, for he was not only a member of the Section's Executive, but also one of the chairmen. It had been forgotten till I went to see Wahnschaffe specially and asked him solemnly to issue the invitation according to our wishes. Wahnschaffe gave exactly the same answer as the Chancellor had given a few days before: "Yes, of course, if it is so desired. We generally invite the chairmen. We hardly know Herr Ebert." The Chancellor could be implicitly relied upon; Ebert had only been elected to the Reichstag in 1912, and till 1914 had not been in the public eye. Every member of the S.P.D. knew him, as every German should know him to-day. Only in course of the War did Ebert become known beyond the circles of the S.D. Party, and later, naturally and particularly, as President of the Empire. On 5th November a meeting took place at Delbrück's, who represented the Chancellor, to which Dr. David, Haase and I were invited. My request that Ebert should always be invited had not yet reached Delbrück. On 6th November the meeting was continued. Between the two meetings there was a discussion in the Executive, in which Haase and Ebert came to loggerheads, and I had to side with Haase, who had written an inoffensive article. Ebert, who was very irritated, wanted to lay down a rule that no member of the S.P.D. Executive should write to the papers before submitting his article to the Party Executive. Such a demand, which Haase opposed vigorously, seemed to me unreasonable; such a practice would be intolerable to me. Wels, who edited the *Fackel*, an agitating weekly organ in the Province of Brandenburg, and at heart supported me on this question, whispered to me that I shouldn't play into Haase's hands. I wrote at the time in my diary: "If Haase is in the right he will find me backing him all right." N.B.—There was a general talk about newspaper articles. I had certainly written most of them. At the time no one thought that a member of the Executive would ever publish a protest against his own Party, certainly not Ebert or Haase. If that had been thought possible, Ebert's demand would have had no point, for a man who is ready to show up his Party will not trip over trifles that are intended to keep him out of an editor's job.

The unseemly wrangle came to an end at that sitting, like the Hornberg shooting case. Later the argument took a practical turn and—against me. After the enforced retirement of the Radical editors of the *Vorwärts,* I had sent in to that paper a few articles, at the request of the new editorial staff. Ebert's unfriendly attitude after each of these articles appeared, against which not the slightest objection from the Party standpoint could be taken or ever was taken, attracted my notice. There was no talk about it, as Ebert did not say a word to me. One day Comrade Dietz of Stuttgart gave me a hint, which I understood only when Richard Fischer came one day into my room to ask me (*entre nous*) not to send any more articles of mine to the *Vorwärts* with my name attached: "Ebert (who had never been employed on a paper) won't stand it." For the sake of peace I now only wrote at special request, or when the subject seemed so important that I would gladly risk a personal rumpus in order to serve the general good with the clearest of consciences.

More than once during the War did Ebert leave meetings of the Executive, threatening to resign if he could not have his way, but neither David nor Gradnauer nor I could say he was always right. I recollect David exclaiming in despair.

"Fancy having to put up with such trifles at a time like this!"

No one appreciates more fully than I Ebert's great qualities. But I do not see any mark of true friendship in trying to make a superman out of one who was remarkably gifted. When historical characters are concerned, sincere friends should in the first place stick to the truth and avoid hearsay—who did not have enough of this about the Hohenzollerns? A perfect fellow without spot or blemish would never have done what we have to thank Ebert for.

Ebert in Festive Mood

Ebert was splendid company among those who were out to enjoy themselves. Then he would talk for hours on business and politics, and let himself go. Before and throughout the War we used to go in turn to the Weihen-Stephan in the Friedrichstrasse and to Ruperti's (later the Krausenhof), nearly opposite the Klaussner in the Krausenstrasse. Our colleagues who had not to go away on business met in one or other of these places to talk over their experiences and the fine times they had in their younger days.

We had the best of good times almost without a break between Christmas and New Year in Upper Bavaria before the War. On Christmas Day evening some of us would regularly start off for Munich, and from there to Garmisch on a few days' walking tour if the weather was fine, either over the Fernpass or Mittenwald and Scharnitz to Innsbruck. We always arranged to be back home on New Year's Eve. On Boxing Day, 1913, on arriving in Munich in mist and rain, Richard Fischer proposed we should have "weisswürste" for breakfast. As we knew the best place for these, we had no reason for discussing the pros and cons. A quarter of an hour after our arrival, we were sitting down at a clean table with a pint pot of fresh beer and excellent white sausages. Richard Fischer, though a thorough Bavarian, was a poor beer-drinker right up to his death. His coarseness, always well meant and never offensive, can be described as characteristic. Although in Bavaria the weather was not fit for "swine," *i.e.* rain and mist, we started off for Garmisch-Partenkirchen, hoping that the weather would improve in the mountains and we could carry out the trip we had planned.

On the way nothing of the mountains could be seen. When we got to Garmisch it was raining cats and dogs. We decided, therefore, to have another breakfast to strengthen us for the journey before us. After finishing our meal about 3 P.M. we tried to go on to the Fernpass, with an occasional rest in between. We started with our knapsacks on our backs, and reached safely, though rather late, the "Schanz" on the Tyrol border—a small inn, where we intended sleeping. Though we had shelter now and again in hospitable public-houses (where the beer was excellent), we were wet to the skin. We should have naturally put up for the night much earlier, but we wanted to walk ourselves tired, and Ede Bernstein had stated—and we all agreed—that "exercise was the best thing out." In our walk from the "Werdenfelser Michel" in Garmisch, via the "Kainzen Franz," the "Hussar" and the "Post," to the "Schanz," we were, to outward view, in a deplorable condition. The water was merrily oozing out of our boots. Richard Fischer whispered in my ear that even his glasses were wet through.

A kindly couple were living at the time in the "Schanz," and welcomed us warmly as being their only guests. As beyond a shirt or two we had no change of clothing, we were clothed in the garments of our hosts. Our own clothes were hung up to dry on the pegs in the kitchen and bar par-

313

lour. As the landlord was a head shorter than I, the knee breeches he gave me were little more than bathing drawers. There was no possibility of buttoning them up, for the landlord was not only shorter, but also much thinner than I. Anyone else of our party would have looked much better owing to his smaller build. The third fellow was best disguised in a woman's garment, as there were no more men's trousers to be had. We led off with Tyroler red wine, and sang German folk-songs and Bavarian ditties that we made up, to the accompaniment of the landlord's zither. No Goethe or Schiller could have composed such verses.

The second day after Boxing Day was already dawning when we went to our bedrooms; Ebert and I had our beds in the same room; Richard Fischer, our senior, slept alone in the next room. Fresh snow had fallen in the night. Our senior colleague, who had not slept particularly well, got up early, and bombarded our tightly closed window-shutters with snowballs. Any more sleep was out of the question; we agreed not to utter a sound and pretended to be still fast asleep. As a matter of fact, we were dressing and shaving. We heard Fischer talking to the landlord and blackguarding the Prussian swine. A snowball occasionally hit our shutters. When we came downstairs we reproached him for not waking us and told him we had not heard a sound. As he had called us Prussian swine to our hosts, I went into the kitchen, breathing vengeance, and quite innocently told the landlord, who had no notion who we were, that Herr Fischer was a famous Jew. At breakfast we, of course, talked about the foul weather of yesterday. In course of conversation the landlord remarked to Richard Fischer, "Now just imagine how unlucky you would have been last night if you had got into an Anti-Semite pub, and they'd refused to put you up for the night." Fischer opened his mouth wide, lifted his nose, looked first at the landlord and then at us, and roared out, in his inimitable rudeness, "You damned Prussian swine." On my modestly saying that he couldn't take the landlord's words amiss, as there could be no question about his looking rather like a Jew, which was no disgrace, the beer mats began to fly around. . . .

The S.P.D. for Peace

While the opponents of the S.P.D. on the Right had made, in the course of the War—and especially after it—slanderous charges about our not having done enough for the country, increasing its difficulties and doing it great harm through our propaganda for a peace by agreement, our opponents on the Left accused us of being fire-eaters, Social patriots and An-nexationists who did nothing for peace. The former con-demned us as traitors to our country, the latter as traitors to our people and working men. The policy of the S.P.D. was judged more fairly abroad than at home. In England and France we were fêted as keen patriots, as English and French Socialists were amongst us, and this is the more important in face of the dishonourable abuse from the Right in our own land—a pro-Marxist organ, like the *Populaire du Centre,* one of Longuet's papers, wrote on 22nd January, 1917, after hav-ing acquainted itself with our "collection of proofs"—to be mentioned later on:

"We have read Scheidemann's Parliamentary speeches. Even at the risk of being attacked by many people, we state without any hesitation that we have rediscovered in these speeches the truest Socialistic spirit. So many of our comrades might well take an example from them."

Our policy in the War is so clear to the eyes of the world

that we need waste no words on these charges, made against their better knowledge by the Left and the Right. The charges from the Right are reduced to absurdity by every official shorthand report of the Reichstag on the speeches of our S.D. leaders; they are confuted by every division on the War Credits. The charges from the Left are as easy to disprove. One thing certainly we have not done; we have not attacked our country in the rear to "end the War." We have rejected what could only lead to prolonging the War and finally accomplishing our defeat—U-boat warfare; this we knew would force the U.S.A. into the War against us. From the beginning of the War we have always pressed for an understanding with our enemies and have stretched out our hand again and again across the Vosges and the Channel, without finding, alas! anyone to take it. What was the answer to our Party demonstrations, our Reichstag speeches, our resolutions in Berlin, Vienna and Stockholm? That answer was crushing. We did not lose our heads, however, and again emphasized our readiness for peace, but not in the way demanded by Radicals, Communists and Bolshevists—peace at any price. No member of the Social Democratic Party had agreed to such an unscrupulous policy that tramples underfoot the real interests of Germany, and through which the workers would be seriously injured in every respect. We were, on the other hand, ready at all times for a peace that would guarantee political independence to the German people, the inviolability of the Empire and its economic progress. After Haase had declared the policy of the Section on 4th August and 2nd December, 1914, we declared publicly our will for peace more than thirty times—by official manifestoes, Reichstag speeches and interpellations. To be added to these are our still unpublished memoranda to the Chancellor, the demonstrations of the S.P.D. and those made jointly with the Austrian and Hungarian Social Democrats. None of these manifestoes, declaring our readiness for peace, was lacking in clearness; some instances taken at random can prove this. At a joint demonstration of the German and Austro-Hungarian Party on 13th April, 1915, this pronouncement was made:

"All Social Democratic Parties, that have always worked for the brotherhood of nations both traditionally and fundamentally, are the recognized heralds of the love of peace, that is derived from popular will and the power of self-assertion, not from any feeling of weakness. It necessarily follows that only such a peace is possible that humiliates no nation, and only such a peace can guarantee the lasting co-operation of all civilized peoples.

"The parties represented at the Congress stand firm on the basis of the resolutions passed by International Socialist Congresses, and consider in this sense the following guarantees necessary to the conclusion of peace:

"The extension of compulsory International Arbitration Courts with a view to the settlement of all disputes between individual States.

"The submission of all State treaties and agreements to the democratic control of popular assemblies.

"The International limitation according to treaty of Armaments with a view to universal disarmament.

"The recognition of the right of self-determination of all nations.

"The representatives of the S.D. parties in Germany, Austria and Hungary further declare: the fact that the S.D. parties of those countries are defending their people and country should be no hindrance to the maintenance of international

relationships or the continuance of their international arrange=
ments."

The introductory clauses that the German Section of the
Reichstag and the Select Committee drafted and published
on 16th August, 1915, are on all fours with the above Austro-
German manifesto. In a declaration, 23rd February, 1917,
it was stated:

"Through the refusal of peace negotiations offered by Germany and her allies, the Government of the enemy Powers
have taken upon themselves the heavy responsibility of continuing the War. They intend to carry out their openly expressed policy of annexations that will mean the ruin and
lasting subjection of the Central Powers. In view of this
situation, the German Social Democratic Party once more
declares its firm determination to fight on till a peace ensuring the vital interests of the German people has been reached.
With the same determination with which we pledge ourselves
to defend our country, we once more express our readiness
for peace. We expect the Imperial Government to adhere
unflinchingly to their wish for peace as announced in their
Note of 12th December, 1916, and be ready at any time to enter
upon negotiations with a view to a peace that respects the right
of all people to live, and contains the guarantee of duration.
Because of these considerations we approve of the Credits
asked for."

Before the Stockholm Conference, which must be separately
described, I spoke again on behalf of the Section in the Reichstag on 15th May, 1917. I attacked the policy of the Annexationists who in scorn called the peace by agreement advocated
by us "Scheidemann's Peace," a peace of humiliation and surrender.

"When Professor Schäfer and Count Reventlow howl and

CARICATURE OF SCHEIDEMANN BY KARL HOLTZ

write, then you hear, 'Fight on! No peace by agreement; annihilation of the enemy—for then we can dictate peace to him.' This is their plan. 'Victory, glory, loot!' This is their slogan. Through this bull-in-a-china-shop, Pan-German policy we have been foolishly suspected of being a nation of robbers —that is to say, a nationally organized robber gang of seventy millions. Through these antics our opponents in Germany bring down upon us all nations of the earth, and certainly get the comforting satisfaction that, in their opinion, nothing can be done. It would be a blessing for all Europe if we could have a treaty by agreement in double-quick time: 'For the defence of our land, for the defence of our hearths and homes, the people will and must come in. Our people will have nothing to do with a war of aggression. We Social Democrats will oppose it tooth and nail—make no mistake.

"The Pan-Germans pour scorn on the peace by agreement, of which we have been always in favour, as if it were a 'peace of surrender.' What does it mean, and what are we surrendering? We refuse to continue the War; we refuse to go on killing hundreds of thousands and maiming hundreds of thousands; we refuse to go on spending daily hundreds of millions; we refuse to go on devastating Europe; but we refuse to give up one bit of German territory or one bit of German property; we refuse what we do not possess; we refuse to be deluded by the notion that war will bring us advantages we cannot claim and for which we must make fresh and horrible sacrifices; we refuse to terrorize and oppress other nations, but we do not refuse to believe that the Germans will emerge from this ghastly War a free people. The Pan-German calls this a peace of surrender. What we will surrender is the Pan-German and his silly talk."

I put the matter as plainly as I could in this speech. In

the first place, my object was to get the Government to state definitely how they stood with the Annexationists and ourselves, supporting peace by agreement; and, in the second place, to stir up the Socialists in enemy countries before the Stockholm Conference and get them to put pressure on their respective Governments. I said, among other things:

"If the English and French Governments should now renounce annexations, as the Russian Government has done, and the German Government, instead of ending the War by a similar renouncement, should intend to continue it for the purpose of self-aggrandizement, then, mark my words, gentlemen, you will have revolution in this country."

Though this remark was quite obvious to us, it seemed monstrous to our opponents in the Reichstag. President Kämpf, who certainly had not understood the sentence, called me to order. The Press of the German world-conquerors treated me as if I had been guilty of and condemned for high treason.

Every attempt made to accuse the S.P.D. of having neglected its duty to the country had come to nought, as well as the reproach of its not having done its best to bring about peace. All efforts to make the S.P.D. responsible for the policy of others who had seceded from it because they thought its policy wrong and struck out a policy for themselves, were unfair and bound to fail when brought up against facts that could be proved by chapter and verse.

The secessionists from the S.P.D. had founded a separate party. This association was as independent of the S.P.D. as the S.P.D. was of it. Obviously no one could make any one of these organizations responsible for the policy of others.

The Search for Possibilities of Peace

It was, of course, utterly impossible to report all our interviews with the Chancellor, even in most confidential circles, let alone in the Press. A typical instance may show how such interviews with the Imperial Chancellor, von Bethmann-Hollweg, were conducted. On 8th November, 1915, Wahnschaffe, Under-Secretary of State, asked me to go in the evening to the Chancellor, as he urgently wanted me to see him on that day. He left it to me to bring Ebert. Ebert and I went at the appointed time to the Wilhelmstrasse. The Chancellor was in the most serious mood. He asked us to help him to fight the pessimistic views that were being made use of abroad to an increasing extent and were injurious to our country. He had recently stated to Haase, Molkenbuhr and myself what Sembat had said. He had got another report, according to which Sembat and another French Minister declared that they must fight on at all costs in view of the present state of things in Germany. A Minister in London had told Vandervelde that the Belgians should resign themselves to the fact that their country would not be freed of the enemy before 1917. We explained to the Chancellor that the foreign Press in no way relied exclusively on Social Democratic utterances. The instructions and statements of the Government were quite sufficient to enlighten foreign countries on the situation in Germany. We really poured out our hearts to him, referred not only to the food shortage, but also to the strong desire for peace that was prevalent among the whole people. We were, however, convinced it was pretty much the same in other countries. The Chancellor answered that he had been for a long time making inquiries abroad about possibilities of peace, "though I have had to deny it in St. Petersburg, London and Paris. In Russia the War Party had entirely the upper hand. In Paris there is no inclination to peace. And in London? Sir Edward Grey sent me word through a neutral who he knew would repeat it, saying that he saw no basis for peace negotiations. After this news from the Entente countries and from speeches in London and Paris, I cannot make any public peace offers. I should get the exact opposite of what I, with you, desire to get—a speedy peace."

We replied that we clearly saw the difficulties of the position. Yet two facts stood out: first, our armies were in a better position than those of the Entente; secondly, if the offer of our willingness for peace was rejected, the whole of the German people would again close up their ranks, and the foreign Press would hardly be able to make useful quotations from German papers. He would be doing a great work if he could only touch the right spot. He expressed his hope that a point of contact would soon be found. With the object of discussing the whole situation, Ebert, Müller and I went off to Vienna soon after the interview. We arrived on the evening of 17th November, and had a thorough talk with Victor Adler the same night. The official meeting with our Austrian Party friends took place on 18th and 19th November. In these parleys the question of annexations was again naturally brought up. "It is with you rather different than with us. With us it is almost a slogan, and we can do nothing with it," said Dr. Victor Adler. A few days after this Vienna meeting, on 23rd November, the Chancellor again asked us to a talk. He had hoped that after fighting in Serbia was over he could talk openly about his willingness for peace. He had recently received news from which it appeared that the Entente were trying to cover up their war plans. What they intended in Salonia and Gallipoli was entirely obscure. One could also certainly reckon on a French offensive in the West at a very early date. "Our reserves in the West are now so strong that our positions will not be seriously threatened, though we must be prepared for the French being successful in forcing in our line here and there." He intended to state in the Reichstag his willingness for peace in clearer words than the *Norddeutsche Allgemeine Zeitung* had recently done. After the speeches Asquith had made at the Guild-hall in answer to two speeches in the Lords and Rénaudel's in the Chamber of Deputies, he must now go to work very cautiously if he did not want to achieve the exact contrary to what he intended. He still hoped to realize his idea, as before 10th December—the day he was to address the Reichstag—the situation might have again materially altered.

After once more returning to the point that he wished to express his willingness to negotiate a peace as clearly as possible, we repeatedly and distinctly reminded him that war-weariness was certainly equally great in all countries. The clearest assurance of his readiness to negotiate was imperative. It was important for him to break away in his speech from the policy of Annexation. The more emphatically he did this, the better it would be. He promised most definitely that he would express his willingness for peace as far as he could, with due regard to the whole situation.

Any doubts of Bethmann-Hollweg's determination to seize every opportunity of serving the cause of peace were unjustified. We were much less satisfied with his attitude over the democratic reforms we were always pressing upon him. Here his ideas seemed to us to be wholly antiquated. At an interview with him on 27th November, 1915, I demanded most emphatically the introduction of electoral reform in Prussia. He replied: "In Germany when the Diet opens there is a speech from the Throne. I will see how far one can go. In the Reichstag I cannot speak about Prussia's electoral law." To ease his conscience I will state that later on prominent members of the Centre and the Progressive Party took the matter up, using the same argument. The Reichstag had nothing to do with the Franchise Act in Prussia.

The S.D. Party did not let 1915 pass by without issuing declarations about Germany's readiness to make peace. We interpellated on 9th December. Landsberg and I were put up to speak. I was to begin, and Landsberg was to speak on the answer to the interpellation. Herr von Bethmann-Hollweg had an earnest conversation before the debate in the Reichstag with Landsberg and me. He knew several days before what we would say and we knew what he would say. As so many times before, I thanked the soldiers, who had done marvels by their courage and sacrifice—the slaughter was getting worse and worse, and there had been sacrifices enough. The question was justified: How much longer was it going to last?

"Our aims for our own security are attained, as far as protection against a break through is concerned. Now the vital question is whether our enemies are ready for peace. The Power that can and should speak first is the Power whose military position and economic strength permit it to regard with calm confidence any misinterpretations of its willingness for peace as a sign of weakness; on this text we will speak of peace; on this text we must preach peace."

I quoted every pacific opinion abroad—there were unfortunately very few—and then continued:

"If the opportunity is offered to the Government of making a peace that can ensure for the German people its political independence, the inviolability of the Empire, and its economic progress, then we ask the Government to make peace. If it sees the possibility of entering into peace negotiations on this basis, then it must do so in the interests of the civilized world. We will then stand by the Government and exert our whole strength in pushing those into the background who refuse such a peace."

The Chancellor from his point of view spoke sensibly, and like an honest man, quite in the way he said he would. He began his speech by referring to the hopes of foreign countries that Germany was weakening because she was talking of peace. "But I trust and believe that the remarks in the interpellation we have just heard as a whole will not encourage, but rather discourage our enemies in their joyful expectations. In the words of the first speaker I fancied anxiety was expressed that we might avoid the possibility of an honourable peace and decline the reasonable peace offers that might be made us, because we intended to occupy all lands we had conquered and others as well." The rest of the speech was devoted to prove that the German Government did not wage war to threaten small nations. "We do not wage this War that has been forced on us to subjugate foreign nations, but to protect our lives and freedom. For the German Government this War has always been what it was from the beginning and what it has never ceased to be in all our manifestoes—the defensive War of the German people."

The Chancellor by this speech had broken away once again from Jingo politicians, who were persecuting him more and more with their hatred. Landsberg's speech was quite excellent. Only a few sentences can be quoted:

"To my great satisfaction I have not heard words from the Chancellor like those M. Briand and Mr. Asquith have spoken. Had I heard such words, even one word about the destruction of French militarism—for such have been spoken—or about

English navalism, or had I heard words that called to mind a well-known petition (the annexationist demands of the Farmers' Union), had the Chancellor used expressions that it contains, and in which one catches the tone adopted by M. Briand and Mr. Asquith, I can assure you, on behalf of my entire Section, that we should have offered the strongest opposition. For we intend to prevent the destruction of our land, but do not intend to destroy any country."

Although Landsberg made by far the better speech, he was sharply attacked in the Section by some of his colleagues, who considered him a Radical, whereas Haase expressed his appreciation of mine—I had spoken well, effectively and with tact; I had also represented the minority point of view. Such praise I had not received before, and I was utterly nonplussed. Why Haase had been obliged to praise me is clearly explained by what follows. At a meeting of the Section on 17th December it appeared that a number of the members of the Section had drafted a statement which would have been made in the Reichstag on 9th December, in case my speech should not find favour in the eyes of my colleagues concerned. Probably making this statement in the Reichstag at the time seemed out of place to Haase, and so he preferred to express his satisfaction with my speech. This adequately explains why he was so appreciative.

At the end of December Ebert and I went off to The Hague, where we had been invited to attend a meeting of the most trusty members of the Party. The sitting took place in the Hotel Victoria. Our Dutch colleague Wibaut told me that Vandervelde was coming from France to The Hague on 5th January, 1916. It was perhaps possible to persuade a few French and English to come likewise. Were we prepared to appear at The Hague also? We naturally said we were, but expressed our doubts about the English and French coming. On our asking whether Wibaut thought a talk in common could be arranged between the lot of us, he was doubtful. However, we were prepared to stand by immediately if we were wanted. We said we were agreeable, provided we were told to come back from Berlin. We could not expose ourselves to the risk of being told that they would have nothing to do with us after waiting here outside the door. All present at the conversation considered our contention obvious. We spoke our minds very clearly about our attitude on Alsace-Lorraine, which was, and would remain, German territory. This rather nonplussed them—the more so as we were now informed that Rénaudel had demanded the restitution of Alsace-Lorraine in the Chamber of Deputies. Wibaut denied it. We insisted that the French official short-hand reports should be fetched from The Hague Tribunal library. These confirmed what we said. Wibaut had made Rénaudel talk sounder stuff in the *Werkblad* than was the case in the shorthand reports. Next day we went back to Berlin. The journey there and back took nineteen hours.

On arriving at Berlin I at once got to work on making a record of our "Efforts for Peace";[1] this had been suggested by me and approved by the Executive. The record was sent to the I.S.B. (International Socialist Bureau) with the request that all other Socialist parties should be urged to collect similar records, so that later on one could see with ease what our comrades in every single country had done in the interests of peace. No answer was given in reply to what I admit was rather a malicious suggestion. The Social Democrats of no other country could have shown such a record.

At the close of 1916 came a message from the W.T.B. (Wolf's Telegraphic Bureau) about the resolutions of the French Social-

---

[1] "German Social Democracy on War and Peace," Berlin, 1916.

ist Congress that had met in Paris. A few extracts may here be given:

"The Party will continue fighting in the War till the whole land is freed of the enemy and the conditions of a lasting peace are fully secured. Among the conditions for a lasting peace the Party understands one to be as follows—the small martyred nations of Belgium and Serbia, which shall rise again from their ruins, must be restored again to their economic and political independence. The manifesto requires the Governments of the Allies to reject any and every policy of annexation. A solid development of the Rights of the People seems to be the imperative necessity for a lasting peace.

"The Socialist Party rejects the political and economic destruction of Germany, but considers necessary the annihilation of Prussian militarism, which is a source of danger to the security of the world and to Germany itself. The resumption of relations with German Social Democrats will be considered only if this is likely to add strength and life to the principles of the International. The Congress authorizes the Socialist Deputies to ensure further the means of attaining victory and of participating in national defence by voting for the Credits. It declares, with a reference to making no separate peace, its adhesion to the words spoken by Asquith in the House of Commons."

The French along with the German Socialists rejected Annexations; the natural incorporation of Alsace-Lorraine with France was not considered an annexation. They negatived the economic and political destruction of Germany, but insisted on the destruction of Prussian militarism. They said not a word about French militarism. Until the destruction of Prussian militarism was accomplished their deputies were to vote the War Credits, and they expected German Socialists to refuse the supplies necessary for the defence of their country!

1917—*the Decisive Year*

In the course of 1917 the War should have been brought to an end if Germany was to be preserved from total collapse. Between the beginning of ruthless U-boat warfare at the start of the year and the dishonourable and short-sighted policy of our official representatives towards the Russians at the end of the year at Brest Litovsk, all chances of coming to an agreement were either ignored or deliberately destroyed. One must be a brazen-faced idiot to say now that no one seriously anticipated America's declaration of war should unrestrained U-boat warfare begin. All but those who cannot put two and two together must, if they are honest, admit that the chances were ninety-nine to one on America declaring war—it had also been expected, and not last of all by the Government. America's warnings and threats had been clear enough. Count Bernsdorff, German Ambassador in Washington, foreshadowed with absolute certainty the U.S.A. declaration of war in case there should be any extension of U-boat warfare. Many Americans friendly to Germany, with wide connections both here and there, had no doubts of what would result if U-boat warfare were intensified. Everything was staked on a single card by world-war gamblers who could hardly have believed in a happy ending to this frightful struggle. Ludendorff, and all "plungers" who thought like him, saw it was neck or nothing. Ludendorff tried to deceive himself and others with ridiculous references to the Americans' unfitness for war, and the Conservative German National leader, Hergt, pathetically asserted: "They can't fly, they can't swim, so they won't come."

The Conquerors of the World, men of the stamp of Count Westarp, who had pressed for beginning intensive U-boat action, repeatedly misfired with their demands in the Chief

Select Committee of the Reichstag. General Ludendorff, who certainly never doubted his godlike characteristics, but may occasionally have had misgivings on a successful end to the War, worked harder and harder for an intensified form of submarine attack. It is perhaps to be understood from a soldier's point of view, but it is unpardonable that Government officials who had a voice in this matter should have given way to Ludendorff's insistence.

I may be permitted here to say that many are wrong in pointing only to Hindenberg and his victories, and talking of Ludendorff only when things have gone wrong, either politically or in the field. If Hindenberg without demur took to himself all the credit he should have shared with Ludendorff, it at least logically follows that he should have taken his share of the abuse that was showered on Ludendorff. Herr von Hindenberg after the War was much better advised than his fighting comrade, Ludendorff. While the latter fled abroad and lived there as a refugee under the name of Lindström, and sharpened his arrows to fire at Ebert and Scheidemann and the Party of "traitors to their country," Herr von Hindenberg entered the service of the Government under those two rascals, Ebert and Scheidemann, and worked with them excellently for many months, first from headquarters in Wilhelmshöhe, near Kassel, and when headquarters were transferred to Kolberg, from there. Herr von Hindenberg, who in every way was the least active of the two generals, "lay very low" after his retirement, whereas Herr Ludendorff, advised by equally excitable and ignorant friends, spoke, wrote and plotted on every occasion. With his passive temperament, the Imperial General Field-Marshal von Hindenburg became President of the Republic, while Ludendorff, the real General, became the colleague in the Reichstag of the Anti-Semites, Ahlemann, Kube and Stöhr. While Herr von Hindenburg, on being invited to stand for the Presidency, honestly and openly declared he had never interested himself in politics, and also had never read any but military books since his cadet days, Herr Ludendorff after his return to the ruined Fatherland fell upon the stupid old book, "Die Weisen von Zion," a ridiculous twopenny half-penny work of the worst kind, in order to educate himself politically. Thus equipped with the political knowledge of a fourth-standard boy in a Kendell School, the General drew his sword against Jews, Catholics, Socialists and Freethinkers. Barred by many of his war comrades more out of pity than hate, he turned his back, loud in his complaints, on the Evangelical Church—a disgruntled and pitiable man.

Intensification of U-Boat Warfare

Zimmermann, Secretary of State, asked me on 17th January, 1917, to come to see him, in order to tell me that the die had been cast. On 1st February the U-boat ruthlessness would begin. Hindenburg and Ludendorff had stated that, apart from other reasons, they would make use of this increased activity at sea as a means of encouraging the soldiers. "In the strictest confidence, the morale of the troops has alarmingly deteriorated. What we experienced a few weeks back was the worst blow in the whole War. Four French divisions routed five German divisions or took them prisoners." During our conversation Zimmermann stated, in answer to my question, that Hindenburg and Ludendorff distinctly hoped to prevent any break through in the West. All was secure in the East. "The greatest precautions have, of course, been taken by us. Our troops will be mainly withdrawn to a prepared position that is described as impregnable."

From Zimmermann's further information I had to conclude that we were in a bad way. As I referred to the ominous decision as a gambler's last throw, Zimmermann replied, "You know what Helfferich, the Chancellor and I thought of the U-boat question. Now we have no choice. At headquarters in Pless everything has been thrashed out, both 'pros' and 'cons.' Ultimately the Chancellor said that he would say neither yes nor no to the Kaiser, but would place himself in the Emperor's hands. Naturally, a Chancellor crisis resulted; it was good luck it was prevented. A dead-set is being made against Bethmann-Hollweg."

Then I got on to the immediate consequence of U-boat war—the impending declaration of war by America. Then Zimmermann said, "We will work our hardest, naturally, to keep America out of the business. We are going to write on 1st February, the day the War begins, a very friendly note to Wilson, in which we shall refer to his noble-hearted efforts for peace. We shall explain to him that we were not able to give up using submarines after the great alteration in the military position. We shall make him definite proposals with regard to American ships." Zimmermann admitted that the probability of war with America was increased, but there were various forms the row might take. Perhaps Wilson would be content with breaking off diplomatic relations. "Things are like this; if the War lasts another year we must accept any sort of peace; we must therefore try to force a decision before that."

I naturally did not mince words during this conversation. I emphasized most strongly the danger all round of this mad venture, and asked finally what he expected neutrals to do. Zimmermann tried to calm me down.

"I shall first go to Vienna and get their approval, so that the Emperor Charles cannot say later it was only a German proposal. Holland has taken precautions, and will probably not take any active steps against us; the same is true of Denmark and Sweden. Switzerland is a big query. What is Switzerland to do if she is treated like Greece? She will be forced to take up arms for the Entente to force a quick decision and protect herself from starvation." On my interjecting that the situation was really desperate, Zimmermann continued, "Of course all steps have been taken for holding either Holland or Denmark in check. When the possibility of war with Switzerland was mooted at the Council of War, the old gentleman said: 'That would not be so bad; we could then roll up the French front from there.'"

At the end of a very thorough talk, Zimmermann said, "No matter what may happen, wild men like Bassermann will later furiously attack the Government. If all goes well they will say all would have gone well much earlier if there had not been such a long delay. If things go ill, then they'll say, 'It's the Government's fault; it hesitated so long.'"

I left Zimmermann in no doubt as to the attitude of the S.P.D. with regard to this unhappy decision.

At the meeting of the Chief Committee on 30th January and 1st February there was a searching debate on submarine warfare. The S.P.D. took a strong dissentient attitude. Their speaker was Dr. David, whose speech in abstract was communicated in confidence to the whole of our Party Press and our responsible members. David not only cut to ribbons Dr. Helfferich's impossible theories and showed up the equivocal policy of this man in the U-boat question (Helfferich had previously declared the opening of ruthless submarine warfare as impossible and ominous for Germany), but also stressed the aggravation of the situation through America's entry into the War. The end of David's speech ran as follows:

"Now that the decision has been taken with regard to U-boat warfare, its political supporters cannot be thinking of making difficulties for carrying it out. They will observe the caution in their public utterances that is required through the grievous plight of our country, now fighting against a world in arms. One should also not make things more difficult for its opponents, so that the only thing we can save—viz. the staunch moral unity of our people—may not be jeopardized."

These words and these actions were those of the Social Democrats—"fellows without a country."

On the evening of the same day when Zimmermann had a private talk with me, an interview with Ebert and me took place at the Chancellor's. Bethmann-Hollweg, an opponent of intensive U-boat warfare, had knuckled under. "Should I have gone?" I had to ask myself how I could best serve the people. He was quite clear that the S.P.D. could not have maintained their policy if he had gone, owing to the U-boat question.

To complete the story it must be here stated that Hans Delbrück, the Privy Councillor and well-known historian, and I tried to move heaven and earth to get the Government, in view of the increased naval activity, to "leave this and do that" on the off chance of dissuading America from declaring war. I had many connections with America. Gerard, the American Ambassador, had put me on a committee, of which Rathenau and Dr. Peter Spahn were members, that administered a fund for German war widows, collected in America. Along with a German-American Noeggerat and the American journalist Swing, I drew up a manifesto for the American Press appealing to Wilson. Hans Delbrück entirely approved of the wording. Swing was a splendid fellow, whose fair-mindedness, I should say, and love for German art and learning, were not shattered even after being torpedoed in the Mediterranean by a German U-boat. When Swing, who was a good American and wished to stop America entering the War, had to leave Berlin with the Staff of the American Embassy, he had actually managed to insert in a popular Paris paper some remarks in favour of a peace by agreement which we concocted together.

Germany's fate was sealed by the opening of unrestrained U-boat warfare. This was the opinion of all active members of the S.P.D., who were now working harder than ever for an agreement. No less a man than the English War Premier, Lloyd George, said on unveiling a memorial at Finchley on 20th October, 1927, that unrestrained U-boat warfare was the salvation of England:

"The Statue represents the liberation of mankind from the tyranny and enslavement of Europe by a great military despotism. That great military despotism was nearer success in the Great War than some people imagine. At the end of the third year of the War four of the seven Allied nations were knocked out and their armies scattered. If German statesmanship had been up to the standard of German military ability, America would not have come into the War at all, and England and France alone would have been opposed to the most frightful military machine ever known in history."

These few words speak volumes against the Imperial Government and the German "conquering heroes" who had kicked over every chance of peace.

Soon after intensive war at sea was opened, American soldiers were embarked for France. The strength of the American troops in the Western theatre of war was as follows, according to official figures:

End of	May	1917	.	.	.	.	1,308
"	" December	1917	.	.	.	.	183,896
"	" March	1918	.	.	.	.	329,005
"	" June	1918	.	.	.	.	897,293
"	" September	1918	.	.	.	.	1,783,955
"	" November	1918	.	.	.	.	2,057,675

No German U-boat succeeded in sinking a single enemy troop-ship.

Simultaneously with the weakening of our position abroad began the deterioration of conditions at home. Abroad a dwindling prospect of a tolerable ending to the War; at home an ever-increasing dearth both in quantity and quality of food-stuffs. In addition, a rising discontent owing to a general refusal to introduce reforms long overdue—especially electoral reform in Prussia. At the same time it was becoming more and more evident that the spirit of democracy would have to go hand in hand with the S.P.D. in their efforts to secure a peace by agreement.

Time for Action

In March, 1917, I made, independently of my speeches in the Reichstag, a new step forward with an article in the *Vorwärts,* under the heading "Time for Action." A long discussion of the question as to why almost the entire world was in sympathy with our enemies is not needed. The answer is easy. Everybody saw that a form of democracy, more or less developed, existed among our enemies and was deciding the issue, while the only thing we had to show was—Prussia! Russia had quickly made up her mind to clear her decks, and had swept up all her dust and rubbish with a very large broom. With us the time was five minutes to the zero hour; yet Bethmann-Hollweg did not intend to start his reforms in Prussia till after the War. In Russia all sorts of reforms were promised *post bellum*. But for the Russians the War was lasting too long, and the worse they were starved the more intolerable was the delay. They said to themselves, "if bread and potatoes cannot be got by all, what hinders us from getting at least equal rights?" Then came the 11th of March; then abdication of the Czar, and then

337

popular government. Why put off till to-morrow what is absolutely necessary, and was declared by the King himself to be
the most urgent necessity years ago, if we can get it to-day?
Now is the time for decisive action. "The difficulties that may
arise, if the Government now demands electoral reform for
Prussia, are the veriest trifles when compared with the difficulties
that may arise if a Bill to this effect is not brought forward.
Members of Parliament and Party politicians who still dare to
say no in the Diet, if the Government forcibly demand the Equal
Franchise, can be put out of the way in a trice. One has only
to mean business and stick to it."

This article not only angered the Government and all reactionary parties, but also the Progressives and the Centre. Even
Ebert, who in principle was in favour of my challenge, reproached me for it. There was a very candid discussion, in the
course of which I said I would rather resign all my functions
than my inalienable right of speaking my mind under my
own name.

Payer, a member of the Reichstag, as well as Erzberger, told
me they could not admit of the Reichstag's meddling with the
franchise. The Chancellor was inconsolable. He sent me word
through Wahnschaffe that he knew I did not intend mischief,
but they had had to hear all sorts of things from the Right—that
I was preaching revolution and wanted to belittle the Kaiser's
prerogative. I explained that my object was to remind the
Chancellor that, in his great anxiety for the Right, he should
not forget his small respect for the people. I wanted to warn
him and urge him to decisive action. If the Government
would only firmly demand the Reichstag Franchise for the
Diet, the National Liberals and the Centre would not dare to
say that they refused equal rights to soldiers, now fighting
for the country.

It would be a mistake to suppose that this article made bad blood all round. On the contrary. Discontent with an ever-wobbling Government, that was, however, agreed on our policy of agreement and strongly opposed Ludendorff's faction, had deeply penetrated the citizen classes. Numerous letters of approval encouraged me further. I have already described, but without mentioning names, one of the most interesting visits I received at the time. Now in this particular case I need have no reserve! One day I was called upon by the former Chief Burgomaster of Posen, Privy Councillor Dr. Witting, a brother of Maximilian Harden, in the Zeppelin Room in the Reichstag, Wittkowski was the real name of both of them. Witting assured me, in the presence of a friend, that I did not know how great my influence was among the citizen classes. I should personally make a bold move, throw out the Government and take command. The great majority of the town voters would support me as well as the whole of the working classes. The whole people would be keen on any step likely to stop the War. I replied that I would stick at nothing if I were convinced that I was doing something to stop the War and end the misery of our people. I had unfortunately no such conviction. The bold move he wanted me to take meant Civil War and Germany's ruin. Witting, P.C., left me very disappointed.

The Wreckers of Chancellors

At this time of grievous anxiety for all lovers of peace, the wreckers of Chancellors had their special worries. How could Bethmann-Hollweg be got rid of? Hosts of abusive "rags," slanging the Chancellor, had not met with the desired success. His enemies met together in the Hotel Adlon on 25th February, 1917. They intended going into the whole question. In a report or rather an act of indictment they attacked the Chan-

cellor in the most virulent way. The Emperor should be requested to subordinate politics entirely to the conduct of war;
this was best achieved by appointing Field-Marshal von Hindenburg Imperial Chancellor. "The amount of work would not
be increased; all diplomatic business would be taken over by the
Army Command. What remained of political and diplomatic
odds and ends could be done by the secretaries and Heads of
Departments in the Foreign Office. The Imperial Chancellor,
von Bethmann-Hollweg, had, in his fatal blindness, alienated
the best and loyalest circles." In the draft of their petition to
Ludendorff it was stated that the Field-Marshal was indispensable, and the Kaiser's favour or disfavour could not touch him.
Hindenburg must be set up in opposition to Bethmann-Hollweg; then the disappearance of Bethmann-Hollweg would be a
certainty.

One must grant that the notorious "Funeral Pyre" letter of
the Court Chaplain, Stöcker, that was to upset Prince Bismarck,
was more refined in its tone than those missives from agitating
industrial magnates and Saxon attorneys. Yet who, for devilish
cunning and intrigue, could have beaten this political dabbler
and Court Chaplain? At a Reichstag meeting (2nd March,
1917) Conrad Haussmann revealed who were behind all these
Pan-German tricks, and had been present at the meeting in the
Hotel Adlon: Privy Councillor E. Kirdorff (Mühlheim-Ruhr),
Privy Councillor B. Körting (Hanover), Privy Councillor Duis-
berg, Admiral von Knorr, Prince Otto zu Salm-Hortsmar, Professor Dr. Metger (Hanover,) Count Luxberg (Weimar) along
with the barristers Petzoldt (Plauen) and Freigang (Chemnitz). There were altogether twenty-nine gentlemen present
at this meeting of conspirators—thirty with Count von Westarp,
who, though he said at first he would come, finally cried off.
Besides the plan of overthrowing the Chancellor, these gentle-

men had others: "No substitution of the Prussian Diet Franchise by the Reichstag system, but the abolition of the Reichstag system by the Diet Franchise, as being up to date." They were typical representatives of those cliques that brought misery and death upon Germany.

General Strikes

War profiteers, in spite of all the distress and emergency orders, were able to procure just as they chose, even in the worst of times, all the necessaries and luxuries of life. They took every chance given them. None of them or the members of their families suffered from hunger in the War. This was well known among the populace, for the women who dropped from exhaustion after buying a few ounces of bread, fat and meat were never the wives or daughters of employers, but without exception the wives of working men and suchlike humble folk. In the factories it was the working men who collapsed, not their masters. Conditions had been always bad; in the spring of 1917 they had become intolerable. In addition to starvation, lack of coal, clothes, underlinen, boots and shoes, there was a growing feeling of embitterment against the Government. If they cannot give us anything to eat why do they refuse us political equality? Why is not peace made? Because the war-mongers want to make further conquests! Hunger, embitterment and despair are bad counsellors. The general atmosphere was most depressing. That it would soon come to outbreaks, great and small, and that the workers would strike here and there, was as plain as your hand. The Unions worked with all their might against strikes, likewise the members of the S.P.D. Finally it was, however, announced that thousands of workmen would come out on 16th April.

On 14th April Wahnschaffe, on behalf of the Chancellor,

341

invited Ebert and me to his house to tell us of his troubles. We told him why all attempts at avoiding the strike would be futile. The reason was literally hunger, that could not be satisfied by cutting down the bread rations at the most critical time. He should see to it that the local authorities did not play the fool. Wahnschaffe told us he had already consulted the Commissioner of Police, von Oppen; he took a very calm view of things, and was trying to keep the gangs of strikers out of the centre of Berlin. I asked Wahnschaffe to tell the Chancellor in our name to take a strong line of stern measures against the Right, which the great majority of the people insisted on thinking the only possible way to peace, food and democracy. As long as absolutely equal rights were not conceded, there would be no peace in the country. The psychology of the people had altered in the War, especially since the Russian Revolution. I could not help making this remark. What would not the Czar be prepared to grant to-day! Wahnschaffe said he agreed.

The strike assumed the gravest proportions in Berlin and Leipzig. In Berlin about 125,000 were on strike, in Leipzig about 18,000. Representatives of the Unions and the S.P.D. did all that was humanly possible to influence the Government as well as the strikers. On 20th April workers in the munitions and arms factories came to see us at the Executive meeting, and declared the continuation of the strike to be lunacy, which was also our opinion. We advised them at the meeting fixed for the afternoon to organize a secret ballot; then the majority would probably vote for a return to work. The workmen saw that they could not get either bread or soap, or boots or under-linen, through striking. It was our job to represent their political demands. That we were trying our hardest to do our job, the workers belonging to the S.P.D. knew well. We had a heated argument with the Government at noon on the same day, after hearing that a meeting decided on by the workers on strike had been forbidden, and that the factories of the strikers had been taken over by the military. Any concern that had been "militarized" was under military jurisdiction and martial law. This could not be successful and would create bad blood.

Any fair-minded man who can to some extent realize things as they were then and estimate their effect on working men coming from the trenches hungry and cold, or threatened with being sent back there, will see in this strike of January, 1918, only briefly alluded to here, a venture he will understand but not approve. So much has been written and spoken about the strike, and so many people have been prosecuted, that no new facts can be given. Those interested are referred to the following works:

Brammer, "The President's Legal Action," 1925.

Scheidemann, "The Collapse," 1922.

Scheidemann, "For People and Fatherland," 1925.

The three books are published by the Sociological Press (Verlag für Sozialwissenschaft).

The policy of the S.P.D. Executive during the strike was not only wholly free from objection—it was obvious. Three members of the Party Executive, Ebert, Otto Braun and Schiedemann, represented at times by other colleagues, were invited, at the request of their comrades who had been forced to strike, to join the Strike Committee in spite of Ledebour's violent protest. Why had they been asked by their friends to join, and why had Ledebour so violently protested? Their friends knew they would do all in their power not only to run the strike on peaceable lines but also to bring it to a speedy conclusion by negotiating with the Government. But Ledebour's friends did not want this at all. Because Ebert and his friends finally joined the Strike Committee, after refusing at first, to serve their country, they were later indicted for treason. Ebert, who, as President of the Empire, was especially vilified, had more confidence in a German law court than, for instance, Dr. Marx, later Minister of Justice and Imperial Chancellor. He instituted legal proceedings against a man called Rothart who had accused him openly of treason. Ebert must have been bitterly sorry for putting his trust in a German court of law. After proceedings that lasted for days, in which Ebert's enemies tried to convict him, with evidence of the most dubious kind, of treason, the following verdict was given by the Court, with Bewersdorf as President, who gained great notoriety through this trial: "The accused is sentenced to three months' imprisonment for slander."

In summing up the evidence, however, Bewersdorf said, "The Court has to inquire whether it has been proved by evidence that the plaintiff has committed treason. This inquiry is to be regarded solely from a criminal law point of view, and not from a political, historical or moral standpoint. This conduct, which can be defended politically and morally, can, however, constitute a criminal offence. . . . Not only did workmen on strike commit treason, but all others who aided, abetted, organized, encouraged and supported the strike were guilty of the offence if they knew of the harm done to the country's defence by the strike, and were, notwithstanding, actively concerned in organizing, encouraging and supporting the strike. Has it been proved that the plaintiff has done any of these things? The Social Democratic Party and the plaintiff have not instigated the strike. It occurred without their co-operation. But the plaintiff has taken an active part in organizing and conducting the strike according to the wishes of the strikers. He has attended many meetings of the Strike Committee, and has aided in drawing up resolutions that contributed to prolong the strike. All these proceedings he supported as such, although he saw clearly that his attitude would be harmful to the defence of the realm. He has therefore acted deliberately contrary to Section 89 of the Criminal Code, and it is proved thereby that he is guilty of misdemeanour. The accused can therefore not be convicted under Section 186, but comes under Section 185 for slander. The most serious of all charges that have been found to be slanderous is treason in the opinion of the Court." Because the defendant had accused the President of the Reichstag of treason he was sentenced for slander to three months' imprisonment under Section 185. For the seriousness of the charge of treason (Section 186) he could not be punished, because the Court found that this charge had been proved against Ebert in accordance with the Criminal Law.

There was a yell of fury throughout the Republic when this verdict was known. By this sentence a most grievous blow had been dealt against the justice of the law, and the German's confidence in German jurisprudence was badly shaken. The man who had been called the worst of firebrands and Social patriots by all Communists, Spartacists and Bolshevists, was said to have committed high treason! This Ebert, a traitor to his country, because he took part in a Strike movement by request, from pure love of his people and his country, in order not to surrender the field to Ledebour and his Radical gang!

In a heated discussion with the opponents of our policy—among whom Ledebour was the moving spirit—Ebert spoke thus at a General Conference in the Reichstag of the S.P.D. in the Committee Room of the Household Select Committee in September 1916: "At a time when English munition workers give up their holidays and their Sundays (*Hear, hear*), when the entire world is turning out with all its might and main munitions and war material for the Entente, when the Entente is bringing one country after another into the War, when all enemy statesmen are opposing on principle any willingness for peace, and our sons and brothers on all fronts are being exposed to the most awful and murderous fire—should German workers strike at a time like this? (*Shame!*) Is it not pure lunacy?"

This was not only Ebert's opinion in September, 1916. It coincided with the attitude of the whole of the S.P.D. directorate. If Germany did not break down, till Hindenburg and Ludendorff uttered their despairing cry for an armistice at the end of September, 1918, it was owing first and foremost to the German Social Democrats. The outcry provoked throughout the country by the Magdeburg judgment could not have been expected by Bewersdorf and his brother judges. The Imperial Chancellor, Dr. Marx, a fine judge himself, the ex-Ministers Schiffer, Radbruch and Landsberg, the retired Vice-Chancellor Friedrich von Payer, an old and respected jurist, Professor Kahl, an ornament of the Berlin Law Faculty, numerous other lawyers and professors in all Faculties, as well as Republican and Commercial Unions and the entire Press of the world, were openly up in arms against the impossible verdict.

Poor is a people that loses a war and feels day by day for years and years the hand of the victor on its throat—poor it is, but not without hope. A land is only without hope when it has no strength left to restore its shattered confidence in its legal system.

Just one word on the effect of the strike as far as munitions were concerned. It was said at the time that Ludendorff was hoarding shells. The output of war material greatly exceeded the demand. Not only could that be seen in the frequent dismissals of workers, but also in the number of men not working full time. Factories were often compelled to shut down for

346

want of coal. Generally speaking, the strike brought about this result—that those who were out of work owing to coal shortage were kept together, and afterwards were able to go full speed ahead. After the strike was over thousands of workmen were out of work. The *Germania,* the chief paper of the Centre, wrote among its comments on the strike on 31st January, 1918:

"Berlin working people were also to a considerable extent put out of work owing to the coal shortage. Owing to the Berlin strike, coal shortage will be shortly at an end, with the result that big Berlin employers will save a round hundred million marks that they would otherwise have spent on compensation for the workmen out of work owing to want of coal."

The *Deutsche Bergwerkszeitung,* a typical big manufacturers' organ, said at the time that no harm could have been done through the strikes to war industries, because in January more than half a million tons of ammunition could not be despatched, and the stocks in the sheds had now increased to more than three million tons.

This proves the silliness of the talk about the strike having done great damage to the Fatherland. The rigid attitude of the S.P.D. to strikes in the Great War, as defined in Ebert's own words, was not in the least affected by the question whether damage had been done at the time to the defence of the country or not.

Prolongers of the War

In a previous chapter we saw how the Annexationists intended to win the War at their writing-desks and on the platform, like Herr Stresemann, who wanted a German Gibraltar and would have liked to perpetuate his hatred against England, and yearned for a dictated peace. Victor Marguérite, the witty father of the "Garçonne," has stated quite rightly in his book,

347

"Les Criminels," that criminals have been everywhere. Where the greatest have been will be confirmed when all records are open to examination. Had he only said that, he would not have said more than many have said in Germany, especially the Social Democrats at the end of 1918. Victor Marguérite, however, had the pluck to attack French Ministers and diplomats, though a Frenchman *par excellence*. Particularly impressive are his descriptions of the days the French President spent in St. Petersburg directly before the outbreak of war. No mercy on evildoers, no matter where they are; that is his text—no sparing French, English, Russians or Germans.

What . . . "German criminals!" Have not we heard thousands of times that the criminals were all on the other side, and that the innocents were on the German side? Yes, we've had it with numberless variations. We all believed it in 1914, and to this day we protest against the scandalous statement that Germany alone was responsible for the outbreak of war. It is an infamous libel on a peace-loving people to throw this accusation in their teeth. M. Clemenceau did so at Versailles!—handed them this charge in black and white—that they alone have to bear the terrible load of guilt, that they alone are responsible for millions of dead and crippled, for millions of widows and orphans, for the cruel destruction of fertile lands, prosperous villages and towns and things that cannot be replaced!

One Word on War Guilt

Just as firmly as we repudiated the sole responsibility for the War that was fastened on Germany at the outbreak of the War, so with the same firmness did we Social Democrats repudiate the contrary assertion of Germany's entire innocence. We know we are at one with Social Democrats all over the world, as well as with Victor Marguérite in saying, "Open the records so that the truth may be told." It is foolish beyond words when German Nationalists keep on alluding to the question of War guilt, before a more favourable atmosphere is created or the records of other countries are opened. As long as neither this nor that can be proved, Germany will always be the black sheep. We could print the contents of whole libraries—a beginning has already been made with the publications of the Foreign Office—to prove our innocence or our comparatively insignificant guiltiness. What is gained by this? Nothing, for thousands of German attempts to clear ourselves are regularly followed by a damnatory quotation from some marginal note by the ex-Emperor to the reports of one of our diplomatists, and all efforts to establish our innocence prove unavailing! Just think of the Kaiser's remarks, known to everybody, to the reports of the German Ambassador in Vienna, Herr von Tschirschky, though these are not the worst. Herr von Tschirschky sent to Berlin shortly before the outbreak of war the following communiqués, to which the Emperor wrote remarks in quotations marks (in parentheses) signed with a W:

"I hear the wish expressed from reliable people here that the Serbians should be seriously taken in hand. (Now or never. —W.) One should draw up a number of demands on the Serbians, and should they not accept them, go for them heavily. I will utilize every occasion to issue a calm, but explicit and solemn, warning against taking precipitate action." (Who authorized him to do that? That's very stupid. It's got nothing to do with him, as it is Austria's job to do what she likes in the matter. Afterwards if things go wrong people will say: Germany refused! Tschirschky must be asked not to write nonsense like this. The Serbians must be cleared out and quickly.—W.)

The ex-Kaiser made many similar comments. But what he thought of the Austrian Note, before he had read the Serbian reply, is clearly shown by his remarks on a telegram from Belgrade on 24th July which he read the next day. It stated:

"The firm tone and precise demands of the Austrian Note have come as a very great surprise to the Serbian Government." (Bravo! One couldn't have expected more from Vienna.—W.)

The telegram goes on:

"The Cabinet Council has been sitting since early this morning under the Presidency of the Crown Prince-Regent." (It seems His Majesty has backed out of it.—W.)

The noble German lord had no suspicion that many crowned heads would have to "back out of it," and quite in another way!

The telegram further reported:

"The Cabinet Council can, however, come to no decision." (The proud Slavs!—W.)

At the bottom of the telegram he wrote: (How hollow the whole of the sovereign State of Serbia appears to be. It is just like this with all Slav States. Only tread firmly on the feet of the rabble!—W.)

This is the language of the Emperor of Peace directly before the outbreak of war.

What our Ambassador in London Lichnowsky telegraphed to Berlin on 22nd July, 1914, was also embellished by the Emperor with marginal notes in parentheses.

"I come across here the hope that our influence in Vienna has succeeded in suppressing all impracticable demands." (How could I do that? It is no concern of mine. These fellows have revolted and committed murder, and must eat humble pie. It is a monstrous piece of British "cheek"! I am not called upon, like Grey, to instruct H.M. the Emperor of Austria how to preserve his honour.—W.)

The Emperor adds to the same report other marginal remarks. Among others are these:

(. . . Grey makes the mistake of putting Serbia and Austria on the same footing. That is preposterous! The Serbians are a gang of robbers who must be arrested for crime . . .!—W.)

He says in another place of the English:

(I will never make a Naval agreement with such scoundrels. —W.)

A statement like this coming from the Kaiser is of such importance for Entente propaganda that the Foreign Office, with its hundreds of records, can hardly explain it away. The Entente Press devoted about ten or fifteen lines to each of these marginal notes, and the Jingos and Chauvinists did, or undid, a hundred times more than our Pan-Germans, with their fat folios, that were sometimes favourably mentioned in the foreign Press.

No matter how the responsibility for the outbreak of war may in the future be distributed among the individual Governments, or what load of guilt may be laid on the shoulders of the "criminals," it is more expedient (and also easier) to "spot" where the guilty parties are who planned to change a war of self-defence, that the entire German people were prepared to wage, into a war of aggression, and who, by kicking over all chances of peace, prolonged the War for more than four years, till Germany's collapse.

While the stay-at-home warriors and Annexationists, Westarp, Traub, Dietrich Schäfer and all the rest of them, were still prepared to shed the last drop of blood—of those who were fighting away from home—in order to be able to incorporate with Germany the North of France and the border states of Russia, by a dictated peace if possible, we Social Democrats saw the ghastly end approaching if we failed to come to an agreement with our army still intact, still able to fight on with success, "for all the world to see," and absolutely unbroken. Directly after a start was made with so-called unrestricted U-boat warfare at the beginning of August, 1917, further fighting, as well as the final result of a struggle now becoming more unequal, appeared to us to be like a simple sum in arithmetic. Our losses could not be replaced; all casualties of the Entente could be at once replaced by American soldiers—well-fed, healthy fellows with the best equipment, supported by fine guns and hosts of aeroplanes, and splendidly trained, moreover, for attack by tanks. Another vastly important contrast between the German and American soldiers was their totally different morale. Our brave sons and brothers were downhearted and half starved. Marmalade made from turnips, called satirically "food for heroes," was certainly not calculated to encourage them to fresh deeds of courage, and on the top of all came an increasing and consuming feeling of hopelessness. Frederick the Great summed up a similar situation in these notable words: "If my soldiers were to begin to think, not one would remain in the ranks!" On the enemy side, however, hardy, athletic Americans were fighting, and the feeling among them was that only a small effort was needed to defeat us.

If we wanted peace by agreement, *i.e.* a peace of humiliation and renunciation—a Scheidemann's peace, as our Jingos called it in scorn—we could have that at any time. But they wanted to win and dictate: Calais—a German Gibraltar—Lithuania—Courland——

The great error, as unintelligible as it was unpardonable, of our Annexationists was that they thought one could make an agreement any time. Could one really expect enemies whose lands had been the theatre of war and had been more or less laid waste, to come to terms with an adversary, hitherto victorious, when the wind changed, and when they had their foes firmly at last by the throat. Ludendorff at any rate did not share this blind belief. The fact cannot be doubted that the possibility of an opportune agreement did exist. Professor Hans Delbrück in his book on the causes of war is quite convinced that even in the spring of 1918—before the great offensive—the possibility of an agreement was by no means out of court. He points to speeches by Wilson and Lloyd George, and then actually says, "Subsequently we heard that Lloyd George, however improbable it may sound, was really and truly ready to negotiate." In the *National Review* (September, 1919), Leo Maxse, one of the most furious enemies of Germany, let the cat out of the bag—Lloyd George, he says, was so absolutely pessimistic the whole time from July, 1917 till July, 1918 that he would have been ready to entertain any reasonable peace offer. "Let us openly confess," he adds, "that we again and again owe our salvation to our enemies." Had there been no Supreme Command and no Fatherland Party, Berlin would have given an answer (July, 1917) that would have enabled our panic-mongers to get to work again until all our war aims would have been sacrificed. . . . Had the enemy given a satisfactory reply about Belgium, negotiations would have commenced, and the mischief done before the public got wind of the intrigue. Real danger did exist for the Entente till unrestrained U-boat warfare opened. From that time they could breathe again; nay more, they could be sure of victory; now the big strong brother, the American, had to come in."

XVII

ATTEMPTS AT AGREEMENT

HOW was it possible to come any nearer to an agreement? The Chancellor's statements were unfortunately not always as straightforward as we wished. Pan-German talk, whether from the Conservative or National Liberal side, was not so important as the attitude of the Chancellor. Because Bethmann-Hollweg had not the pluck to break away from the Right, he favoured both sides for the sake of a mythical peace at home, although, as we often saw, he did not disguise his own aversion in private conversation from the demands made by these warlike fanatics. The Opposition, from whom nothing else was to be expected, only noticed the remarks which were ambiguous, and maintained a negative attitude. Our aim, then, had to be to get at the Governments concerned through the Socialists in Entente countries. The way could only be prepared by meetings. Various Inter-Parliamentary Conferences had been held; these had been arranged for by Socialists in neutral countries—an unsatisfactory one in Switzerland, the other in Stockholm. The cause of peace could, however, not be served by conferences at which S.D. Parties from the countries at war were not present. We made discreet moves in Holland and Denmark, and one day had the great pleasure of welcoming our Dutch comrade, Troelstra. He was off to Stockholm to try to arrange a conference with the International Socialistic Bureau

(I.S.B.) which Socialists from countries at war might attend. We eagerly jumped at the plan, and found ourselves in perfect agreement with some Austrian and Hungarian comrades, who had been asked by us to Berlin as representatives of their Parties. In a very short time we accepted Troelstra's proposals about the work to be done at such an International Congress— one thing only was talked of: how could we get peace as quickly as possible? National Party disputes, as well as the question of War Guilt, were to be kept in the background. Our hearts were beating quicker—we had been grasping at straws for a long time. Troelstra went off to Copenhagen and Stockholm, and Victor Adler to Switzerland to inform our Russian friend, Axelrod. Our warmest good wishes went with both on their journeys.

We had now more to do than before, for we were accustomed to organize these conferences thoroughly (I may say that of the S.P.D. Executive). Now for this Conference, that should at any rate bring us nearer to peace! It was taken for granted that Socialists from all countries at war with the Entente would be there. But would the Social Democrats from France, Belgium, England and Italy come? We fondly hoped so. No matter, we intended going to Stockholm well prepared. The whole world, apart from our allies, was up against Germany. The hostility of everybody was a fact we had to reckon with. Attacks, both violent and unjustified, would rain down upon us if the Entente Socialists were present. We had therefore to put on all our armour if we were to stand firm against them. To stand firm meant: (1) to make it clear to Socialists in Entente countries that we, belonging to a peace-loving country, could not, and therefore did not, desert our Fatherland in the hour of her greatest trial, and (2) that we as International Socialists had not forgotten to carry out our duties towards the Socialist International. The first remark, that will seem superfluous to many, was, however, necessary because many Socialists in Entente countries really thought that the duty of defending one's country existed only for them and not for us. Dr. David spoke very soundly on this question in Stockholm later on. It has been stated in another place that the Party Executive had decided on printing a collection of documents concerning our work in the War. I enthusiastically collected from the shorthand reports of the Reichstag, from Party Select Committees and Minutes of the Conferences, full accounts of our efforts to promote peace. A document was produced, as simple and unassuming in its form as convincing in its content. With this evidence in our hands we would go to Stockholm and ask the others, "Where have you put on paper what you did for peace?"

If our hopes of Stockholm are to be rightly understood the whole situation at the time must be borne in mind. It shall here be briefly given. The quarrels over unrestrained U-boat warfare have already been described. The excitement caused by the fatal decision lasted for a long time and could not be allayed by its great success, which was naturally exaggerated by the War Information Department.

The Polish question at the time played a great part. Ludendorff wished to secure by his Polish policy a big recruiting ground "with no compulsion." The result was too utterly tragic and funny—just a few dozen Polish volunteers came forward, as had been announced in a secret session to the Reichstag. This venture of Ludendorff's was a mere flash in the pan, like his famous letter "to the dear Jews in Poland," that certain circles would like to suppress. This will never succeed, and many thousand copies of the letter were circulated.

As an instructional document from "a great period" it is here given in extracts. The letter was issued in the autumn of 1914.

"TO THE JEWS IN POLAND

"The heroic Armies of the great Central-European Powers, Germany and Austria-Hungary, are in Poland.

"The mighty march of our Armies has forced the despotic Russian Government to run away.

"Our soldiers bring you liberty and freedom, equal civil rights, religious freedom, liberty to work undisturbed in all branches of economic and social life according to your inclination.

"You have fretted too long under the iron Muscovite yoke!

"We come as friends to you; barbaric foreign rule is over.

"Equal rights for the Jews shall be established on a firm basis.

"Your holy duty is now to co-operate with all your strength and work together for freedom.

"All the might of your people must be exerted, and you must help the good cause as one man.

"We expect you to show your good sense and devotion by your deeds.

"Apply with the greatest confidence to the commanders of our army in those places where you live.

"All supplies of goods will be well and promptly paid for. Prepare the way for victory throughout the whole of Ssaune and bring the Nizochaun liberty and justice.

(Signed) "THE SUPREME COMMAND OF THE
ALLIED ARMIES OF GERMANY AND
AUSTRIA-HUNGARY."

The forcible evacuation of Belgian workmen from their homes produced lasting ill-feeling against the Germans. It was a measure carried out at the suggestion of Hugo Stinnes, who had much influence at headquarters. If any non-German in any part of the world dared to say a good word for Germany, these deportations promptly silenced him. The so-called Flemish question was being constantly mooted, especially by Stresemann, because the National Liberals thought that Belgium would be divided by this means and prepared for incorporation with Germany—*divide et impera!* The Belgium problem had become a general subject for discussion throughout the entire world. The deportations provoked a regular howl of indignation. It is no good looking for reasons for this proceeding. There is no excuse for this stupidity. It was the work of capitalist and military psychology—the policy of force *à la* Stinnes and Ludendorff.

At a meeting of the Chief Select Committee on 3rd March, 1917, I discussed the whole Belgian problem. I warned them against any attempt at talking anything except peace anywhere in Belgium. We had damaged our position in the East by our Polish policy, and we had done the same in the West over the Flemish question. Then I took the opportunity of bringing up the case of deporting working men from Belgium to Germany. We should let these men go home at once. On the whole the debate took a line favourable to my views. Only Count Westarp dissented.

The political tension was increased by the news of the Russian Revolution and the victory of Tscheidse and Kerenski. From my notes (21st March) I addressed that evening a telegram of congratulation to Tscheidse and the Duma, to be forwarded by Stauning (Copenhagen) to St. Petersburg. My colleagues, Müller and Molkenbuhr, approved of the draft, which I sent at once to the Party offices so that Ebert and the rest of my colleagues might give their opinions. The tele-

gram was sent as I had written it. At a conversation next day
with Ebert and Wahnschaffe it appeared that Ebert, for reasons with which I could not agree, objected to sending the
telegram, but that Wahnschaffe was highly pleased. Even the
Chancellor, whom the chairmen of the Section were consult-
ing on the forthcoming Budget, as well as the speakers of the
Sections taking part in the debate (of the S.D. Section Noske
and I were present), spoke hopefully of events in Russia and
thought them of international importance. And should we
not have ecstatically welcomed this revolution? At this meeting Bethmann-Hollweg scored off Count Westarp in splendid
style. Westarp had referred to an article of mine in the *Vorwärts* in which Russia had been referred to and protested
violently against it. Whereupon the Chancellor said, "I must
ask you not to say anything (at the next meeting of the
Reichstag) in favour of the old régime in—Russia."

This and a lot more happened during the time we were
preparing to go to Stockholm. Stockholm was our great hope
—not only with us Social Democrats and in the trenches, but
also among all classes of the population in town and country.
On 4th April, 1917, we were informed by our Party friends,
Janson and Dr. Helphand, coming from Sweden, where they
had been in touch with the Russians, of events in Russia—
shortly Borgbjerg, our Danish friend, was to go on an "instructional" tour to St. Petersburg—we could imagine what
that meant—and then would come direct to Copenhagen to
talk over matters. Our passes were got ready for us overnight
on instructions from Zimmermann, Secretary of State, whom
we had let into our confidence, by the Foreign Office. The
Secretary of State was delighted with our plan and wished us
bon voyage and the best of luck. Peace! peace! that was his
refrain. With the Poles it cannot fail, surely! Ah, if it is pos-

sible—a little rectification of frontier here and there on the Narew. We can act differently with a *free* Russia—but who will guarantee it remains so? We made it clear to him that we would act with all necessary caution, but would prefer peace to any rectification of boundaries that might prolong war.

In these days Ebert was in a highly nervous condition. He was now sorry for being up against sending the telegram to Tscheidse and the Duma. The General Committee of the Trades Unions, with which we were cordially co-operating, proposed Gustavus Bauer as our travelling companion to Stockholm. The Executive sent Ebert and me. We arranged to start on 6th April. The day began well. When I got to the Stettin railway station, about twenty minutes before the train started, Ebert was standing on the steps with a face as white as a sheet, and told me he had left the passes behind at home and we could not start. As I cannot have looked especially pleased, Ebert assured me that Rostock was a very fine town to spend a day in; Bauer and I might expect him there next day. Ah, good Lord! If any one of us had come to him with a proposal like that! I replied that we had no intention of admiring Rostock, but that Borgbjerg was expecting us in Copenhagen with his bag in his hand.

Meanwhile Dr. Helphand (Parvus) joined us. He had already reserved a carriage. Scarcely had we told him of Ebert's bad luck when one of Fritz's sons came tearing along with the passes. Everybody was relieved but Ebert, who, after discovering he had left the passes behind in Treptow, had deposited his luggage in the cloakroom at the Friedrichstrasse Station. We prevailed on him to travel without his luggage. We arrived in the evening at Copenhagen. On the platform

we separated to avoid the numerous spies and secret agents.
We met again in the Hotel Central.

We were invited to supper in Copenhagen at the house of a
well-known Party friend, where we had a chance of filling
our stomachs at last. Ah, who would have believed that so
much food existed! Fruit on every table and flowers. Happy
Denmark, land of peace. . . .

In the carriage and on the trip across the Baltic we discussed
over and over again what we should say to the Russians
through Borgbjerg. Though we knew that Borgbjerg would
turn up after supper (he could not come before owing to his
newspaper work), and we were to give him full instructions,
Ebert explained everything during supper in full detail, though
besides ourselves, who had travelled with him, only our host
and his wife were present. Hardly had we settled down to
smoke after our meal in another room when Borgbjerg arrived, and we had to hear the same story all over again. I
always envied Ebert's ability for repeating the same thing in
the same way time after time, *e.g.* in the Executive, Party
Select Committee, in the Reichstag Section, etc., and finally
perhaps before the Committee of Control. If this had been a
proof of strong nerves in Berlin, it was a proof of very weak
ones in Copenhagen. What had we given Borgbjerg to take
with him on his journey? According to what we had arranged
it was this: he could tell the Russians we wished for peace
without compulsion. Poland would be no hindrance; we
knew we were at one with the Government in this—no annexations in Courland or Lithuania; a desire did exist, perhaps on both sides, of making some small rectifications of
frontiers, but these could easily be settled at the peace negotiations; things were more difficult in the Balkans; Macedonia,
Dobrudska, Serbia, Bulgaria, Roumania, etc., we only needed

362

to talk about to know at once that Victor Adler did not think our formula of "no annexations" covered everything. Hence all these questions of agreement should be reserved; an agreement would certainly be arrived at. I asked Borgbjerg, and strictly authorized him, to tell the Russians that no offensive from the German side would be undertaken against Russia. In case of need they should merely ignore what had happened on the Stochod. Even the Army Command had not said they had gained great successes on the Stochod and taken thousands of prisoners. Only when the Russians had made a great fuss about it in their own reports had it been acknowledged on the German side that a victory had been gained. Dr. Helphand, an old Russian revolutionary, would discuss the demands of the Entente and their wish "to get freedom for Germany." Borgbjerg might draw Russia's attention to the fact that the German worker had at the time duties to perform different from those of the Russian worker. To depose the Czar with the assent of citizen classes was child's play compared with the fight that had to be fought in Germany against the Capitalist and the big manufacturer. What in Russia was the chief thing, *viz.* the form of government, was in Germany relatively of minor importance. However, for future struggles we should need the masses at home; therefore the Russians should make peace so that our masses could return home from the trenches.

Borgbjerg's plan was this: he intended travelling via Stockholm to Haparanda and then to St. Petersburg; he intended also going into the country, and above all to Moscow. His accounts of the difficulties in obtaining passports was interesting. The Danish Government were rather reserved, and advised him to travel as a private gentleman without special credentials from the Danish Government. The Government referred him to the Russian Legation. The latter behaved to Borgbjerg as if it had always represented revolutionary Russia; it gave our friend the passports, but only on condition that he should first present himself to the English Legation; the latter questioned him for a long time, and then told him there was no objection to his going to Russia. Borgbjerg proposed starting next day, though his wife's confinement was hourly expected. His wife herself begged him to start, as it was a matter of urgency. Why did our friend's wife refer to urgency? It was very simple. Branting was on his way to St. Petersburg! We not only feared, but also our Danish friends, that he might make things awkward for us before Borgbjerg arrived in St. Petersburg, owing to Branting's Entente sympathies. Next day Borgbjerg was two hours distant from Copenhagen when his wife presented him with a healthy baby girl, who received the Russo-German name of Tatjana Margarete, in memory of her father's journey undertaken by him on behalf of the peace of Europe. On 9th October, 1917, I was present at the christening. I shall always think of it with pleasure. The ceremony took place in a church opposite Borgbjerg's house. The pastor was a worthy servant of the Lord, squinted a little and had watery eyes. He had a terrible voice; a verger, who helped him, did not sing quite so well. In spite of the bad singing Tatjana Margarete grew happily into a beautiful girl and was her good parents' pride and joy.

Immediately after Borgbjerg's departure Stauning, who had had urgent business abroad, arrived in Copenhagen. Ebert told him at length what he had told Borgbjerg, but was out of temper because Stauning only said yes or no a few times. Ebert thought later his message for Stauning should have been translated into Danish, as he may not have understood him fully. I left the matter for him to do next day, and asked to be allowed to go to the Thorwaldsen Museum while this was being done, as I really could not have heard the story all over again.

Lenin Sent from Switzerland to Russia

On Easter Monday evening Dr. Helphand made us the following proposals: In the next few days about forty Russian exiles would be coming from Switzerland via Germany to Malmö. He would be going there to welcome the Russians. Among them would be Lenin, Axelrod, Martov, and many other well-known Socialists. As it was not improbable that one of the more influential Russians might like to talk to us, somebody should stop behind in Copenhagen and come, if summoned, to Malmö. Ebert was against the proposal, because we had business in Berlin, and the Russians would certainly not talk matters over with us. I did not believe either in a regular conversation with us, but thought it probable we should be reproached for having gone away. We eventually agreed on giving Dr. Helphand a kind of authorization for interviewing the Russians in the shape of a letter. He knew our views quite well from our talks with Stauning and Borgbjerg, at which he was present. Dr. Helphand's meeting with the Russians did not come off. I found out much later that Lenin and his friends' journey from Switzerland through Germany to Russia was Dr. Helphand's arrangement, about which he had informed few people, while he never said a word to us about it. Probably he wanted to keep us out of the firing line if things should go wrong. Helphand's idea was this. As Lenin was a more pushing fellow than Tscheidse and Kerenski—he would at once brush the two of them to one side and be ready without delay for peace; it

365

would then only depend on Germany to make a reasonable peace with Russia.

Without an understanding with the more responsible authorities in Germany, Dr. Helphand would naturally never have carried his plan through. However cunningly the plan had been devised and thought out in all details, it was stupidly shattered by the German diplomatists at Brest-Litowsk. April 10th, 1917, saw us again in Berlin. On the 13th came Victor Adler, Carl Renner and Seitz from Vienna. They approved of our conduct in Copenhagen. Adler reported a conversation with Count Czernin. The Count had talked in the same way as Bethmann-Hollweg and Zimmermann had to us. The desire for peace was equally strong in Berlin and Vienna, but neither here nor there had any one the pluck to take a firm line. For truth's sake it must be said that Czernin was much more inclined to go further than his German colleagues, the Berlin diplomatists, on the strength of his own conviction. Yet it must be remembered that Czernin had to reckon with less opposition from Annexationists than had his Berlin colleagues.

It was in the meantime telegraphed from Haparanda that the English had not let our friend Borgbjerg pass the frontier. They let Branting through all right, but Borgbjerg's friendship with us had not been unknown to the English spies. Only with considerable trouble did Borgbjerg get permission to pass the Russian frontier.

Borgbjerg's Report

Although very important events were happening between whiles, we must state what Borgbjerg reported about his Russian trip. The report was read in Stauning's house in Copenhagen on 25th May, 1917. We were stopping in Copenhagen on our way to Stockholm.

Borgbjerg had been very well received in St. Petersburg. He first spoke with Tscheidse, who listened attentively and invited him to a meeting of the Workers' and Soldiers' Council. All there listened to his interview with Bauer, Ebert and me with great interest. Most of what he told them about the policy of the majority was new to them, or at any rate appeared to them in a new light. When he repeated his report at a meeting of the Workers' and Soldiers' Council he was asked many questions, as, for instance: "Is the Chancellor in agreement with what Scheidemann and his colleagues have told you?" To this he replied: "I cannot say, but I think so. The German Social Democrats are not the governing body and do not represent the majority in the Reichstag." Next question: "Is the resolution of the Social Democratic Section approved by other groups and parties?" "Some not unimportant groups are, without a doubt, in perfect agreement with it." Next question: "That means there are important groups in agreement with it." "Between what I said and the last question there is a difference, but I cannot explain it."

Borgbjerg then described the preliminaries of the Dutch and Scandinavian Parties and asked us to attend the Stockholm Conference. Other questioners went as far as to ask whether there was any chance of a revolution in Germany. These he answered by saying it was very improbable; in wartime a revolution would certainly not break out. If after the War, all would depend on how the War ended and what attitude the Government took on the internal reforms demanded. Then he drew attention to the difference between conditions in Russia and those of the Western States of Europe. "In Russia the revolution is the culmination of great efforts made to sweep away intolerable conditions, like the revolutions in England in the seventeenth, and in France and Germany in the eighteenth or nineteenth centuries." To make the matter quite clear he referred to Denmark. "There a revolution would be absolutely senseless, because Denmark has a democratic constitution. Though there is a lot to reform in Germany, a revolution there, as in Denmark, would only be a social one, which would aim at the complete confiscation of the capitalist means of production." Such a revolution could not be expected for a very considerable time, etc. The debate was to the point and very quiet. Finally Borgbjerg was told that their resolutions would be sent him in a few days. Two days later a delegate of the Workers' and Soldiers' Council came to him and began with the words: "Your mission has succeeded. The Workers' and Soldiers' Council has decided—as has been announced in the Press—to issue invitations to a Conference. It will be easier for the English and French to take part. A clashing with the other conference is then out of the question."

What Borgbjerg further told us of his experiences at the Workers' and Soldiers' Council in St. Petersburg—among other things, that the new "Peace Loan" had been approved—put the Russian Socialists in such a favourable light that I said: "The Russian Socialists are now adopting the view that we took from the start: 'We have something to defend, then let us defend it.'" Stauning and Borgbjerg fully agreed with this sentiment.

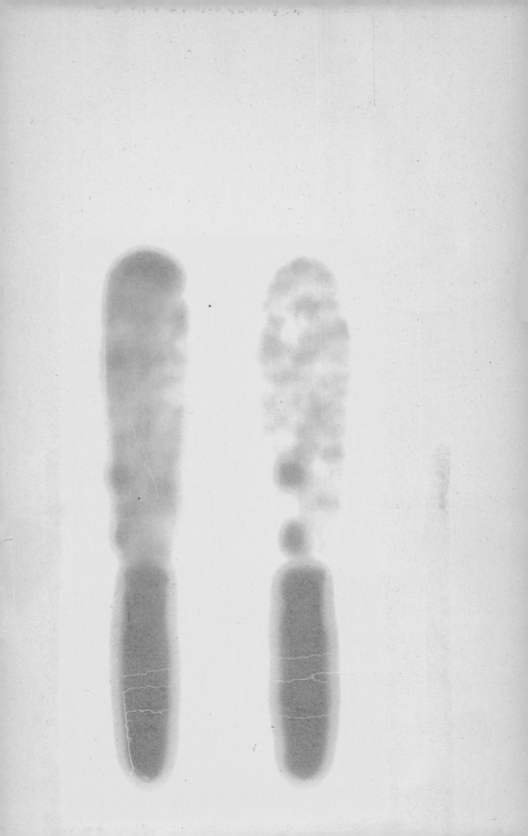